Towards the Private Funding of Higher Education

An almost universal driving force for contemporary change in universities is the shifting view of higher education as more of a private than a public good. *Towards the Private Funding of Higher Education* presents a contemporary global picture of this move towards the privatization of higher education, and examines how these shifts in ideology and funding priorities have significant policy implications.

The resulting developments, such as the imposition and escalation of student tuition fees and the emergence of online providers of higher education, emerge out of a combination of economic, political and ideological pressures, further enhanced by technological changes. By using multiple international and regional examples to analyse the various pressures for privatization, this book examines the different forms privatization has taken, while offering an analytical interpretation of why the privatization drive emerged, why it has been resisted in some instances and what forms it is likely to assume in the future.

Towards the Private Funding of Higher Education illustrates and challenges the emergence of a new relationship between the university, government and society. It is an essential read for higher education professors, university managers and higher education policy makers across the world.

David Palfreyman is Director of the Oxford Centre for Higher Education Policy Studies (OxCHEPS), New College, University of Oxford, UK.

Ted Tapper is a Visiting Fellow at the Oxford Centre for Higher Education Policy Studies (OxCHEPS), New College, University of Oxford, UK.

Scott Thomas is Professor and Dean of the College of Education and Social Services at the University of Vermont, USA.

International Studies in Higher Education
Series Editors:
David Palfreyman, OxCHEPS
Ted Tapper, OxCHEPS
Scott Thomas, University of Vermont, USA

Towards the Private Funding of Higher Education: Ideological and Political Struggles
Edited by *David Palfreyman, Ted Tapper and Scott Thomas*

Global Rankings and the Geopolitics of Higher Education: Understanding the Influence and Impact of Rankings on Higher Education, Policy and Society
Edited by *Ellen Hazelkorn*

Organizing Academic Work in Higher Education: Teaching, Learning and Identities
Edited by *Liudvika Leisyte and Uwe Wilkesmann*

Access and Expansion Post-Massification: Opportunities and Barriers to Further Growth in Higher Education Participation
Edited by *Ben Jongbloed and Hans Vossensteyn*

International Trends in University Governance: Autonomy, Self-Government and the Distribution of Authority
Edited by *Michael Shattock*

Diversity and Inclusion in Higher Education: Emerging Perspectives on Institutional Transformation
Edited by *Daryl Smith*

Affirmative Action Matters: Creating Opportunities for Students Around the World
Edited by *Laura Dudley Jenkins and Michele S. Moses*

The Physical University: Contours of Space and Place in Higher Education
Edited by *Paul Temple*

Student Financing of Higher Education: A Comparative Perspective
Edited by *Donald Heller and Claire Callender*

Enhancing Quality in Higher Education: International Perspectives
Edited by *Ray Land and George Gordon*

The Global Student Experience: An International and Comparative Analysis
Edited by *Camille B. Kandiko and Mark Weyers*

Universities and Regional Development: A Critical Assessment of Tensions and Contradictions
Edited by *Rómulo Pinheiro, Paul Benneworth and Glen A. Jones*

Tribes and Territories in the 21st Century: Rethinking the Significance of Disciplines in Higher Education
Edited by *Paul Trowler, Murray Saunders and Veronica Bamber*

Universities in the Knowledge Economy: Higher Education Organisation and Global Change
Edited by *Paul Temple*

Towards the Private Funding of Higher Education

Ideological and Political Struggles

Edited by
David Palfreyman, Ted Tapper
and Scott Thomas

LONDON AND NEW YORK

First published 2018
by Routledge
2 Park Square, Milton Park, Abingdon, Oxon OX14 4RN

and by Routledge
711 Third Avenue, New York, NY 10017

Routledge is an imprint of the Taylor & Francis Group, an informa business

© 2018 selection and editorial matter, David Palfreyman, Ted Tapper and Scott Thomas; individual chapters, the contributors

The right of David Palfreyman, Ted Tapper and Scott Thomas to be identified as the authors of the editorial material, and of the authors for their individual chapters, has been asserted in accordance with sections 77 and 78 of the Copyright, Designs and Patents Act 1988.

All rights reserved. No part of this book may be reprinted or reproduced or utilized in any form or by any electronic, mechanical, or other means, now known or hereafter invented, including photocopying and recording, or in any information storage or retrieval system, without permission in writing from the publishers.

Trademark notice: Product or corporate names may be trademarks or registered trademarks, and are used only for identification and explanation without intent to infringe.

British Library Cataloguing-in-Publication Data
A catalogue record for this book is available from the British Library

Library of Congress Cataloging-in-Publication Data
A catalog record for this book has been requested

ISBN: 978-1-138-68978-7 (hbk)
ISBN: 978-1-315-53741-2 (ebk)

Typeset in Minion
by Florence Production Ltd, Stoodleigh, Devon, UK

Printed and bound by CPI Group (UK) Ltd, Croydon, CR0 4YY

Contents

	Contributors	vii
1	The funding of higher education: the oscillating balance between the public and private financing of the university DAVID PALFREYMAN, TED TAPPER AND SCOTT THOMAS	1
2	Distance learning and the rise of the MOOCs: the more things change, the more they stay the same ROBERTA MALEE BASSETT AND ALEX USHER	6
3	The ecology of state higher-education policymaking in the US JAMES C. HEARN AND ERIK C. NESS	19
4	The Australian hybrid: public and private higher education funding ANDREW NORTON	48
5	The United Kingdom divided: contested income-contingent student loans GARETH WILLIAMS	72
6	The robust privateness and publicness of higher education: expansion through privatization in Poland MAREK KWIEK	90
7	Germany: resistance to fee-paying BARBARA M. KEHM	112
8	Is higher education in Latin America a public good? Issues of funding, expansion, stratification and inequity ALMA MALDONADO-MALDONADO AND JOSÉ HUMBERTO GONZÁLEZ REYES	124

9 Higher education development in China: fast growth and governmental policy since the Chinese economic reform of 1978   143
SHUMING ZHAO AND YIXUAN ZHAO

10 Whither the Japanese system of higher education? Higher education as a public and private good – differentiation and realignment   162
FUMI KITAGAWA AND AKIYOSHI YONEZAWA

11 How inexorable is the shift from the public to the private funding of higher education?   177
DAVID PALFREYMAN, TED TAPPER AND SCOTT THOMAS

Index   185

Contributors

Roberta Malee Bassett, PhD, is a senior education specialist working in the World Bank's Global Practice in Education, providing technical expertise for projects related to higher education reform initiatives around the world. Roberta is the author/editor of numerous articles, reports and books on topics related to international higher education including *The WTO and the University: Globalization, GATS and American Higher Education* (Routledge, 2006); *International Organizations and Higher Education Policy: Thinking Globally, Acting Locally?* (co-editor with Alma Maldonado-Maldonado, Taylor and Francis, 2009) and *The Forefront of International Higher Education: A Festschrift in Honor of Philip G. Altbach* (co-editor with Alma Maldonado-Maldonado, Routledge, 2014).

James C. Hearn is professor and associate director at the University of Georgia's Institute of Higher Education. His primary research interests centre on tertiary education policy, organization, and finance.

José Humberto González Reyes was born in Mexico City. He studied sociology at the National Autonomous University of Mexico (UNAM). He holds a Master's Degree from the Educational Research Department at the Center for Research and Advanced Studies of the National Polytechnic Institute (CINVESTAV-IPN). His research topics are: private higher education, higher education access and educational inequities.

Barbara M. Kehm is Professor of Leadership and International Strategic Development in Higher Education at the Robert Owen Centre for Educational Change, School of Education, University of Glasgow (United Kingdom). From 2003 until 2011, she was Professor of Higher Education and Director of the International Centre for Higher Education Research (INCHER), University of Kassel (Germany). She has published more than 30 books and over 300 book chapters and journal articles on a broad range of topics in the field of higher education studies. Her particular areas of expertise are internationalization in and of higher education, new forms of governance and professionalization processes in higher education. Barbara M. Kehm is also an active member of several academic advisory boards and two boards of trustees of German higher education institutions. She is a reviewer for several journals in the field as well as for grant applications to national research councils in a number of different countries (Europe and beyond).

Fumi Kitagawa currently lectures entrepreneurship and innovation courses at the University of Edinburgh Business School. She has held international research and teaching positions including Senior Research Fellow at the Department of Higher Education at National Institute for Educational Policy Research, in Japan; Assistant Professor at the Centre for Innovation, Research and Competence, Lund University, Sweden; and Lecturer in Enterprise Studies at the University of Manchester. She has worked with the OECD's projects on the contribution of higher education to regional development, and has recently been involved in the projects funded by the European Commission on developing entrepreneurship training for researchers at HEIs, and measuring the contribution of higher education to innovation capacity.

Marek Kwiek, a UNESCO Chair in Institutional Research and Higher Education Policy, a director of the Center for Public Policy Studies, University of Poznan, Poland. An international higher-education policy expert to the European Commission, OECD, World Bank, UNESCO, OSCE, Council of Europe and USAID. His research interests include university governance, academic entrepreneurialism, and the academic profession. He publishes mostly internationally (Science and Public Policy, Higher Education, Studies in Higher Education, Comparative Education Review, Journal of Studies in International Education, etc.). A Fulbright 'New Century Scholar' 2007–2008. An editorial board member of Higher Education Quarterly, European Educational Research Journal, British Educational Research Journal and European Journal of Higher Education. Kwiekm@amu.edu.pl; www.cpp.amu.edu.pl.

Alma Maldonado-Maldonado is a researcher at the Educational Research Department of the Center for Research and Advances Studies (CINVESTAV). Previously, she was an assistant professor at the University of Arizona's Center for the Study of Higher Education in the US Maldonado was born in Mexico City; she studied at the National Autonomous University of Mexico (UNAM). Later, Alma earned her Ph.D. at the Boston College's Center for International Higher Education. Her research focuses on comparative higher education, international organizations, higher education policy and research in Latin America and issues regarding globalization, mobility and internationalization of higher education (institutions, faculty and students).

Erik C. Ness is associate professor at the University of Georgia's Institute of Higher Education. His primary research interests include public policy effects, especially on students, institutions and state systems, and the public policymaking process, specifically the political dynamics associated with state-level higher education policy adoption.

Andrew Norton is the Higher Education Program Director at the Grattan Institute. He is the author or co-author of many articles, reports and other publications on higher education issues. These include University fees: what students pay in deregulated markets; The cash nexus: how teaching funds research in Australian universities and a reference report on higher education trends and policies, *Mapping Australian higher education*. He has worked as a ministerial adviser on higher education and as a university policy adviser. In 2013–2014, he was the co-author of government-commissioned review of Australia's demand driven student funding system, and in 2016–2017 served on an expert panel advising the Australian education minister on higher education reform. He is an honorary fellow at the Centre for the Study of Higher Education at the University of Melbourne.

David Palfreyman is Director of the Oxford Centre for Higher Education Policy Studies (OxCHEPS), New College, University of Oxford, UK. He is a Member of the Board of the Office for Students, the new regulator of English universities.

Ted Tapper is a Visiting Fellow at the Oxford Centre for Higher Education Policy Studies (OxCHEPS), New College, University of Oxford, UK.

Scott Thomas is Professor and Dean of the College of Education and Social Services at the University of Vermont, USA.

Alex Usher is President of Higher Education Strategy Associates (HESA), a consulting firm which advises governments, institutions and corporations in the higher education sector on policy and strategy. One of Canada's most-recognized experts on student financial aid, his policy work spans issues such as access to education, higher education finance, measurement of institutional performance and rankings. He works frequently for the European Commission, World Bank and other development agencies in Asia and Africa. Mr. Usher is a Fellow-in-Residence at the CD Howe Institute and writes a popular daily commentary on Canadian higher education called One Thought to Start Your Day.

Gareth Williams is an emeritus professor at the UCL Institute of Education University of London, where he founded its Centre for Higher Education Studies in 1986. Earlier in his career an OECD economist, he has worked mainly on the economics of education and higher education policy analysis, particularly finance, labour market issues and strategic management. His books include The Academic Labour Market; Changing Patterns of finance in Higher Education and Higher Education as a Public Good (edited with O Filippakou).

Akiyoshi Yonezawa is Professor and Director, *Office of Institutional Research, Tohoku University*. With a background in sociology, he mainly conducts research on comparative higher education policy – especially focusing on world-class universities, internationalization of higher education, and public-private relationships in higher education. He established his expertise in higher education policy and management through working experience at universities and public organizations such as Nagoya University, OECD and the University of Tokyo. He is a board member at Japan Association for Higher Education Research. He is a co-editor of the Book Series Higher Education in Asia: Quality, Excellence and Governance series (Springer Book Series).

Shuming Zhao is Senior Distinguished Professor and Honorary Dean of the School of Business, Nanjing University, China. He serves as President of the International Association of Chinese Management Research (IACMR, Third Term), President of Jiangsu Provincial Association of Human Resource Management, Vice Chairman for the Steering Committee for National Business Degree Programs of the Ministry of Education of China and Vice President of Chinese Academy Management. Dr. Zhao's research area is human resource management, multinational business management and entrepreneurship. He has been chairing several research projects for the National Natural Science Foundation of China and has published more than 10 books and over 300 academic papers and articles. Professor Zhao graduated from the English Language and Literature Department, Nanjing University in 1977. He holds a master's degree in linguistics and education (1983) and Ph.D. in higher education and human resource management (1990) from Claremont Graduate University in the United States. He was a post-doctoral fellow of human resource management at the College of Business, Florida Atlantic University in the United States in 1990–1991.

Yixuan Zhao is Assistant Researcher at the Department of Human Resource Management School of Business, Nanjing University, China and Post-doctoral Fellow of Nanjing University-Daqo Group, Nanjing, China. She received Bachelor Degree with Honours from the College of Business, the University of Missouri-St. Louis, USA (2004); International MBA from Marshall School of Business, the University of Southern California, USA (2009) and Ph.D. in Human Resource Management from the School of Business, Nanjing University, China (2016). Her research area is human resource management and millennial employee management. She has published several papers in top Chinese and international journals.

Cambridge# 1
The funding of higher education
The oscillating balance between the public and private financing of the university

DAVID PALFREYMAN, TED TAPPER AND SCOTT THOMAS

Introduction: higher education as a public good?

As much as we may want to believe that higher education institutions are worthy bodies that promote desirable ends – furthering knowledge, enhancing desirable cultural values and expanding the socio-economic opportunities of those fortunate enough to have been embraced by the experience of the university, and 'speaking truth to power' – it is also important to remember that higher education is a complex and expensive entity that has to be financed. Historically, within most societies the university has been granted a privileged position and nurtured by the state and most governments. This nurturing has taken various forms ranging from the essentially symbolic (that universities are those bodies which tell us what is to count as high status knowledge) to the very practical (for example, the granting of direct public financial aid and/or the recognition in law that they are deserving of being awarded financial rewards and monopoly privileges because they are reputable bodies pursuing worthy public good goals).

Changing contextual realities

The support for the public funding of higher education is dependent upon a range of variables that vary in importance both over time, and from one national setting to another. However, the comparative national pictures appear to be bounded by a common time frame. For example, in the two decades following the Second World War, once postwar reconstruction commenced (from approximately 1950 to the late-1960s), higher education systems seemed to expand steadily and were underwritten on a wide front by public funding. In the past two decades, although in many nations higher education has continued to expand, it has done so often without that same commitment of public funding – either public funding has been withdrawn or has failed to grow proportionately in line with the expansion of student numbers. Political decisions were made to the effect that, if there was to be higher education expansion, it had to be achieved through private rather than public funding. In the latter case the implication is that higher education may be a good that should expand but governments have reached the decision that they lack the resources to fund it. Of course, governments may well decide to make selective strategic funding decisions – for example, to underwrite the costs of what are considered to be important research initiatives but require students to meet their tuition costs, while subsidizing certain supposedly economically beneficial degree courses.

Perhaps the more interesting examples are those nation states that have over time moved away from the previous commitment to the public funding of higher education; moving most frequently to requiring students to meet some or even all of their tuition costs. The continuous non-funding of higher education is undoubtedly easier to explain than the withdrawal or more selective application of prior public funding. In the former case there are clearly political decisions that suggest, while expansion may be desirable, it could not be afforded out of the public purse. The question then is why expansion should have been promoted in the first place? Was it an unavoidable political necessity? As several of our chapters will illustrate there are varying pressures that have underwritten such a course of action, including pressures that suggest the need to provide – even if belatedly once the expansionist movement is under way – at least a measure of public funding.

Again, as several of our chapters will demonstrate, differing combinations of factors have led to the withdrawal of public funding in many nation states and invariably, it is a protracted and sometimes uneven, process. Clearly underlying any such move is a relative political decline in the perceived importance of higher education as a social good that merits public funding. This can take different forms. First, higher education has failed, at least in the eyes of those controlling the political process, to deliver expected returns. Alternatively, it may have become politically more important for governments and states to secure the more adequate provision of other social goods. Governments may have to make choices when public resources are constrained and it could be judged politically more expedient to fund health care or even schooling over higher education. So a combination of political and economic variables will shape the patterns of public funding with the priorities for governments changing over time, although obviously the political colouring of the governments will have a bearing on the decisions that are made. But the question remains, what responsibility, if any, do higher education institutions themselves, along with their representative bodies, bear for the downgrading of their political importance? How political adroit, or maladroit, have they been in sustaining or not their access to public funding?

Perhaps most interestingly, there have also been significant challenges to our initial perception of higher education as promoting significant economic, cultural and social benefits – that higher education is a public good and thus deserving of public funding. This challenge received perhaps its most serious manifestation in the UK during the 1980s, the years of Thatcher Governments, although it has to be said that Parliament during those years resisted the imposition of tuition fees upon home-based students; that development was first imposed by Blair's Labour Government with fees being then substantially increased by a Conservative/Liberal Democratic coalition government (fees have risen from £1,000 to £3,000,and then to £9,000 and now to £9,250 per annum with further increases at some selected institutions to come). But the more substantive point is that, if acquisition of higher education was seen as enhancing individual opportunities, why should there then not be an obligation upon those in receipt of it to pay for it? The questions that then follow are: how it is to be paid for; whether all recipients should be required to pay; and if higher education were also to remain at least in part a public good what, if any, should be the level of public funding and on what terms would it be distributed to the universities?

Different models of change

As has already been implied the privatization of higher education can take different trajectories. The public funding of universities may be steadily withdrawn and institutions may then be forced to seek private funding to sustain all or part of their established functions. For example, there could be state withdrawal from the payment of student tuition fees, either across the board or on a selective bases; while public support for the payment of the university's research agenda could continue, either across the complete range of its academic activities or on a selective basis with some areas of knowledge continuing to receive public support while others were denied it. Alternatively, it may be thought politically advisable to encourage the foundation of new privately-incorporated and privately-funded institutions which, possibly on a selective basis, could apply for public funding to underwrite some of their activities whether that should be research or teaching. In recent years we have seen many examples of both developments, which fudge the distinction between the public and private sectors of higher education. While within the established academic community there is frequently a tendency to decry such developments as an undermining of the idea and ideal of the university, it is difficult not to conclude that in many countries it now makes more sense to see higher education as comprising a broad tertiary model rather than conforming to a narrow university system – a product as much of the market as of the state, a mixed-economy delivery of what was once wholly a public good or private service.

Most of these developments are the consequence of policy changes initiated by central governments, invariably using the state apparatus as a regulatory mechanism to impose the guidelines within which the new procedures should operate. However, there has also been some movement from the bottom up within universities (invariably initiated at the departmental level), which fudges the distinction between public and private funding. In order to sustain their research activities, some departments have sought private funding to sustain their work, which may incorporate the provision of scholarships for graduate students hired to undertake some of the research. In some cases, this has resulted in the intervention of the university intent on regulating such activities in order to preserve its interests (its good name and payment for the use of university-owned facilities). Such developments not only blur the distinction between private and public funding but also could possibly bind higher education institutions more closely to the economic structure, which would have widespread political, although not necessarily, academic support.

A key consideration in the relationship between the university and the market is how much independence the higher education institutions have in forging that relationship? With respect to the possible imposition of tuition fees we want to know whether there is something of a free market with universities imposing their own fee levels which they could possibly vary by academic programme and year of study. Or is the fee structure imposed by the state? If there is at least a measure of discretion that the university can employ, then how does it decide on fee levels? Are mechanisms employed to determine accurately the costs of running programmes? Is there a temptation to maximize profits? Is cross-subsidisation a possibility so that profitable programmes can help to subsidize unprofitable programmes? Why are degree programmes terminated? Are degree programmes ever terminated because they are financially unprofitable to run? While private funding may help higher education institutions to escape the possible constraints of public funding, does it not also impose its own burdens? In particular do the demands of managing a university effectively take precedence over the sustaining of quality academic programmes? In a nutshell, what is the basis for academic planning? Of course, whether privately or publicly funded, this is always an issue with which universities have had to grapple but one can anticipate that institutions will behave differently in this respect if the decision is in part dependent upon their sources of funding. However, even when tuition costs are publicly funded an academic unit will need to sustain at least a stable student base if it is to remain viable but one suspects it may be more difficult to argue the case for sustenance if there is also an economic cost (possibly increasing over time) to its preservation. Moreover, it is likely that the introduction of new degree programmes is influenced at least in part by their presumed financial viability – that these are programmes likely to attract a sound, hopefully expanding, student base.

The politics of change

Historically, at least in those countries strongly influenced by western political values and exhibiting a strong measure of economic development, the political support for the public funding of higher education was most vigorously pursued by governments underwritten by social democratic values, although the consensus that saw the university as espousing a public good had much broader political support. In a world marked by increased demands upon the public purse and a stronger recognition of higher education as a private good, the university finds itself more isolated politically in part because the social democratic impulse has itself changed. Consequently, the support for the public funding of higher education is weaker and the outcomes more problematic.

We are, therefore, experiencing a time in which the university has a greater need to justify its public funding; it is no longer something that it can take more or less for granted. The university appears to have to demonstrate that it is a public good: that it is socially inclusive and offers opportunities to individuals from across the social spectrum, that it both serves the needs of and helps to develop the economy, and that it is a culturally innovative as well preserving force – looking forwards as well as backwards. The picture which is most likely to emerge is one in which a combination of public and private funding will prevail, that henceforth the university will be carried forward by a combination of the state as well as the market. And as a final reflection that states the sentiments of the editors of both this book and of the series, if not the chapter authors of this book, those universities that ignore this message, while they may not fail, nor will they prosper either academically or in terms that will serve the wider needs of their societies, let alone higher education.

2
Distance learning and the rise of the MOOCs
The more things change, the more they stay the same

ROBERTA MALEE BASSETT AND ALEX USHER

Some historical context

The history of higher education can be defined by a fascinating tension between the traditional and the innovative. Higher education is notorious for being conservative – committed to historic norms of operations and delivery, instruction and teaching modalities, student engagement, governance structures, academic hierarchies, physical spaces and campuses, etc. One is able to trace higher education back over a millennium into the past because there are some universal characteristics of higher education that serve as markers from institutions of the past to those of today. The endurance of traditional higher education makes it one of the oldest organizational models in existence.

Institutions of higher education – and their academic staffs and students in particular – are, on the other hand, regularly criticised for being too liberal. Universities have been spaces for radical thought, transformative ideas, and even revolutionary thinking. While the pedagogical and architectural models of universities may trace their origins back millennia, academic thought has pushed the boundaries of social acceptance for generations. Indeed, when governments and leaders feel threatened by movements against their power, one of the first organizational structures often to face their wrath is higher education. Academic freedom – freedom of teaching (Lehrfreiheit) and freedom of learning (Lernfreiheit) – has underpinned the modern university since its founding in Germany as inspired by Wilhelm von Humboldt in 1818. Such freedoms are understood today to be absolutely vital to the enterprise of higher education, but this does not mean that such freedoms do not remain fundamentally 'radical'. Governments around the world continue to seek ways to contain and control these freedoms – through financial controls, via limitations on hiring and firing and by codifying governance modalities in ever-changing laws on higher education, for example. There is no doubt that higher education – and its populace of critical thinkers and motivated students and staff – can be seen as threatening to the 'establishment'. Innovation and questioning the status quo remain foundational elements of higher education across the globe.

The form of the university

This recognizable, fundamental form with a constancy of evolution in ideas and institutional structures has, therefore, become an especially interesting concern with the rise of modern forms of delivery of instruction. Institutions of higher education have been in a state of perpetual evolution within their framing forms from their earliest iterations. From the days of the first western universities in Paris, Bologna and Oxford, institutions of higher learning featured learned men offering tutorials/lectures on philosophic questions to small groups of students from elite families. In time and as the economic, social and political environments began to require exposure to knowledge and information among a broader segment of society, courses developed in specialised fields of study.

Teaching became coupled with research, and the modern university was born in Berlin in 1818. Then, as the demand for access to higher learning expanded, diversification of mission and purpose created stratified and articulated systems of higher education, with institutions of varied curricular offerings, degree awarding, and research capacity forming broad systems of post-secondary opportunities. The introduction of 'A Master Plan for Higher Education of California: 19601975'[1] provided one of the most comprehensives and innovative structures for codifying, rationalizing and optimizing a diversified yet integrated and articulated system of higher education institutions. Featuring institutions with fundamentally different missions as related to teaching and research – with funding and administrative models to match, the Master Plan serves as an illustration of a global tension between striking the appropriate balance between teaching and research in the delivery of elements of higher education.

This tension can be seen most acutely in the decades-long investigation into teaching students in non-traditional ways. Since the industrial revolution scholars and institutions have experimented with options for delivering instruction to students not present full-time on their physical campuses – via satellite campuses, travelling faculty, short-term programs with self-learning modalities in between teaching sessions. In the twentieth century, with its explosion in communication technology, the opportunities for reaching more students via distance modalities seemed nearly endless.

Independent and distance learning

> A good educational system should have three purposes: it should provide all who want to learn with access to available resources at any time in their lives; empower all who want to share what they know to find those who want to learn it from them; and, finally, furnish all who want to

present an issue to the public with the opportunity to make their challenge known . . .
Learners should not be forced to submit to an obligatory curriculum, or to discrimination based on whether they possess a certificate or a diploma. Nor should the public be forced to support . . . a huge professional apparatus of educators and buildings which in fact restricts the public's chances for learning. It should use modern technology to make free speech, free assembly, and a free press truly universal and, therefore, fully educational.

Ivan Illich. Deschooling Society[2]

With this, Illich captures the essence of the drive for distance learning and expanded access. Everyone should have the chance to learn when and what they want to learn, to share what they learn and to use that learning to whatever end they deem valuable. The radical environment of the 1960s and 1970s allowed for this concept to flourish in the push for alternatives to traditional higher education.

M.G. Moore (1973) presented one of the first comprehensive assessments of the history and promise of what he described as 'independent learning and teaching' (ILT) as a major initiative of modern higher education. His observations at the time remain prescient today[3]:

Independent Learning and Teaching is an education system in which the learner is autonomous and separated from his teacher in space and time, so that communication is by print, electronic or other non-human medium.
Independent learning and teaching is a system consisting of three sub-systems: a learner, a teacher and a method of communication . . . (T)o understand the teaching system, we must modify traditional concepts of teaching according to both the restraints and opportunities that are consequences of distance and autonomy.

(pp. 663)

In higher education, the University of Chicago established the first known major correspondence (ILT) program at an elite university in the United States in the late nineteenth century, though such early efforts of educators like William Rainey Harper (president of the University of Chicago at the time) were either ignored or ridiculed by similarly elite institutions in the US. These early forms of ILT, which were designed to provide educational opportunities for those who could not achieve admission nor afford full-time residence at an educational institution, was perceived as inferior education, undermining the status of elite universities such as the University of Chicago.

Many educators regarded – and continue to regard – correspondence courses as simply profit-drivers or ways for the institutions to make side money (not unlike perceptions of the open enrollment summer session, continuing education, or other non-degree programs offered at elite institutions today). Distance learning for a broader, more diverse, less elite student body was a democratization of higher education that was opposed by the entrenched elitism of traditional higher education at the time.[4] While quality assurance of the education product being delivered via indirect communication technologies (in the earliest days via post and in its current format of electronic media) remains a very real concern, educational opportunities for the broadest possible student population is fundamental to global democratic ideals, leading to a perpetual evolution of distance learning modalities.

Like Moore a decade earlier, Desmond Keegan (1980)[5] further identified six key elements of ILT/distance education:

- Separation of teacher and learner
- Influence of an educational organization
- Use of media to link teacher and learner
- Two-way exchange of communication
- Learners as individuals rather than grouped
- Education as an industrialized form

Interest in the possibilities of individualized distance learning continues to grow as the development of each new communication technology provides greater and potentially more enriching learning opportunities.

The technological revolutions of the postwar era amplified opportunities for non-traditional education delivery. According to the Handbook of Research for Education Communications and Technology (2001), radio and television were used in schools to deliver instruction at a distance from the 1920s, while the major expansion of distance education came with the advent of audio and computer teleconferencing. These new technologies have ultimately offered options for the delivery of instruction in public schools and higher education, among other economic activities. With the establishment of the Open University in Britain in 1969, opportunities for distance learning became increasingly attractive as genuine alternatives to traditional modes of higher education delivery[6] in the United Kingdom. Indeed, as noted by Juliana Marques (2013):

> An influence to many other ideas in the future, the Open University revitalized distance education because it combined correspondence instruction, supplementary broadcasting and publishing, residential short courses and support services at local and regional levels. Its founders believed communication technologies could be explored to provide high-quality degrees.[7]

The rapid development of computer- and mobile technology-related applications has captured the interest of the public and has been responsible for much of the attention being paid to certain distance educators – mainly those affiliated with major universities and/or Silicon Valley. Growth in the use of technology for distance education is not solely a western phenomenon, however as the global demand for expanded access to higher education has promoted the search for innovative approaches wherever possible. But, as with many education issues in the late twentieth and early twenty-first centuries, the US, UK and other western countries continue to command a central position in the global discourse on higher education – including the delivery of higher education through ever-changing modes of technology.

What are MOOCs?

With this historical perspective on the long-time search for effective and sustainable models of delivering higher education to as wide an audience of students as possible via ILT, distance learning ideas and opportunities have culminated today in the modality of the MOOC – Massive Open Online Courses. In the first decade of the twenty-first century, MOOCs became the latest trendy modality for distance education. Indeed, beginning in 2008, MOOCs became the hottest topic in disruptive innovations in higher education. Predictions began to emerge that MOOCs would utterly change the face of global higher education. As with every other technological innovation introduced into higher education in the preceding century, however, the results remain mixed and the future of MOOCs uncertain.

First, some background on MOOCs. The term MOOC originated in Canada in 2007, with the delivery of a course from the University of Manitoba to a campus-based class of twenty-five credit-seeking students and 2,300 online students, taking the course for their own edification.[8] Three years later, a Stanford instructor named Sebastian Thrun offered an online class in computer science which he dubbed a 'MOOC'; over 160,000 individuals signed up. This was, in fact, a notably different 'beast' than the Canadian MOOC of a few years earlier. It was a one-to-many broadcast enterprise rather than the more collaborative and constructivist approach of the Canadian version.[9] It also worked because, as a computer science class, there were objectively correct and incorrect answers that made automated marking of the coursework possible.

Based on some enthusiastic reviews of Thurn's course, MOOC numbers began to balloon. Thurn himself started a company called Udacity, which developed and delivered MOOCs on its own. Two other Stanford professors who had worked on Thrun's initial course started another company called Coursera. Their business model involved signing up prestigious universities to develop their own MOOCs and deliver them via the Coursera website. Finally, a third major platform, called EdX, emerged from a joint collaboration between MIT and Harvard. Other companies emerged in different parts of the world (notably, the UK's Open University's *FutureLearn*), but within 18 months of Thrun's experiment, there were these three globally-dominant players—

Udacity, Coursera and EdX—all based in the United States, each with a different ownership and operating model.

The MOOC phenomenon emerged coincidentally with the aftermath of the 2008 financial crisis, at a time when many governments were undergoing a period of austerity and in many cases enacting cuts to their higher education systems. There was, therefore, a great interest in a technology which promised to deliver higher education at a fraction of the cost at existing institutions. In the early days of MOOCs, the figures were impressive: Udacity founder Sebastian Thrun's original course at Stanford University enrolled more than 160,000 students, and in the first year or so course enrolments of 50,000 or more were common.[10] For cash-strapped governments, the potential of MOOCs to reduce delivery costs was enticing.

But, while the raw statistics were impressive, there were questions from the outset about who exactly was enrolling in these courses. The case for using MOOCs as a substitute for traditional delivery could be made effectively only if enrollees were traditional-aged students. Otherwise, it would be seen as a complementary but separate medium of delivery. In the early days, comprehensive data about student demographics and reliable statistics about MOOC enrolments were unavailable, because the companies and institutions whose platforms hosted the courses were mostly private and, therefore, not bound to release data to the public. Indeed, many providers were not required nor sought to collect demographic information like the age, gender and prior education of their students. Where such data did exist, it was collected on an ad hoc basis by host institutions. Eventually, however, some piece-meal evidence of enrollment patterns began to emerge.

The first significant data release of MOOC demographic data came in 2013, from the University of Pennsylvania, which at the time of release had offered thirty-two sessions of twenty-four unique courses through the Coursera platform, accounting for roughly 20 percent of all Coursera users to that point.[11] It consisted of the results of a voluntary survey which was emailed to all participants in those courses; 34,779 students responded to the survey, which made for a response rate of 8.5 percent. The data showed that nearly two-thirds of respondents were from outside the United States (a finding verified by an analysis of IP addresses). Within the United States, respondents were roughly equally split between men and women, but outside the US, the ratio was over 60–40 male, with the imbalance most pronounced in the BRICS – Brazil, Russia, India, China and South Africa – countries. But perhaps a more important discovery was that only about 10 percent of MOOC users were actually students, and that over 50 percent were employed full-time and that over 80 percent of all participants already had a degree. Half said they had enrolled in the course 'just for fun' while 44 percent said they were interested in gaining specific job-related skills.

Further evidence of this type came from a survey of US-based enrollees of EdX MOOC courses offered by Harvard University in 2014.[12] Correlating enrolment information with information from the American Community Survey, this paper determined that MOOC users were from neighbourhoods which were substantially more affluent than the national average. They also noted that MOOC users tended to come from families with much higher levels of parental education. In sum, MOOC enrollees looked somewhat different from the core traditional higher education population: on average, they were older, wealthier and more likely to be male.

On its own, this finding was not enough to make MOOC enthusiasts think twice about the potential of MOOCs to be put into more general use. Rather, it was the growing awareness of the rate of MOOC completions that changed the conversation about MOOCs. As it turned out, a very large percentage of people who 'enrolled' in a MOOC never actually participated in the course. One of the first explorations of this phenomenon came from a Duke University course on bioelectricity offered in the fall of 2012[13]. Of the 12,725 students who enrolled in the course, only 7761 (61 percent) even opened the first video and 3658 (29 percent) ever took a quiz. By the 5th week of the course, fewer than 1000 enrollees were opening the videos, and in the end just 313 (2 percent) passed the final exam and earned a certificate. A larger survey of MIT and Harvard-based MOOCs a few months[14] later put certification results a little higher (in the 5–6 percent range), but otherwise revealed similar patterns. A broader study conducted in 2015 aggregating data for multiple platforms showed an average completion rate of about 12 percent, with substantially higher completion rates in courses that were fully auto-graded (i.e. courses which exclusively use multiple-choice grading, and which tend to be used in science and engineering fields) than those which were not. This was a major issue in the policy debate about MOOCs. Public investment to achieve course enrolments in the tens of thousands appeared sound; public investment in courses with 5 percent completion rates, less so.

A live 'experiment' in the use of MOOCs for teaching students-at-risk definitely changed the debate about MOOCs within the United States, however. In January 2013, Udacity signed a deal with San Jose State University (SJSU) to provide on-line delivery of three mathematics courses traditionally taught in-person. Students received a substantial discount (the cost per course was $150) and – unlike most MOOCs – students would receive university credit for completing the courses.[15] Within 6 months the experiment was called off, however, citing poor results. A report from *Inside Higher Ed* at the time suggested that pass rates in the online version of the course were almost one-third lower than in the classroom version.[16] It was this failure, in part, which drove Udacity to get out of the business of delivering degree-level courses in partnership with major universities. Thrun at the time said that, 'these were students from difficult neighbourhoods without good access to computers, and with all kinds of challenges in their lives. It's a group for which this medium is not a good fit'.[18]

The poor results of MOOCs among disadvantaged students should not have come as a surprise. At roughly the same time of this Udacity-SJSU experiment with MOOC delivery, Columbia University' Teachers College released the results from two studies, which provided significant evidence that students with lower levels of academic preparation were much more likely to drop-out of online courses.[18] The reason was obvious: students with lower levels of social capital and academic preparedness need support to complete their studies. They need close contact with teachers and peers to obtain the knowledge needed to navigate and complete courses. By the very nature of delivery, this is more difficult to achieve in an online environment rather than a physical one. In a MOOC, where the student-teacher ratio is in the thousands or tens of thousands, it is impossible. Even those studies which were most positive about the results of online education (and in which teacher-student contact was much higher than it is in MOOCs), the data still identified negative impacts for lower-performing students.[19]

Apart from the inherent limitations of online education with respect to disadvantaged students, as mentioned above, the value-proposition being offered to students via MOOCs is also a major challenge concerning uptake and expansion. MOOC platforms promoted their courses as being offered by prestigious universities, but this was offset by the fact that there was no recognizable credential attached to the learning. Students might receive certificates if they paid a small fee, but the certificates were essentially meaningless, since the external environment for MOOC courses and credentials – the labour market and other educational institutions in particular, had no basis for recognising the learning outcomes from the MOOC courses. Not only would they not be recognized for credit by a local university, but the institution which offered the course did not offer degree-program credit either.[20] It was something of a catch-22: students could only be attracted to MOOCs if prestigious universities' names were attached, but, precisely because they were prestigious, they would not countenance offering credit to simply anyone who signed up for a course on the internet. Even the development of more sophisticated proctoring services,[21] designed to eliminate the possibility of fraudulent test-taking, did not alter these institutions' stance.

MOOCs continued to evolve after 2013 and in some ways began to hybridize into slightly more fit-for-purpose entities. MIT created a 'micro-Masters MOOC' in Supply Chain Management. Individuals could take the series of courses for free, or for a small fee opt to pay to join a certificate stream. Those who obtained a certificate also received the right to enrol at MIT for one semester in order to obtain a full Master's degree.[22] The Georgia Institute of Technology's Computer Science Department partnered with Udacity and AT & T to create an online 'MOOC' version of its existing Master's program, which had about 300 students.[23] The new version, which was lightly selective, cost $7,000 compared to $45,000 for the in-person version and ended up enrolling 1700 students (70 percent of whom were American). Subsequent analysis of application data by Harvard researchers using data from the National Student Clearinghouse showed that most of the MOOC participants did not apply to any other school, meaning that it was demonstrably expanding opportunity to people who would otherwise not have access to this kind of education.[24]

Neither of these success stories were necessarily endorsements of MOOCs as alternative delivery vehicles, however. The Georgia State MOOC was a MOOC in name only, since it both cost a significant amount of money and had entry selection criteria. The MIT mini-Master's had open enrolment, but attaining the real credential still depended on attending MIT and paying $40,000. This is not to deny the considerable success of either program; it is, however, notable that their success cannot be translated to a 'traditional' understanding of MOOCs as a whole. Specifically, their advantage seems to lie in the fact that they cost a great deal of money (which is used to provide services such as direct interaction with instructors) and that they provide real credentials. In sum, they succeed because they exhibit some key characteristics of traditional on-campus and online programs and not like the idealised version of MOOCs.

The future of MOOCs

MOOCs clearly have some successes worth noting. Mainly, they fulfill a market niche for cheap continuing education and accessing education opportunities from formerly inaccessible elite institutions. The cache of courses from an Ivy League or similarly respected institution was the initial draw. But, the practicality of the medium has become increasingly important. MOOCs for professional development and lifelong learning are building in relevance. Adults with degrees looking to pick up a particular skill are well served by the medium, as are people who simply wish to learn something for enjoyment (the so-called 'edu-tainment' market). . . .

Moreover, corporations and industrial fields are also looking to MOOCs to fill a learning and training gap. 'Tech sector corporations like Microsoft, AT&T, and Comcast play an increasing role in this proliferation of MOOC providers and technical skills-based courses, as they have begun designing, creating, and using MOOCs with employee learning in mind . . . AT&T, Microsoft, and McKinsey & Company (are) already show(ing) promise in these arenas (of utilising internal MOOCs for professional development), as completion rates for their corporate MOOCs are either at or above 80 percent'.[25] At a time when labour market surveys repeatedly show employer dissatisfaction with the skills of post-secondary education graduates (while concurrently decreasing corporate spending on traditional on-the-job training modalities), MOOCs may just be one potential tool for promoting greater productivity among workers.[26]

Perhaps in the future, if systems for measuring specific competencies come to augment (or perhaps supplant) the current degree system, then MOOCs might come to be seen as an excellent delivery vehicle for smaller, competency-based credentials. And there is no doubt that many of them produce course material which is exciting, entertaining and delivered in a novel way. If they were openly available as a form of Open Education Resource, they would no doubt be enormously useful to students across the globe, particularly in the developing world where access to materials of this quality is limited.

> The advent of Massive Open Online Courses was accompanied by enormous enthusiasm about their potential to democratize access to high-quality education in poor countries. But it wasn't long before MOOC hype gave way to MOOC hate, or at least intense skepticism, from critics who see these free online courses as poorly tailored to non-Western cultures and even as instruments of neocolonialism.[27]

This debate still rages, as to how valid a mode of deliver MOOCs can be for those outside of the western centre of higher education. To date, MOOCs have been western courses developed by western faculty for a majority western student population. And while mega-universities exist in the developing, lower-middle to lower income countries (such as in Turkey and Thailand, for instance), the delivery of courses via a MOOC platform requires a level of infrastructure and technology that remains somewhat challenging to countries with lower levels of development. So, with the western prevalence of MOOC course development and delivery came a push-back on the idea of MOOCs as a mechanism for expanded access to higher education.

Notwithstanding issues around neo-colonialism and 'who owns knowledge',[28] MOOCs are conceivably a way to extend education at very low cost in developing countries. The delivery of education outside physical educational institutions is nothing new to developing countries, which often have large, developed open universities of their own. In fact, from the human capital point of view, MOOCs can be seen as a step backwards because for the most part they do not ladder into a credential of value as courses offered by national distance education providers do. But undoubtedly they convey some types of course material in a much more attractive way than local courses do, and they often have very prestigious names attached to the courses (if not a credential), and this makes them attractive to a certain type of students: statistics from all major MOOC providers show a very large proportion of students coming from India and other low-income countries.

The challenge is turning this novel and free form of instruction into a credential of value. One experiment by a Rwandan NGO, Kepler, shows one potential way to establish MOOCs as the instrument for achieving more traditional outcomes. Kepler advises students on how to put together a set of MOOCs in such a way that the student can pass 'challenge' exams for competency-based degrees, such as those offered by places like Southern New Hampshire University (SNHU) in the United States. The MOOCs can be delivered by any provider; Kepler's role is to create a coherent curriculum out of the many hundreds of MOOCs on offer, and SNHU's role is to certify that competencies have been obtained. If more developing countries were able to come up with their own challenge-based exams to obtain credit or even degrees in the manner of China[29] or South Korea[30], then it would be easier to see MOOCs as a pathway to credentials and possibly a way of reducing the cost of higher education delivery thereby expanding access, at least for some students.

MOOCs will remain tools which appeal mostly to policymakers and entrepreneurs with eyes on cost savings and achieving desired education outcomes. Utilisation of innovations for education reform are as dynamic an influence on policymakers as has been witnessed at any time in the history of global education reform. Though quantifiable returns to MOOCs remain elusive for key stakeholder groups, a sense of optimism remains that this particular innovation will bring solutions to a sector facing reduced public financial support at a time of explosive demand for access to all of the benefits from higher education. On a spectrum of options for reforms and innovations, MOOCs remain a vibrant opportunity awaiting proof of its long-term viability.

In terms of participation in MOOCs, people with at least some degree of auto-didacticism will remain its core student base. But, higher education needs to cater to a wider audience than this. The evidence flatly suggests that the students who benefit least or outright lose in a switch to online or MOOC learning are students from poorer, less-privileged backgrounds: precisely the people that public policy on higher education should be doing the most to assist. MOOCs may have their place in a wide lifelong learning eco-system, but they cannot replace the core functions of physical educational institutions—particularly for those most in need of the benefits afforded by achieving further education. As has been true throughout the history of expanded education opportunities, establishing a genuine balance between known education delivery models and innovation in education remains the key to serving the broadest possible stakeholder community—students, institutions, the economy and society.

Notes

1 Kerr, C. and the Master Plan Survey Team. (1960) 'A master plan for higher education of California: 1960–1975'. Downloaded 3 February 2017 from http://ucop.edu/acadinit/mastplan/MasterPlan1960.pdf
2 Illich, I. (1971) 'Deschooling society'. Downloaded 17 February 2017 from http://ournature.org/~novembre/illich/1970_deschooling.html (Quotes from Chapter 6).
3 Moore, M.G. (December 1973). Toward a theory of independent learning and teaching, Journal of Higher Education, XLIV(12): 661–679.
4 Pittman, V. (1991) 'Rivalry for respectability: collegiate and proprietary correspondence programs,' in *Second American symposium on research in distance education*, University Park, PA: Pennsylvania State University.
5 Keegan, D. (1980) 'On defining distance education', *Distance Education*, 1(1): 13–36.
6 The Association for Educational Communications and Technology. (2001). The handbook of research for education communication and technology. Downloaded 24 January 2017, from http://www.aect.org/edtech/ed1/13/13-02.html

7 Marques, J. (2013). A short history of MOOCs and distance learning. Downloaded 20 February from http://moocnewsandreviews.com/a-short-history-of-moocs-and-distance-learning/
8 Daniel, S.J. (2012) 'Making sense of MOOCs: musings in a maze of myth, paradox and possibility', *Journal of Interactive Media in Education*, Downloaded from http://jime.open.ac.uk/2012/18.
9 Bates, A.W. (2015) *Teaching in a digital age: Guidelines for designing teaching and learning*, Vancouver, BC: Tony Bates and Associates
10 Waldrop, M.M. (2013) 'Online leaning: Campus 2.0' *Nature*, 14 March 2013. Downloaded from https://scientificamerican.com/article/massive-open-online-courses-transform-higher-education-and-science/ (accessed 26 March 2017).
11 Christensen, G., Steinmetz, A., Alcorn, B., Bennett, A., Woods, D. and Emanuel, E.J., 'The MOOC phenomenon: who takes massive open online courses and why? Downloaded 18 November 2016 from SSRN: https://ssrn.com/abstract=2350964 (accessed 6 November 2013).
12 Hansen, J.and Reich, J. (2014) 'Socioeconomic status and MOOC enrolment: enriching demographic information with external datasets. Paper delivered at the fifth international learning analytics and knowledge conference, 2014'. Downloaded 26 March 2017 from http://harvardx.harvard.edu/files/harvardx/files/ses_and_mooc_enrollment_lak_colloquium_hx_working_paper_submission3.pdf
13 Belanger Y and Thornton J (2013) 'Bioelectricity: a quantitative approach'. Downloaded 26 March 2017 from http://dukespace.lib.duke.edu/dspace/bitstream/handle/10161/6216/Duke_Bioelectricity_MOOC_Fall2012.pdf
14 Ho, A.D., Reich, J., Nesterko, S., Seaton, D.T., Mullany, T., Waldo, J. and Chuang, I. (2014) HarvardX and MITx: the first year of open online courses (HarvardX and MITx Working paper no.1) Downloaded from https://papers.ssrn.com/sol3/papers.cfm?abstract_id=2381263 (accessed 27 March 2017).
15 Fain, P. (2013) 'As California goes' Inside higher ed, 16 January 2013 downloaded from https://insidehighered.com/news/2013/01/16/california-looks-moocs-online-push (accessed 26 March 2017)
16 Rivard, R. (2103) 'Udacity project on pause' Inside higher ed, 18 July 2013. Available online at www.insidehighered.com/news/2013/07/18/citing-disappointing-student-outcomes-san-jose-state-pauses-work-udacity
17 Chafkin, M. (2017)'Udacity's Sebastian Thrun, Godfather of free online education, changes course. Fast Company', December 2013/January 2014. Downloaded from https://fastcompany.com/3021473/udacity-sebastian-thrun-uphill-climb March 26
18 Xu, D. and Smith, J. S. (2014), *Adaptability to online learning: Differences across types of students and academic subject areas*, Columbia University.Teachers College Community College Research Centre Working Paper No. 54 downloaded from http://ccrc.tc.columbia.edu/publications/adaptability-to-online-learning.html(accessed 28 March 2017).
19 Joyce, T.J., Crockett, S., Jaeger, D.A., Altindag, O. and Connel, O. D. *Does Classroom Time Matter? A Randomized Field Experiment of Hybrid and Traditional Lecture Formats in* Economics. NBER Working Paper no.20006. Downloaded from http://nber.org/papers/w20006 (accessed 2 April 2017).
20 There was one exception here: namely, Colorado State University. CSU announced . . . . A of X, no student had actually taken them up on the offer.
21 Kolowich, S. (2012) 'MOOCing on site' Inside higher ed 7 September 2012. Downloaded from https://insidehighered.com/news/2012/09/07/site-based-testing-deals-strengthen-case-granting-credit-mooc-students on March 28, 2017
22 Massachusetts Institute of Technology (2016) 'New MicroMaster's MOOC teaches supply chain design'. Downloaded from http://news.mit.edu/2016/micromasters-supply-chain-management-program-0516(accessed 28 March 2017).
23 Carey, K (2016) 'An online education breakthrough? A Master's Degree for a mere $7,000' New York Times 28 September 2016. Available online at www.nytimes.com/2016/09/29/upshot/an-online-education-breakthrough-a-masters-degree-for-a-mere-7000.html

24 Goodman, J., Melkers, J. and Pallais, A. (2016) 'Can online delivery increase access to education? Faculty research working paper series RWP 16–035'. Downloaded from https://research.hks.harvard.edu/publications/workingpapers/citation.aspx?PubId=11348&type=WPN (accessed 27 March 2017).
25 Online Course Report (2016). 'State of the MOOC 2016: a year of massive landscape change for massive open online courses'. Downloaded 15 April 2017, from http://onlinecoursereport.com/state-of-the-mooc-2016-a-year-of-massive-landscape-change-for-massive-open-online-courses/
26 McGowan, M.A. and Andrews, D. (2015). 'Labour market mismatch and Labour productivity: evidence from PIAAC data economics department working papers no. 1209 OECD'. Downloaded 15 April 2017 from https://oecd.org/eco/growth/Labour-Market-Mismatch-and-Labour-Productivity-Evidence-from-PIAAC-Data.pdf
27 Wildavsky, B. (2014) 'Evolving toward significance or MOOC ado about nothing?'. Downloaded 15 April 2017, from http://www.nafsa.org/_/File/_/ie_mayjun14_forum.pdf.
28 Altbach, P. (2013) 'MOOCs as neocolonialism: who controls knowledge' in *Chronicle of Higher Education* 4 December 2013.
29 Latchem, C. and Xinzheng, L. (1999) 'China's higher education examinations for self-taught learners"' *Open Learning: the Journal of Open, Distance and e-Learning*, 14(3).
30 Usher, A. (2014) The Korean academic credit-bank: A model for credit transfer in North America? Toronto: Higher Education Strategy Associates.

3
The ecology of state higher-education policymaking in the US

JAMES C. HEARN AND ERIK C. NESS

Nearly a century ago, US Supreme Court Justice Louis Brandeis observed that, in their freedom to create and implement policies independently of their peers, the country's individual states can serve as separate and independent 'laboratories of democracy'. The metaphor applies aptly in the case of tertiary education. The fifty US states exhibit remarkable diversity in the ways they organize, govern and fund higher education. These variations shape state actions affecting colleges and universities. This essay draws on existing research to present a conceptual framework for understanding and investigating the factors driving states' distinct approaches. The framework highlights four critical classes of influence: a state's socio-economic context, its organizational and policy context, its politico-institutional context and its external context.

Critical in these distinctions is the degree to which individual states rely on the workings of markets, private non-governmental actors and decentralized authority for coordination and direction of their tertiary systems. Although the US as a whole has, by almost any measure, one of the most privatized systems of higher education in the world, this orientation plays out distinctively in each individual state owing to significant intrastate contextual differences. The essay concludes with consideration of the factors driving these variations and their implications in the face of changing international attitudes and expectations for higher education.

The fraught notion of 'System' in US higher education

In a formal legal sense, the phrase 'higher-education system' conveys worldwide an association with governmental control, oversight and coordination. Thus, most nations employ ministries of education to make critical policy and budgetary choices and ensure quality and accountability to citizens. These central education agencies have formal authority established in law and regulations if not in national constitutions, and exhibit substantial power in steering countries' efforts in education across the continuum from pre-primary to post-degree levels. To be sure, there is some movement worldwide towards decreasing educational centralization (Schugurensky, 1999; McLendon and Hearn, 2009), in keeping with broader trends in public management (Bozeman, 2007). Still, the absence of substantial formal, national authority in higher education is rare (Hearn, Warshaw and Ciarimboli, 2016).

Nations vary extensively in the extent to which they establish and empower higher-education authority at the subnational (provincial) level. Germany stands as an example of a nation with notable authority at both levels, mixing and integrating two forms of governance. The United States, however, is distinctive in its heavy reliance on subnational (i.e. state) authority. The US constitution does not mention education, thus effectively leaving to the individual constituting states this important responsibility. With no formal national system of higher education,[1] each of the fifty states has established publicly supported institutions and systems and maintained some form of control over them (Glenny, 1959).

Even at the state level, however, authority is highly variable. States take disparate approaches to structuring and governing their institutional arrays. As will be discussed later in this chapter, those variations play significant roles in policy agendas and choices. In many states, the extent of the states' legal authority falls very far short of what would be typical for a national ministry of education.

In the absence of both national authority and consistent significant state authority, and in the presence of large numbers of non governmental (private) institutions, is the notion of 'system' apropos in any sense to US higher education? After all, US higher education lies towards the lowest end on any continuum of formalized national centralization (Ben-David, 1992). And, non-governmental actors play large roles in the governance of state-supported public institutions (McGuiness, 2011, 2016), buffering those schools somewhat from political and agency influences (McLendon and Hearn, 2009). Still, a nation's higher education efforts can be controlled and coordinated through means other than formal bureaucratic mechanisms at the national and provincial levels.

The sociologist Burton Clark (1979, 1983) observed four 'pathways' for control and coordination of higher education: bureaucratic, professional, political and market. In the US, voluntary professional monitoring is long established and legitimized as a means of quality control: powerful accrediting organizations and disciplinary associations largely have substituted for a significant governmental role in quality control. Similarly, while national and state political leaders have historically used what has been called 'the bully pulpit' to persuade and shame colleges and universities into favoured directions, institutions have remained largely shielded from the ebbs and flows of different political views.[2] It is the fourth of Clark's forms, the market, that has been and remains the dominant force in establishing and maintaining systemic qualities in US higher education. The nation continues to rely more on competitive markets for students, faculty and funding than on national or subnational governments to steer higher education.

These features of US higher education are distinctive internationally, but are not disqualifying for the designation of 'system'. The US abides under a socially constructed and highly institutionalized set of agreements and norms around higher education, changing organically rather than by central fiat (Meyer et al., 2007). One may view this approach as a model to be emulated or to be avoided, but it merits consideration as a system.

By definition, a more marketized and less bureaucratically driven system will attend especially closely to developments 'on the ground'. Importantly, the supply of education needs to be attuned closely to the contemporary demand for it, rather than determined philosophically or politically by removed government agents. The nation's population diversity and size demand extensive market variation and market segmentation in higher education, and institutions must adapt efficiently to shifts in these markets. Market differentiation is necessarily geographic and political, reinforcing the nation's allegiance to preserving state authority and control in education. Because the states are more sensitive to local market conditions than national agencies, they are central in expressing the public will in higher education. And, in turn, because institutions within states are most sensitive of all to their own students' goals and behaviours, it makes sense that most states have historically allowed substantial institutional autonomy (Glenny, 1959; Berdahl, 1971).

There are some clouds emerging around this deeply engrained conception of the US higher-education system, however. The nation's traditional commitment to state authority and the states' traditional commitment to some level of institutional autonomy appear to be coming into conflict with rising national concern over post-secondary quality and accountability (Schmidtlein and Berdahl, 2011). Both federal and state governments are shifting from their more historically comfortable role of *encouraging* educational improvements, via goal-setting, planning, creating task forces and establishing incentives, to a newer, more aggressive commitment to *intervening* (Hearn and Holdsworth, 2002; Newfield, 2016). Witness, for example, recent efforts by the Bush and Obama presidential administrations to assert greater federal quality oversight and control through implementing academic progress standards for students and institutions that receive student financial aid (e.g. see Smith, 2015).

Interestingly, however, the encourager role appears to be expanding alongside the intervener role. Some states have begun to tie institutional funding more directly to student outcomes (intervening), but many of those allowing individual institutions more discretion in how they act to achieve goals set under state outcomes-based funding, in how they set tuition levels and the like (encouraging) (McLendon and Hearn, 2009; Hearn, 2015). These disparate developments suggest that characterizing trends in coordination, control and privatization in US higher education will continue to be challenging. The US unquestionably has a system of higher education, but the varied actors involved help ensure that holistically characterizing its evolution will remain a daunting task.

The fifty states: heightened privatization, accountability and tension

In the less bureaucratically driven US higher-education system, the fifty states constitute the most significant source of public support for educational operations (Zumeta, 2001). All states have private colleges receiving little or no direct public support, and in fact the country has more private non-profit institutions than public institutions. But all states also have public (state-supported) institutions, and these institutions enrol a majority of all US students. In those public sectors, taxpayer-based funding is the dominant source of revenues.[3] In the US, the federal government provides major support for student financial aid and for research/contract funding, and it enforces a number of equity and safety regulations on campuses, but it does not fund basic educational operations of institutions. That funding comes from the states.

Each of the states provides citizens an array of public institutional options. Most visible are the states' 'flagship' universities, such as the Universities of California, Wisconsin, Texas and the like, but the majority of students in most states attend comprehensive state colleges, 2-year community colleges and technical-vocational institutions. States typically devise distinctive funding approaches for each of their public institutional sectors, and typically play varied roles in maintaining and improving efficiency, equity and effectiveness in the sectors (McGuinness, 2016).

State efforts in tertiary education are currently under enormous pressure (Perna *et al.*, 2014). In constant 2014 US dollars, state funding per full-time equivalent [FTE] student hit its peak in 1987–1988 at over $10,000 and has not approached such heights again – most recent data suggest it currently is under $8000 (College Board, 2016b). The number of FTE students increased from almost seven million in 1984 to nearly 11 million in 2014, but state funding has kept pace with neither rising student demand nor increasing institutional costs in providing educational services (*ibid.*). In response, institutions have raised tuition and fees dramatically. As schools have increasingly turned to students to finance their operations, they have reinforced the notion of education as a private, rather than public, good (Desrochers and Hurlburt, 2016).

Together, these trends have brought decreasing state stakes in public higher education. Former University of Michigan president James Duderstadt (2000: 312) observed only half-jokingly that we are seeing movement from 'state-supported' to 'state-assisted' to merely 'state-located' institutions. Indeed, many states have granted increasing autonomy to public colleges and universities, offering latitude in decision making on tuition, programming and the like in exchange for less direct state financial support. Most prominent of these moves are those in the state of Virginia (Leslie and Berdahl, 2008; Pusser, 2008).

This movement towards disinvestment and sometimes decentralization has come with strings attached, however. As Zumeta and Kinne (2011) have noted, long-past are the times when states left lump-sums of money at higher education's doorstep with few questions asked. Instead, declining governmental funding and increasing autonomy have usually been coupled with heightened accountability for funds received (Woodhouse, 2016). For example, public colleges and universities may be allowed to set higher tuition and fee rates to make up for decreased state funding, but to maintain their discretion they must demonstrate outcomes that serve the public good as perceived by lawmakers.

Most prominent in the new pressures on state institutions are those associated with performance or outcomes-based funding (Burke and Associates, 2005; Hearn, 2015; Snyder and Fox, 2016; Dougherty et al., 2016). The movement to tie state allocations to institutions' measurable performance on key metrics is not new, but increasing numbers of states are increasing the proportion of state operating funds distributed this way, to the point that some are tying as much as 100 percent to such indicators as student graduation rates, numbers of graduates produced in scientific, technical, engineering and mathematical [STEM] fields, and student job placement. Conservative-leaning states have been especially likely to impose such regimes on higher-education institutions (McLendon, Hearn and Deaton, 2006) and the recent surge in Republican control of state governorships and legislatures suggests the trend toward this form of funding is likely to continue.

Writ large, there is a clear trend towards states firmly emphasizing and strengthening the ties between the marketplace and higher education. Whatever bureaucratic control and coordination remains at the state level attends more than ever to serving a market-centred neo-liberal ethic. These developments constitute simultaneous movement towards accountability and privatization, i.e. the framing of institutional and system goals in economic terms; prioritizing student, service and labour markets; transferring formerly governmental authority and decision-making to markets; and corporatizing institutional finance in the direction of cost-sensitive pricing, contingent faculty hiring, responsibility-centred budgeting and revenue-centred structural innovation.[4]

Arguably, the trends towards accountability and privatization may threaten the nation's historic commitment to using public higher education to serve the public good as well as private needs. Since the nineteenth century, public colleges and universities in the US have maintained commitments to producing widely and deeply informed democratic citizens and providing access to all segments of the population in pursuit of all kinds of degrees (Thelin, 2004). With tuitions rising, along with student indebtedness to cover those charges, and with institutions newly incentivized towards admitting and graduating students with especially strong prospects of graduating and contributing to economic development, state investments have begun to tilt towards rewarding students and institutions for attention to practical fields paying the best salaries. Conversely, state support for enrolments in the humanities and such lower-paying helping professions as teaching and social work is shrinking dramatically. In parallel, states' movements towards privatization and accountability may be fostering heightened stratification among students, faculty, fields and institutions (Hearn, Warshaw and Ciarimboli, 2016).

Conceptualizing influences on state higher education policymaking

States do not make their policy choices in vacuums. For example, while almost all states may be moving towards greater attention to accountability, any given state's particular approaches are shaped by a rich mix of historical precedents, prominent personalities, socio-economic conditions, political and cultural leanings, structural constraints, existing policies and the like. The different choices of, say, California and Mississippi, are directed in good part by the startlingly different contexts of those two states. In any state, a new crop of legislators and a new governor rarely imply a dramatically new set of policies, or even a new set of concerns. Instead, policymaking in the states, even in the face of significant ideological or economic shifts, remains constrained by the distinct contexts from which these decisions emerge. We examine those underlying themes in the next section.

In Figure 3.1, we present a framework for considering how conditions within individual states and at the intersections among states may shape policymaking in those settings. Our model conceives of state policy innovation and change as being a product of four distinct sets of forces: (1) the socio-economic contexts of states; (2) the organizational and policy contexts of states; (3) the politico-institutional contexts of states; and, 4) the external contexts of states. Within each area of influence, we employ existing research findings to theorize how specific factors may shape the policies that states consider and choose. Ideally, this discussion will highlight the ways that individual state contexts can moderate and contextually tailor larger national trends toward privatization.

Socio-economic context

A state's demography, educational and economic conditions, play ongoing roles in shaping governmental behaviour. A poorly educated workforce and high unemployment rates, for example, create pressures and priorities on lawmakers and thereby can elevate some potential policy choices while moving others off the table.

Population demography plays a key role in shaping state post-secondary policy outcomes in a number of important respects. The state policy innovation research literature consistently finds that more populous states often adopt programmes and policies of greater technical sophistication (Mohr, 1969; Walker, 1969; Berry and Berry, 1990). In the domain of higher-education policy, it follows that more populous states will have greater need for integrated, longitudinal student unit-record systems – such databases track students across

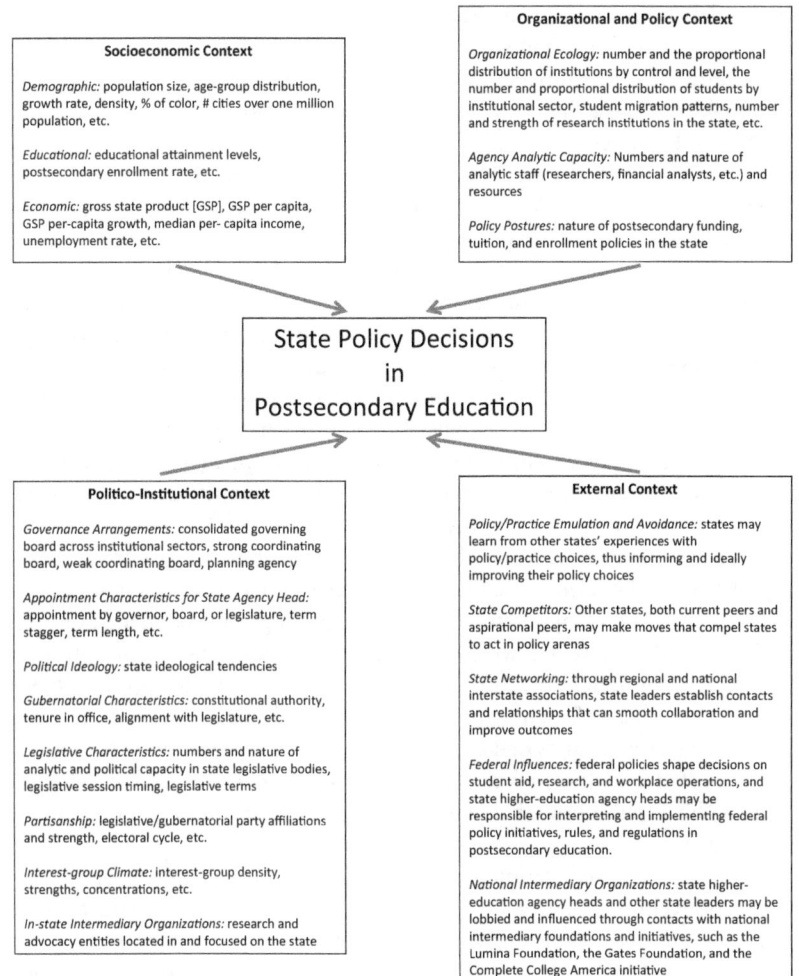

Figure 3.1 The ecology of state higher-education policymaking

all levels and sites on their educational experiences, and thus can help those states address the complexities of larger numbers of students and institutions (e.g. Hearn, McLendon and Mokher, 2008).

The age-group distribution of a state's population can also affect policymaking processes and choices. Work by Doyle (2006) and Tandberg and Ness (2011), for example, suggest that the youthfulness of a state's population can influence state post-secondary policymaking. Beyond size and age distributions, factors such as population growth rate, population density, urban city and racial-ethnic diversity may also be influential. States with large cities may need more commuter-institution spaces, fewer residence halls, and more corporate partnerships than states with few urban centres.

Educational characteristics of the state population can also shape state policymaking. These influences are exerted on both the 'supply' and the 'demand' side. States with a highly educated citizenry benefit from improved economic competitiveness. The growing 'knowledge economy' rests on knowledge production and management and information technologies, and since the 1980s many US state governments have been prioritizing human-capital formation over traditional 'smokestack chasing' (Hearn, Lacy and Warshaw, 2014). In this competition, states with less educated citizenries will tend to lose against more educated states. States' broad-based merit-scholarship programmes are an example of a higher-education policy innovation aimed at enriching a state's supply of human capital (see Hearn and Griswold, 1994; Heller, 2002; Doyle, 2006; Doyle, McLendon and Hearn, 2010). Such programmes represent a shift towards privatization in that they direct state educational support towards economic development rather than towards serving equity or other social ends.

On the 'demand' side, levels of educational attainment in a state can shape the preferences of citizens for education as well as other governmental services. Lower levels of education lead to higher demands for governmentally supported healthcare and welfare services, while higher levels of education appear to stimulate economic activity, thus raising tax revenues and also appear to lessen criminal activity, thus lessening prison costs (McMahon, 2009). In these senses, educational characteristics of a state fundamentally drive not only the kinds of leaders elected and the higher education policies considered and adopted, but also the capabilities of a state to progress educationally, socially and economically.

In shaping higher-educational policymaking, states' economic characteristics can play roles closely tied to states' demographic and educational characteristics. Among the state economic factors, most often considered influential are gross state product [GSP], GSP per-capita, GSP per-capita growth, median per-capita income and the unemployment rate. There is longstanding evidence from the political science literature that solid economic health may expand state expenditures on education and other outcomes and, conversely, economic privation (e.g. declines in gross product or employment rates) can stimulate policy change (e.g. see Dye, 1966). There is also mixed evidence that economic health may facilitate policy innovation (e.g., Berry and Berry, 2014). In higher education in particular, economic disadvantage may lead to state policy experimentation in such arenas as merit-scholarship programs (Doyle, 2006), state-funded eminent scholars policies (Hearn, McLendon and Lacy, 2013), and research and development tax credits (Hearn, Lacy and Warshaw, 2014). Thus, the effects of economic conditions may be contingent: ample fiscal resources may be a precondition for certain reforms while economic disadvantage may prompt other kinds of reforms. State economic well-being not only directly constrains what a state can do – it may also have indirect effects, via lawmakers' sense of comparative advantage or disadvantage relative to other states. In keeping with the focus of this chapter, there is good reason to argue that policymakers' concerns over competitive economic contexts are rising while their concerns over social inequalities and other targets of educational spending are declining, in keeping with overall trends toward privatization.

Organizational and policy context

As noted earlier, states vary significantly in the ways they structure their tertiary offerings and the approaches they take to considering, developing and implementing policies. These variations can be important influences on state governmental behaviour. Here, we focus on three prominent dimensions of states' organizational and policy contexts: organizational ecology, agency analytic capacity and policy postures.

Each state has a distinctive organizational ecology. Most visibly, states differ in their numbers and kinds of institutions. For example, states in the northeastern and midwestern parts of the country tend to have higher proportions of private institutions, while those in the plains and mountainous states of the west tend to rely much more heavily on public institutions for delivering higher education. Similarly, such states as Arizona and Nevada invest heavily in 2-year institutions (community colleges) while some other states have virtually no such institutions. States with a larger proportion of students enrolled in community colleges, for example, would face different financing, access and academic considerations from those facing states with most students enrolled in public and private 4-year institutions. Intersecting those differences are variations in the distributions of students both within states and across state lines. Some states are heavy 'importers' of students, while others are net 'exporters'. And some states can claim as many as five distinguished, highly selective research universities, while some have none.

Many researchers (Hossler *et al.*, 1997; Zumeta, 1992, 1996) have argued that variations among these ecological conditions lead states to face different types of pressures, problems, and opportunities in the delivery of higher education, which in turn can account for differences in policy outcomes and in policy innovations for higher education. As an example, in south-eastern and western states where enrolments in public institutions tend to be higher, statewide merit-based financial aid programmes are especially popular; the converse is true in north-eastern and mid-Atlantic states, which tend to have more developed private institutional sectors and which invest more generously in statewide need-based financial aid programmes (Doyle, 2006; Hearn, Griswold and Marine, 1996). While the US states are unquestionably experiencing a generalized shifting of financial burdens from public to private sources (Ehrenberg, 2006), this variation in states' organizational ecologies persists.

A second element of the organizational and political context is the analytic capacity of the states' individual higher-education agencies. Variations in higher-education agencies' authority and level of centralization can influence the amount, visibility and value of information, data and research the agencies provide policymakers. In particular, the number and level of training of the analytic staff contributes to agencies being able to conduct cost-effectiveness studies, formative and summative policy evaluations, and access and persistence assessments and can influence decisions ranging from tuition rates to presidential searches to institutional mission differentiation (McLendon, 2003). In these ways, agency staff may facilitate not only effective policy development and implementation but also the identification of emerging aspects of post-secondary systems meriting special attention from the state.

The final element of the organizational and policy context encompasses state's post-secondary policy postures, that is, state's approaches to such central and familiar questions of how to price higher education, how to fund higher education, how to structure higher education, who attends higher education, towards what aims higher education will be directed and so forth. Policy postures address such factors as the levels, trends and nature of state appropriations for higher education and the setting of tuition and enrolments at the campus and system levels.

The levels and distribution of state funding for post-secondary education vary across states in ways that may lead policymakers to different ideas or proposals for funding higher education. For instance, many states in the southern and the south-western regions of the US have experienced marked enrolment increases in post-secondary education, which could focus government attention on accountability mechanisms that prioritize college completion and increase educational attainment. Similarly, rapid tuition increases may prompt state officials to consider tightening institutional oversight (McLendon and Hearn, 2013) or to introduce innovative programs to help citizens plan for and pay for college (Mumper, 2001). States' historic policy postures on post-secondary education funding, tuition rates and enrolment patterns influence how government officials go forward addressing emerging issues, focusing their attention and tilting their judgments on the preferability of some goals and solutions over others. Again, this differentiation takes place within broader national trends toward privatization, and shapes the ways those trends play out in specific state conditions.

Politico-institutional context

As Figure 3.1 suggests, a state's political conditions and institutional arrangements represent the third context that shapes state policy decisions in post-secondary education. In line with Tandberg and Griffith's (2013) identification of a 'new institutionalism' path in higher-education policy studies, our conceptualization incorporates not only socio-economic and organizational influences but also the influences of a state's politics and governmental arrangements. For this politico-institutional context, we identify eight dimensions that may help shape state post-secondary education policy decisions: (1) higher education governance arrangements; (2) the nature of the appointment characteristics for the state higher-education agency's executive officer; (3) political ideology; (4) gubernatorial characteristics; (5) legislative characteristics; (6) partisanship conditions; (7) interest-group climates; and (8) in-state intermediary organizations.

A central feature in a state's politico-institutional ecology is the nature of its higher-education governance arrangement. Researchers (e.g. see McGuinness, 2016) most often distil such arrangements into three categories. Consolidated governing boards are highly centralized systems with the greatest authority over higher education institutions. They tend to operate as either the sole statewide higher-education system (such as in Kansas, Utah and some other states with small numbers of institutions) or as two state wide systems representing different sectors (such as in North Carolina which has separate systems for four-year and two-year institutions). Consolidated boards have wide-ranging responsibilities to hire and fire campus presidents, set tuition levels, and approve or eliminate academic programmes. Coordinating boards, the second type of governance arrangement, oversee multiple campus- or system-level governing boards. These coordinating agencies have more limited day-to-day authority, although 'regulatory coordinating boards' (such as those in Indiana and Tennessee) have approval power over institutional budgets and authorization to approve or eliminate academic programmes. By contrast, 'advisory coordinating boards' (such as Texas and Washington) lack these formal powers, but can have significant influence through responsibilities to coordinate the post-secondary education sector, to make budget recommendations and to set a statewide master plan. The genesis of coordinating boards was to serve as a buffer between state government officials and the campuses so as to assist governors and legislators in making informed decisions. Planning agencies, the third and final type of governance arrangement, have the weakest statewide oversight. With limited to no formal authority, the campuses in planning-agency states enjoy the most autonomy. Michigan is perhaps the most notable example because the state constitution specifies clear authority over academic and fiscal affairs by the University of Michigan, Michigan State University, and Wayne State University. The independent authority of some boards is great enough to warrant considering them an autonomous 'fourth branch' of state governments (Glenny and Dalglish, 1973; Lacy, 2013).

To varying extents, therefore, state-level post-secondary organizational and governance arrangements can influence decisions ranging from tuition rates to presidential searches to institutional mission differentiation. These governance arrangements can also influence the value of information, data and research and the extent to which they are provided policymakers. These observations are important both theoretically and practically. Higher-education researchers have consistently found governance arrangements to 'matter' in shaping a state's policy decisions. Several studies (e.g., McLendon, Hearn and Deaton, 2006) have suggested that states with consolidated governing boards tend to be less likely to adopt some harder-edged regulatory policies, such as weaker performance-accountability programmes as compared to higher-stakes performance funding programmes that are associated with the coordinating board states. Other studies have linked the consolidated governing structures with an increased probability of state adoption of newer financing policies such as merit-aid policies and college savings, outcomes-based funding policies, and prepaid tuition programmes (e.g. Lowry, 2007; McLendon, 2003; Hearn, McLendon and Mokher, 2008; McLendon and Hearn, 2013; McLendon, Hearn and Deaton, 2006; McLendon, Heller and Young, 2005; McLendon, Tandberg and Hillman, 2014; Tandberg and Ness, 2011; Tandberg, 2013; Zumeta, 1992, 1996).

Seeking logical mechanisms to explain such findings, some researchers (e.g., McLendon, Hearn and Deaton, 2006) have hypothesized that states with more centralized agency authority will possess more staff and thereby greater analytic capacity, and those capacities may make states to more likely to experiment and adopt new policy innovations. Yet, this reasoning may be problematic because the three types of agencies are not rigidly stratified with respect to the size or resources of their professional staffs. For example, state agencies in coordinating board systems with limited centralized authority may have many highly credentialed analysts and large budgets for data analysis and policy assessments. That is, staffing patterns vary within as well as across different types of state agencies.

It is clear that the influence of governance arrangements varies by policy issue and that those arrangements are not alone determinative. Still, governing structures remain an important element in the contexts shaping state tertiary-education policy decisions.

The second element in the politico-institutional context relates to the appointment characteristics of the state agency head. Historically, most states have asked their corporate institutional board (e.g. board of regents, board of governors, board of trust and state commission of higher education) to make the hire of this executive, regardless of whether he or she is to lead a consolidated governing board, a coordinating board, or a planning agency. Recently, however, some states have begun shifting appointment powers directly to governors – that is now the case in eight states (McGuinness, 2016). Even in states with board appointment authority, governors can have indirect influence through their prerogative to appoint individual board members, as is the norm in statewide higher-education agencies. These gubernatorial influences can be moderated by staggering the terms of board members and by establishing board-member terms in office of 6 or more years, thus exceeding governors' typical 4-year term.[5]

There are certainly exceptions to governors' appointment influences, in such states as North Carolina and Nevada, where the legislature and the general public choose board members respectively. Given the prominent role that governors have played in recent policy activity around state college completion efforts, for example, the varying levels of governors' appointment authority and influence could significantly affect state post-secondary education policy decisions (Gándara, Rippner and Ness, forthcoming).

A state's political ideology, most often arrayed on the conservative-liberal continuum, consists of a set of orientations or beliefs related to politics and policy options. Researchers often distinguish between two types of ideological influence: (1) citizen ideology, which is the mean position on a liberal-conservative continuum of the electorate in a state, and (2) state government ideology, the mean position on a liberal-conservative continuum of elected public officials in a state. Both measures have yielded strong connections between states' ideology and various policy choices (see, for example, Berry, Ringquist, Fording and Hanson, 1998; Barrilleaux, Holbrook and Langer, 2002). For example, states with populations and government officials towards the liberal side of the continuum tend to support broader social services and higher levels of public welfare benefits, while states with more conservative ideologies tend to favour markets-based reforms, abortion regulations and death-penalty statutes (e.g. see Barrilleaux, Holbrook and Langer, 2002).

For higher-education policy outcomes, the effects of political ideology are more mixed. Recent longitudinal studies have found evidence that political ideology can affect higher education finance policy, such as the adoption of prepaid tuition policies, college savings programmes and merit scholarship programmes (e.g. Doyle, 2006; Doyle, McLendon and Hearn, 2010; Hearn, McLendon and Mokher, 2008; McLendon, Tandberg and Hillman, 2014; Nicholson-Crotty and Meier, 2003; Tandberg, 2010, 2013). Yet, the direction of ideological influences has varied. Some studies have found states with liberal ideology more likely to enact financing initiatives and to appropriate more resources to public colleges and universities, while other studies have found conservative-leaning states more likely to do so. Thus, the extent to which ideology may be driving a shift towards more privatizing financial trends for higher education is surprisingly unclear.

A state's gubernatorial characteristics, such as governor's formal and informal authority and influence, can be an especially significant influence on post-secondary education policy decisions. Governors in some states hold strong formal powers, such as the line-item veto, broad appointment powers of cabinet officials and many statewide boards and commissions and substantial tenure potential that allow governors to be re-elected for multiple terms. Governors with more limited powers hold fewer instruments of formal policy control, which can limit their overall policy influence (Beyle, 2004). Although empirical studies of the effects of gubernatorial control are limited and inconsistent in their findings (e.g. see Barrilleaux and Berkman, 2003), one might hypothesize that states with more powerful governors (favouring privatization efforts, for example) may face less influential political and professional resistance from governing and coordinating boards.

Indeed, the few studies of gubernatorial influence in higher education have found some evidence that the extent of governors' formal powers can influence state policy decisions. Namely, stronger gubernatorial powers appear to be associated with an increased likelihood of states adopting dual-degree programmes (Mokher and McLendon, 2009) and creating statewide P-16 councils (Mohker, 2010). Apropos of our special attention here to developments relating to privatization, there is also evidence that stronger gubernatorial powers may be associated with implementing outcomes-based funding (Dougherty et al., 2016) and supporting efforts to spur economic development through research (Hearn, McLendon and Lacy, 2013; Hearn, Lacy and Warshaw, 2014). This limited but growing body of work offers initial support that gubernatorial power influences post-secondary education policy decisions and shows warrant for further inquiry.

The legislative characteristics of a state represent another important politico-institutional element. Squire (2000) operationalizes three primary characteristics to construct a measure of legislative professionalism, which essentially compares each state to the US Congress in regard to: (1) duration of legislative session, (2) number of professional staff, and (3) legislator compensation. This measure arrays states from the most 'professional' legislatures (e.g. California, New York, Pennsylvania), with nearly year-round sessions, salaries in the $100,000 range, and many legislative aides, to so-called 'citizen' legislatures (e.g. Georgia, North Dakota and New Hampshire) with shorter legislative sessions, modest pay and few staff members.[6]

Scholars have studied the effects on legislative professionalism for decades, especially after reforms to enhance professionalization through additional staff with expertise in various policy domains, in forecasting fiscal estimates of policy proposals, and in monitoring and assessing policy effectiveness. Many analysts (e.g. Squire, 2007) have concluded that these changes helped deepen the institutions' capacity to deliberate, develop policy alternatives and enact legislation. There is also some evidence that more professionalized legislatures can have indirect effects by attracting better-educated legislators, who may serve many terms due to higher pay and who may also be more inclined to pursue and support new policy innovations (e.g. Barrilleaux et al., 2002). In higher education, several studies have found largely positive associations between states' levels of legislative professionalization and higher-education policy adoptions (Hearn, McLendon and Lacy, 2013; Lacy and Tandberg, 2014) and between professionalism and their funding of higher education (e.g. Toutkoushian and Hollis, 1998; Nicholson-Crotty and Meier, 2003; McLendon, Hearn and Mokher, 2009; Tandberg and Ness, 2011; Ness and Tandberg, 2013; Tandberg, 2010, 2013; McLendon, Tandberg and Hillman, 2014). Such findings signify likely relevance of legislative professionalism on state post-secondary-education policy decisions.

Compared to other dimensions in the politico-institutional context, higher education researchers have surprisingly disregarded partisanship. Political party control of legislative and executive branches seem likely to influence post-secondary education policy decisions, but perhaps some scholars have implicitly assumed that higher education exists above 'the partisan fray' and that states' demographic and economic characteristics serve as better predictors of state higher-education policy activity. Recently, however, a series of empirical studies in the field has called into question these long-standing assumptions (Dougherty *et al.*, 2016). Specifically, recent studies have found that in states with stronger Republican control of the legislature have been more likely to pass rigorous performance-accountability programs (McLendon, Hearn and Deaton, 2006; McLendon and Hearn, 2013). Dougherty *et al.* (2016) similarly have concluded that Republican strength is associated with accountability initiatives. With regard to state spending on higher education, a growing body of empirical research has often, but not always, found Democratic party strength and control of government to be associated with higher appropriation levels (e.g. Archibald and Feldman, 2006; Lowry, 2007; Hicklin and Meier, 2008; McLendon, Mokher and Doyle, 2009; Tandberg, 2010, 2013). The fact that the Republican party currently controls solid majorities of the states' governors offices and legislatures may make significant increases in higher-education appropriations unlikely.[7]

Timing in the electoral cycle is another element broadly related to partisanship that, although under-studied, holds promise for building understanding of post-secondary education policy choices (McLendon, Deaton and Hearn, 2007). Studies of education policy at the primary and secondary levels in the US, for example, have found that certain school-reform measures were more likely to pass in years closer to a statewide election due to the programs' popular appeal and incumbent legislators' desires to position themselves as education reformers (e.g. see Wong and Shen, 2002).

Interest-group climates in the states comprise the seventh politico-institutional influence on state policy decisions. Although the study of interest-group activity at the state-level has traditionally lagged relative to its examination at the national-level, the tactics and motivations of lobbying activity, the factors propelling interest-group mobilization and the effects of interest groups on governmental behaviour at the state level constitute growing areas of research attention (Gray and Lowery, 1996) in political science in the US Most recently, researchers (e.g. Tandberg, 2010, 2013; Ness, Tandberg and McLendon, 2015) have begun to turn to interest groups as formative elements in higher-education policymaking.

Empirical and theoretical research on interest-group climates centres on three elements: (1) density, or number of total interest groups in a state; (2) strength, or the number of interest groups in a given sector compared to all groups; and, (3) concentration, or the niche of interest groups within a given sector. Tandberg (2006, 2010, 2013) developed measures to examine the influence of interest-group climates on state post-secondary education policy decisions. Borrowing from Gray and Lowery's (1996) pioneering measures of 'relative density', Tandberg's interest-group ratio is derived from the number of higher education interest groups (i.e. registered lobbyists and total number of post-secondary institutions) divided by the total number of registered interest groups in a state. Empirical studies employing these measures have found positive associations between stronger interest-group climates and increased state spending on public higher education. Such findings suggest interest-group activity affects post-secondary-education policy decisions, and should encourage potential further inquiries examining the array of interests operating within the states and their effects on higher-education policies. In particular, this work highlights the ways private and political actors favouring marketization and privatization in education can shape agendas and policy choices in the US system.

In-state intermediary organizations represent the final element within a state's politico-institutional context. As Ness, Tandberg and McLendon (2015) observe, these organizations might be considered interest groups in the tradition of Malen's (2001) 'less obvious actors', but seem distinctive enough to consider separately here. In-state intermediaries might include policy or research organizations, think tanks and advocacy groups such as the Texas Association of Business and the Georgia Budget & Policy Institute. Ness and Gándara's (2014) inventory of a particular type of intermediary – ideological think tanks at the state level – identified fifty-nine conservative-leaning think tanks and forty progressive think tanks. Each of these organizations is associated with a conservative or progressive national network, but operates independently in a single state to promote policy solutions related to state funding, higher-education costs and other issues. The analysis suggests that conservative-leaning organizations were most concerned with efficiency and productivity, which is consistent with the 'market-oriented' mission of their umbrella organization, the State Policy Network. The scope of higher-education policy activity by these intermediary organizations, and the prominent voices they represent suggests that they stand to influence policy decisions and warrant further examination (Gándara and Hearn, 2014).

External context

Despite the decentralized structural context of US higher education, the individual states do not develop policy in a vacuum. They are influenced by factors beyond their borders in numerous ways. Among those impacting forces are the actions of other states regarding similar challenges, the contacts and information gleaned from networks of state actors, the actions of the federal government and the role of national intermediary organizations.

Other states can shape a given state's actions in four noteworthy ways. First, states may borrow ideas from others to simplify the range of alternatives under consideration. That is, states 'learn' from one another's policy behaviours, discerning what has (and has not) worked elsewhere. This learning can be efficient, in that it reduces the costs of states' searches (Dougherty *et al.*, 2013, 2014; Lacy and Tandberg, 2014). Second, states may seek to improve or defend their competitive standing by adopting other states' policies. Actions taken by one state can affect the state's neighbours in ways beneficial or detrimental (and sometimes both), which in turn may prompt those other states themselves to take action. When the state of Georgia adopted a broad-based, merit scholarship programme for state residents in the early 1990s, several of the state's neighbours followed suit in an effort to retain their own talented, college-bound students (Doyle, 2006). Similarly, one state's decision to adopt a research-centred economic-development policy may prompt neighbouring states to adopt similar policies to remain economically competitive within a region (Warshaw and Hearn, 2014). Third, states may adopt others' policies to conform to normatively accepted standards. Such a pattern seems apparent in the domains of open-meetings/open-records laws, civil-liberties legislation, longitudinal student databases and other areas. Normative pressures can drive states to seek greater legitimacy via choices assumed to reflect 'best practices'. Fourth, outright coercion from other states can conceivably influence state choices, although such seems rarely to be the case.

As a group, such influences are termed 'diffusion' in the research literature. Somewhat surprisingly, the evidence for the existence of diffusion effects is mixed. The idea has strong intuitive appeal. Yet, the findings of rigorous quantitative and qualitative studies have widely varied, with reports of no evidence of diffusion, evidence of positive (emulative) diffusion, and even evidence of negative diffusion (avoidance) (Doyle, 2006; Hearn, Lacy and Warshaw, 2014; Hearn, McLendon and Lacy, 2013; McLendon, Deaton and Hearn, 2006; Mohker and McLendon, 2009; Ness and Mistretta, 2010; Cohen-Vogel *et al.*, 2008; Levine, Lacy and Hearn, 2013; McLendon, Heller and Young, 2005; Dougherty *et al.*, 2016).

Why might there be such variation in these findings? One likely explanation lies in the thinness of the modelling and hypotheses employed by analysts. All policy studies face limitations on the amount and depth of data acquired, and this may be especially true for quantitative studies. Short-hand indicators (proportions of legislators belonging to a particular party, or consolidated vs. coordinated state agency power) can collapse complex structures and processes into binaries, ultimately reducing the richness of analysts' insights. To address such constraints, Cohen-Vogel *et al.*,(2008) interviewed policymakers in six states in depth to build understanding of where in the policymaking cycle the influence of a state's neighbours is most felt. While qualitative studies usually have limited generalizability in a statistical sense, they can provide pathways to new knowledge that are not apparent from strictly numbers-driven analyses.

Independently of diffusion processes, US states also can be influenced through contacts and relationships built in networks with other states. For example, various regions of the country are served by voluntary associations through which states gather and share data, discuss policy challenges and ideas, and build connections. In the west of the country, an example would be the Western Interstate Commission for Higher Education. Through such organizations, the professionals who staff the state agencies thus benefit from meeting and working with counterparts in peer states.

Of course, the federal government also shapes the actions of the states in several ways. The foundational need-based student financial aid program in the US is the federal Pell Grant, and most student aid officials at the state, system and institutional levels build their policy and funding approaches off the base of the Pell Grant. The grant is essentially a voucher based both on a student's financial need and the cost of the institution attended. The federal government's institutionalization of those features in the early 1970s represented one of the nation's earliest moves toward prioritizing student choice and thus, indirectly, privatization (Hearn, 1993). Because of the grant's voucher-like aspects, Pell funding can conceivably influence the pricing of state institutions. The federal government also shapes state policy decision making through its research funding priorities and workplace policies (e.g., requiring equal opportunity hiring and imposing occupational safety regulations).

Often, state agency leaders are responsible for ensuring that these policies, programs, and regulations are fairly and uniformly applied across state systems, and that all involved parties have adequate understanding of the federal context. In particular, states often rely on agencies to ensure that all students know of the availability of federal grants and loans and of the significant ways such programs increase the affordability of higher education.

National intermediary organizations represent the final element of the external context. As with in-state intermediaries, these policy organizations (e.g. the Complete College America initiative, the Jobs for the Future initiative, the Education Commission of the States, the State Higher Education Executive Officers association), regional compacts (e.g. the Western Interstate Commission on Higher Education, the Southern Regional Education Board), and foundations (e.g., the Bill & Melinda Gates Foundation, the Lumina Foundation for Education) can influence state-level post-secondary education policy decisions through their advocacy directly to state elected officials and to state higher-education leaders. The role of 'advocacy philanthropy' has increasingly been shown to influence education policies at the primary/secondary (Reckhow, 2012; DeBray *et al.*, 2014) and tertiary (Hall and Thomas, 2012) levels. That philanthropy appears to do so by advancing specific policy solutions through national convenings and by serving as an additional source of revenue as state funding stagnates. A recent empirical study of Complete College America's role in diffusing outcomes-based funding policies diffused across three states offers evidence that intermediaries can provide a 'call to action', can simplify complex issues, and can incentivize states to adopt certain policies (Gándara, Rippner and Ness, forthcoming). This nascent body of research offers initial evidence that national intermediary organizations influence state post-secondary education policy decisions and suggests that much more research is necessary to understand these associations.

Conclusions

State higher-education policymaking in the US is evolving in ways that threaten historic commitments to employing colleges and universities in the service of the broader public good. These trends have been noted in opinion pages (e.g. Dirks, 2016), in scholarly books (Newfield, 2016) and in dramatically framed popular documentaries (e.g., see 'Starving the Beast', 2016). State spending on public higher education is increasingly constrained by the pressing budgetary demands of infrastructure, law enforcement, primary/secondary education and state pension and healthcare plans. At the same time, US taxpayers are increasingly restive regarding the role of government, as opposed to the marketplace, in addressing societal challenges. The federal government has retreated somewhat from both its research support for institutions and its commitments to maintaining college affordability via need-based student aid and student loan subsidization. Together, these pressures have lessened the potential of higher education to address challenges of inequality, shifting labour markets, knowledge growth and economic development.

In this chapter, we have characterized these developments as a collective movement toward privatization in the broad sense. Retreating government support has prompted change at both the system and institutional levels (Ehrenberg, 2006; Newfield, 2016). Most obviously, higher-education leaders have raised tuition and fees dramatically, rapidly scuttling historical commitments to low pricing and shifting the balance of institutional revenues away from governments (College Board, 2016a). In theory, such moves need not reduce affordability, if adequately offsetting student aid is provided for those most needing it, but such has not generally been the case (College Board, 2016b). Less visible but perhaps equally significant have been a series of moves to incentivize efficiency and entrepreneurship on campuses, making institutions more accountable for expenditures and performance. While those goals are unquestionably laudable in the abstract, they can have less salutary operational effects on the public good. Four specific movements exemplify the point: expanding outcomes-based funding, emphasizing practical degrees, abandoning from historic academic employment arrangements and instituting responsibility-centred budgeting.

As noted earlier, increasing numbers of states have adopted *outcomes-based (or performance-based) funding approaches*. These policies strategically tie large proportions of states' institutional allocations to performance on chosen indicators of efficiency and service to state goals. In doing so, they deviate from historic state approaches tying funding to raw enrolments or, more simply, to moneys politically available in state coffers (Hearn, 2015).

Perhaps the single most representative feature of the new outcomes-based programmes is their emphasis on graduation rates and numbers: schools are incentivized to produce maximum numbers of graduates with minimal spillage (i.e. student attrition, delayed time to degree, etc.). Without incorporating effective offsetting incentives into these new performance formulas, states run the risk of discouraging institutions from tolerating college students' exploration of better-fitting degree aspirations. A majority of students in four-year colleges in the US change majors over the course of their studies (e.g. see Allen and Robbins, 2008), and that movement may be developmentally productive for students and ultimately for society, but it is inefficient in the sense that it can delay graduation.

States with heavily outcomes-centred funding also run the risk of lessening the rigor of academic offerings and the value of degrees: student 'pass-through' may be rewarded in the pursuit of mechanical efficiency towards graduation, but at the cost of learning outcomes. Perhaps most troublingly, states focusing on graduation numbers can run the risk of discouraging public institutions from admitting 'at risk' students from disadvantaged educational and socio-economic backgrounds – the inevitable attrition of some proportion of those vulnerable students can lessen graduation rates and numbers.

Parallel to the demands for more performance accountability have come a variety of moves by state governors and other political leaders to privilege *practical, vocationally focused post-secondary education and training* over education in other fields such as the arts, humanities and social services. A particular emphasis in this movement is on favouring science, technology, engineering and mathematics [STEM] fields, under the reasoning that such schooling may be especially likely to foster state economic development. To the extent the public good remains a motivating force behind this state policy emphasis, it is defined as serving the economic development goal rather than other goals.

In 2011, Texas Governor Rick Perry asked state institutions to offer a $10,000 bachelor's degree 'in fields that will provide graduates with the best opportunity for employment', prominently including STEM fields (Hamilton, 2012; Shinn, 2014). Subsequently, Florida Governor Rick Scott announced 'If I'm going to take money from a citizen to put into education then . . . I want that money to go to degrees where people can get jobs in this state' (Anderson, 2011). He later singled out a particular field for criticism, noting that Florida does not need 'a lot more anthropologists . . . It's a great degree if people want to get it. But we don't need them here . . . I want to spend our money getting people science, technology, engineering and math degrees. That's what our kids need to focus all of their time and attention on: Those type of degrees that when they get out of school, they can get a job' (Bender, 2011). Subsequently, a legislative ally observed 'When the No. 1 degree granted is psychology and the No. 2 degree is political science, maybe before we ask $100 million more of taxpayers we should redeploy what we have. That way we make sure we're not sending graduates out with degrees that don't mean much' (Colavecchio, 2010). In short, prominent political leaders are arguing that curricular offerings at public universities should be focused on the currently projected needs of a state's economy.

Needless to say, policy moves in such directions would serve only one aspect of higher education's historic contributions to society. Indeed, they could come at the expense of the less measurable but significant contributions of the liberal arts. Bowen (1996), Pascarella and Terenzini (2005), McMahon (2009), and numerous others have found evidence supporting colleges' contributions to such outcomes as civic engagement, artistic appreciation, cultural expression, geopolitical understanding, and social tolerance.

Further, with instigation from some of the same political leaders, state-supported institutions have been prominent in the movement in the US toward *weakening the security of academic employment*. These efforts have taken place on the 'front and back ends' of academic positions. That is, both hiring patterns and the review of senior academic staff have shifted toward patterns less favourable to employment security. On the front end, public institutions have reduced hiring in tenure-track and tenured positions, committing instead to ramping up contingent academic hiring. Currently fewer than a third of the academic staff at public institutions have tenure, down from over two-thirds in the 1970s (Finkelstein, Conley and Schuster, 2016). In the eyes of state officials and many campus leaders, retreat from offering tenure to productive academic staff provides a path towards greater strategic flexibility in educational offerings, especially toward those favouring economic development. Worldwide, few nations have committed historically as deeply as the US to academic tenure, and from a global perspective, this shift in academic labour markets in the US may be untroubling. Nonetheless, employment security via tenuring has long been considered a mainstay of academic employment in the US tertiary education sector. As emphasis on cost-cutting, performance metrics and strategic enrolments has risen, tenure has been subjected to increased scrutiny and schools have increased their reliance on part-time lecturers, full-time non-tenure line instructors and graduate students instructors. Numerous observers fear negative implications for student learning and institutional governance from the disruptive 'unbundling' of the traditional academic roles of teaching, research, and service (Belkin and Korn, 2015; Hearn and Milan, 2013; Hearn and Warshaw, 2015; Toutkoushian and Bellas, 2003).

The weakening of academic employment security has also taken place on the back end, among already-tenured staff. Increasing numbers of US institutions began requiring regular post-tenure reviews in the 1990s, and now those efforts are developing more 'bite'. In Wisconsin, political leaders and associated board members weakened the protections of faculty tenure in statute, and this year they placed post-tenure reviews more firmly in the hands of top administrators rather than academic staff (Thomason, 2016). As with the move to non-tenure-line staff, these state efforts to lessen the security (and thus the autonomy) of faculty strengthen states' role in shaping what knowledge is pursued, offered and transmitted to students.

In concert, state-supported institutions in the US are increasingly adopting *incentives-based budgeting systems* [IBBS], which are aimed towards integrating budgeting and management decision-making more fully at the level of individual units within institutions (Hearn *et al.*, 2006). Such systems originated in such private institutions as the Universities of Southern California and Pennsylvania, but their appeal to state policymakers propelled their adoption in massive public systems like the University of Indiana and the University of Minnesota (Priest, Becker, Hossler and John, 2002). IBBS approaches decentralize budgeting decisions to the units most affected and the staff presumably most knowledgeable about what is needed, require that those units make economically justifiable decisions and provide rewards and penalties based on the quality of those decisions. In doing so, states and their institutions have aimed to reduce the incidence of subsidies to units without measurable economic returns while heightening the importance of the marketplace in decision making. For example, under IBBS, an academic department would be provided funding based on quantitative metrics of its performance on key indicators, such as enrolments, research grants, degrees granted and the like. Analogous to outcomes-based funding at the state level, IBBS can reward certain outcomes that are strategically valued on campuses, and can ensure that decisions are made by informed officials 'on the ground'. Potentially, however, IBBS can also disadvantage outcomes that are not easily translatable into financial returns and its unit-centred design can decrease cooperation and increase duplication and competition across academic units on individual campuses.

Each of the abovementioned four movements on campuses – adopting outcomes-based funding, emphasizing practical degrees, retreating from tenuring and instituting responsibility-centred budgeting – serves a short-term version of efficiency that, ultimately, may disserve society. To the extent that colleges and universities may be analogized to manufacturing facilities, each of the movements can tighten input-process-outcomes relationships and potentially help ensure that all campus activity is more closely tied to immediately beneficial results for the money spent. Yet the manufacturing metaphor has limits. Higher education's contributions emerge only partly from its role as a provider of highly trained workers at reasonable costs, or its role as a producer of narrow analyses useful for identified corporate and governmental problems.

Joseph Schumpeter, a twentieth-century economist and innovation theorist, observed that 'A system . . . that at every given point of time fully utilizes its possibilities to the best advantage may yet in the long run be inferior to a system that does so at no given point in time, because the latter's failure to do so may be a condition for the level or speed of long-run performance' (1942: 83).

That is, short-term static efficiency may actually detract from long-run dynamic efficiency.

Higher education seems a case in point. The wisdom of particular higher-education spending decisions by policymakers, like the wisdom of major-choice decisions by students, cannot be determined until a time well afterwards. As Roger Brown (2015: 9) has perceptively noted,

> No [decision maker] has, or can have, the necessary information about quality, not least because higher education is a 'post-experience good' ... This means that the information that is really needed is only available long after it can be of any use. William Goldman's famous saying about Hollywood – 'nobody knows anything' – comes to mind here.

Much of what higher education contributes to society comes in forms that are difficult to measure but nonetheless important: engaged and culturally aware citizens, informed voters, critically thinking graduates working in fields fitting their aspirations and talents, serendipitous knowledge discovery and the like. To the extent we commit public funding only, or mainly, towards pursuing efficiency under a manufacturing metaphor, we greatly disserve the larger public good. As trends towards privileging the private over the public, the concrete over the abstract and the short term over the longer term gain speed, responsibility falls to those with remaining power to question and perhaps to resist. In the US, the federal government and many state governments are currently showing no such inclination, and indeed seem intent on limiting government support for general education, science and the arts. The nation's 'fifty laboratories' may remain a source of strength, however. There, alternative formulations of higher education's future may still stir.

Notes

1. The nation's four military academies are the lone exception.
2. For example, boards of institutions and systems often provide their members term lengths staggered so as not to directly coincide with the terms of the political leaders who appoint them. In this way, the boards remain somewhat buffered from vulnerability to political shifts.
3. Although a few especially prominent public universities receive the majority of their support from research dollars
4. Some would define privatization more narrowly, focusing on specific linkages between systems, institutions, private corporations and individual actors. For example, 'outsourcing' of traditionally internal services like food services is sometimes termed privatization. For us, however, the scope of the term is more inclusive both specifically and conceptually.
5. Staggered terms may be becoming less important as an instrument ensuring political neutrality, however, as party control of state governors' offices is solidifying: since 2010, there have been only seven party changes in sixty-six gubernatorial elections (see https://nga.org/cms/elections).
6. The National Conference of State Legislatures (2014) provides a similar classification based on these three characteristics.
7. Data are from NGA and NCLS. https://nga.org/cms/elections http://ncsl.org/research/about-state-legislatures/partisan-composition.aspx.

References

Allen, J. and Robbins, S.B. (2008) 'Prediction of college major persistence based on vocational interests, academic preparation and first-year academic performance', *Research in Higher Education*, 49(1): 62–79.
Anderson, Z. (2011) 'Rick Scott wants to shift university funding away from some degrees.' *Sarasota Herald-Tribune*, 10 October. Available online at http://politics.heraldtribune.com/2011/10/10/rick-scott-wants-to-shift-university-funding-away-from-some-majors/.
Archibald, R.B. and Feldman, D.H. (2006) 'State higher education spending and the tax revolt', *Journal of Higher Education*, 77(4): 618–644.
Barrilleaux, C. and Berkman, M. (2003) 'Do governors matter? Budgeting rules and the politics of state policymaking', *Political Research Quarterly*, 56(4): 409–417.
Barrilleaux, C., Holbrook, T. and Langer, L. (2002) 'Electoral competition, legislative balance and American state welfare policy', *American Journal of Political Science*, 46(2): 415–427.
Ben-David, J. (1992) *Centres of learning: Britain, France, Germany, United States* (2nd edn), New Brunswick, NJ: Transaction Publishers.
Bender, M.C. (2011) 'Scott: Florida doesn't need more anthropology majors.' *Tampa Bay Times*, 10 October. http://tampabay.com/blogs/the-buzz-florida-politics/content/scott-florida-doesnt-need-more-anthropology-majors (accessed 30 November 2016).
Berdahl, R.O. (1971) *Statewide coordination of higher education*, Washington, DC: American Council on Education.
Berry, F.S. and Berry, W.D. (1990) 'State lottery adoptions as policy innovations: an event history analysis', *American Political Science Review*, 84(2): 295–416.
Berry, F.S. and Berry, W.D. (2014) 'Innovation and diffusion models in policy research', in P.A. Sabatier and C. Weible (eds), *Theories of the Policy Process*, Boulder, CO: Westview Press, pp. 307–338.
Berry, W.D., Ringquist, E.J., Fording, R.C. and Hanson, R.L. (1998) 'Measuring citizen and government ideology in the American states, 1960–1993', *American Journal of Political Science*, 42(1): 327–348.
Beyle, T. (2004) 'Governors', in V. Gray and R. Hanson (eds), *Politics in the American States* (8th edn), Washington, DC: CQ Press, pp. 194–232.
Bowen, H.R. (1996) *Investment in learning: The individual and social value of American higher education, second edition*, Baltimore: Johns Hopkins University Press.
Bozeman, B. (2007) *Public values and public interest: Counterbalancing economic individualism*, Washington, DC: Georgetown University Press.
Brown, R. (2015) The marketisation of higher education: Issues and ironies, *New Vistas*, 1(1): 3–9. Downloaded 13 December, 2016 at http://uwl.ac.uk/sites/default/files/Departments/Research/new_vistas/vol1_iss1/vol1_iss1_art1_23April2015.pdf.
Burke, J.C. and Associates. (eds) (2005) *Achieving accountability in higher education*, San Francisco: Jossey-Bass.
Clark, B.R. (1979) 'The many pathways of academic coordination', *Higher Education*, 8(3): 251–267.
Clark, B. R. (1983) *The higher education system: Academic organization in cross-national perspective*, Berkeley, CA: University of California Press.
Cohen-Vogel, L., Ingle, W.K., Levine, A.A. and Spence, M. (2008) 'The spread of merit-based college aid: Politics, policy consortia and interstate competition', *Educational Policy*, 22(3): 339–362.
Colavecchio, S. (2010) Lawmakers stress need for higher ed but warn of cuts, *Tampa Bay Times*, 26 February. http://tampabay.com/news/lawmakers-stress-need-for-higher-ed-but-warn-of-cuts/1076083. (accessed 25 October 2016).
The College Board. (2016a) *Trends in college pricing: 2016*, Washington, DC: The College Board. Available online at http://trends.collegeboard.org/sites/default/files/trends-college-pricing-web-final-508-2.pdf.
The College Board. (2016b) *Trends in student aid: 2016*, Washington, DC: The College Board. Available online at https://trends.collegeboard.org/sites/default/files/2016-trends-student-aid.pdf

DeBray, E., Scott, J., Lubienski,C. and Jabbar, H. (2014) 'Intermediary organizations in charter school policy coalitions', *Educational Policy*, 28(2): 175–206.

Desrochers, D. M. and Hurlburt, S. (2016) *Trends in college spending: 2003–2013*, Washington, DC: The Delta Cost Project. Retrieved from http://deltacostproject.org/sites/default/files/products/15-4626%20Final01%20Delta%20Cost%20Project%20College%20Spending%2011131.406.P0.02.001%20....pdf.

Dirks, N.B. (2016) Flagships must create new models to preserve the public good, *Chronicle of Higher Education*, 16 July. Downloaded December 13, 2016 at http://chronicle.com/article/Flagships-Must-Create-New/237055.

Dougherty, K.J., Jones, S.M., Lahr, J., Natow, R.S. and Pheatt, L. (2016) *Performance funding for higher education*, Baltimore: Johns Hopkins University Press.

Doyle, W.R. (2006) 'Adoption of merit-based student grant programs: an event history analysis', *Educational Evaluation and Policy Analysis*, 28(3): 259–285.

Doyle, W.R., McLendon, M.K. and Hearn, J.C. (2010) 'The adoption of prepaid tuition and savings plans in the American states', *Research in Higher Education*, 51(7): 659–686.

Duderstadt, J.J. (2000) *A University for the 21st Century*, Ann Arbor: University of Michigan Press.

Dye, T.R. (1966) *Politics, economics and the public: Policy outcomes in the American states*, Chicago, IL: Rand McNally.

Ehrenberg, R.G. (ed.) (2006) *What's happening to public higher education?: The shifting financial burden*, Baltimore: Johns Hopkins University Press.

Finkelstein, M.J., Conley, V.M. and Schuster, J.H. (2016) *The faculty factor: Reassessing the American academy in a turbulent era*, Baltimore: Johns Hopkins University Press.

Gándara, D. and Hearn, J.C. (November 2014) College completion, the Texas way: An examination of the development of college completion policy in a distinctive political culture, Paper presented at the annual meeting of the Association for the Study of Higher Education, Washington, DC.

Gándara, D., Rippner, J. and Ness, E. (forthcoming), 'Exploring the "how" in policy diffusion: national intermediary organizations' roles in facilitating the spread of performance-based funding policies in the states', *Journal of Higher Education*.

Glenny, L.A. (1959) *Autonomy of public colleges*, New York, NY: McGraw-Hill.

Glenny, L.A. and Dalglish, T.K. (1973) *Public universities, states agencies and the law: Constitutional autonomy in decline*, Berkeley, CA: Center for Research and Development in Higher Education, University of California, Berkeley.

Gray, V. and Lowery, D. (1996) 'A niche theory of interest representation', *Journal of Politics*, 58(1): 91–111.

Hall, C. and Thomas, S. (2012, April) 'Advocacy Philanthropy' and the public policy agenda: The role of modern foundations in American higher education, Paper presented at the annual meeting of the American Educational Research Association, Vancouver, British Columbia, Canada.

Hamilton, R. (2012) 'Perry's $10,000 Degree Challenge Spreads to Florida.' *The Texas Tribune*, 26 November.

https://texastribune.org/2012/11/26/perrys-10000-degree-challenge-spreads-florida/ (accessed 30 November 2016).

Hearn, J.C. (1993) 'The paradox of growth in federal aid for college students: 1965–1990', in J.C. Smart (ed.), *Higher education: Handbook of theory and research, Volume IX* New York: Agathon, pp. 94–153.

Hearn, J.C. (2015) *Outcomes-based funding in historical and comparative contexts, A lumina issue paper prepared for HCM strategists*, Indianapolis, IN: Lumina Foundation, Available online at https://luminafoundation.org/files/resources/hearn-obf-full.pdf.

Hearn, J.C. and Griswold, C.P. (1994) 'State-level centralization and policy innovation in U.S. postsecondary education', *Educational Evaluation and Policy Analysis*, 16(2): 161–190.

Hearn, J.C., Griswold, C.P. and Marine, G.M. (1996) 'Region, resources and reason: a contextual analysis of state tuition and student-aid policies', *Research in Higher Education*, 37 (3): 241–278.

Hearn, J.C. and Holdsworth, J.M. (2002) 'Influences of state-level policies and practices on college students' learning', *Peabody Journal of Education*, 73(3): 6–39.

Hearn, J.C., Lacy, T.A. and Warshaw, J.B. (2014) 'State research and development tax credits: the historical emergence of a distinctive economic policy instrument', *Economic Development Quarterly*, 28(2): 166–181.

Hearn, J.C., Lewis, D.R., Kallsen, L., Holdsworth, J.M. and Jones, L.M. (2006) '"Incentives for Managed Growth": a case study of incentives-based planning and budgeting in a large public research university', *Journal of Higher Education*, 77(2): 286–316.

Hearn, J.C., McLendon, M.K. and Lacy, T.A. (2013) 'State-funded "Eminent Scholars" programs: university faculty recruitment as an emerging policy instrument', *Journal of Higher Education*, 84(5): 601–641.

Hearn, J.C., McLendon, M.K. and Mokher, C. (2008) 'Accounting for student success: an empirical analysis of the origins and spread of state student unit-record systems', *Research in Higher Education*, 50(1): 665–683.

Hearn, J. and Milan, M.C. (2013) 'Here today, gone tomorrow? The increasingly contingent faculty workforce', *TIAA-CREF Institute: Advancing Higher Education*. Retrieved from https://tiaacrefinstitute.org/public/pdf/institute/research/advancing_higher_education/ahe_contingentfaculty0313.pdf

Hearn, J.C. and Warshaw, J.B. (2015) The evolving organizational character of the public research university, Paper presented at the Institutional Design Futures Conference, Scottsdale, AZ, April.

Hearn, J.C., Warshaw, J.B. and Ciarimboli, E.B. (2016) 'Privatization and accountability trends and policies in U.S. public higher education', *Education and Science*, 41 (184): 1–26.

Heller, D.E. (2002) 'State merit scholarship programs: an overview', in D.E. Heller and P. Marin (eds), *State merit scholarship programs and racial inequality*, Cambridge, MA: The Civil Rights Project at Harvard University, pp. 13–22.

Hicklin, A. and Meier, K.J. (2008) 'Race, structure and state governments: the politics of higher education diversity', *Journal of Politics*, 70(3): 851–860.

Hossler, D., Lund, J.P., Ramin, J., Westfall, S. and Irish, S. (1997) 'State funding for higher education: the Sisyphean task', *Journal of Higher Education*, 68(2): 160–188.

Lacy, T.A. (2013) *Measuring governance: State postsecondary structures and a continuum of centralization*, (Unpublished doctoral dissertation), Athens, GA: University of Georgia.

Lacy, T.A. and Tandberg, D.A. (2014) 'Rethinking policy diffusion: the interstate spread of "finance innovations."', *Research in Higher Education*, 55(7): 627–649.

Leslie, D.W. and Berdahl, R.O. (2008) 'The politics of restructuring higher education in Virginia: a case study', *Review of Higher Education*, 31(3): 309–328.

Levine, A.D., Lacy, T.A. and Hearn, J.C. (2013) The origins of embryonic stem cell research policies in the US states, *Science & Public Policy*, 40(4): 544–558.

Lowry, R.C. (2007) 'The political economy of public universities in the United States', *State Politics and Policy Quarterly*, 7(3): 303–324.

Malen, B. (2001) 'Generating interest in interest groups', *Educational Policy*, 15(19): 168–186.

McGuinness, A.C. (2011) 'The states and higher education', in P.G. Altbach, P.J. Gumport, and R.O. Berdahl (eds), *American higher education in the 21st century: Social, political and economic challenges* (3rd edn), Baltimore: Johns Hopkins University Press, pp. 139–169.

McGuinness, A.C. (2016) *State policy leadership for the future: History of state coordination and governance and alternatives for the future*, Denver, CO: Education Commission of the States.

McLendon, M.K. (2003) 'State governance reform of higher education: patterns, trends and theories of the public policy process', in J. Smart (ed.), *Higher education: Handbook of theory and research*, Volume 18, Netherlands: Springer, pp. 57–143.

McLendon, M.K. and Hearn, J.C. (2013) The resurgent interest in performance-based funding for higher education, *Academe*, 99(6): 25–30.

McLendon, M.K., Hearn, J.C. and Deaton, R. (2006) 'Called to account: analyzing the origins and spread of state performance-accountability policies for higher education', *Educational Evaluation and Policy Analysis*, 28(1): 1–24.

McLendon, M.K., Hearn, J.C. and Mokher, C. (2009) 'Partisans, professionals and power: the role of political factors in state higher education funding', *Journal of Higher Education*, 80(6): 686–713.

McLendon, M.K., Heller, D.E. and Young, S.P. (2005) 'State postsecondary policy innovation: politics, competition, and the interstate migration of policy ideas', *Journal of Higher Education*, 76(4): 363–400.

McLendon, M.K., Mokher, C. and Doyle, W. (2009) '"Privileging" public research universities, An empirical analysis of the distribution of state appropriations across research and non-research universities', *Journal of Education Finance*, 34(4): 372–401.

McLendon, M.K., Tandberg, D.A. and Hillman, N.W. (2014) 'Financing college opportunity: factors influencing state spending on student financial aid and campus appropriations, 1990 through 2010', *Annals of the American Academy*, 655: 143–162.

McMahon, W. (2009) *Higher learning, greater good*, Baltimore: Johns Hopkins University Press.

Meyer, J.W., Ramirez, F.O., Frank, D.J. and Schofer, E. (2007) 'Higher education as an institution', in P.J. Gumport (ed.), *Sociology of higher education: Contributions and their contexts*, Baltimore: Johns Hopkins University Press, pp. 187–220.

Mohr, L.B. (1969) 'Determinants of innovation in organizations', *American Political Science Review*, 63(19): 111–126.

Mokher, C.G. (2010) 'Do "education governors" matter?: the case of statewide P-16 councils', *Educational Evaluation and Policy Analysis*, 32(4): 476–497.

Mokher, C.G. and McLendon, M.K. (2009) 'Uniting secondary and postsecondary education: an event history analysis of state adoption of dual enrollment policies', *American Journal of Education*, 115: 249–277.

Mumper, M. (2001) 'The paradox of college prices: Five stories with no clear lesson', in D. Heller (ed.), *The states and public higher education policy: Affordability, access and accountability*, Baltimore, MD: Johns Hopkins University Press, pp. 39–63.

National Conference of State Legislatures, (2014) 'Full- and part-time legislatures'. Available online at http:/ncsl.org/research/about-state-legislatures/full-and-part-time-legislatures.aspx. (accessed on 17 December 2016).

Ness, E.C. and Gándara, D. (2014) 'Ideological think tanks in the states: an inventory of their prevalence, networks and higher education policy activity', *Educational Policy*, 28(2): 258–280.

Ness, E.C. and Mistretta, M.A. (2010) 'Merit aid in North Carolina: a case study of a "nonevent."' *Educational Policy*, 24(5): 703–734.

Ness, E.C. and Tandberg, D.A. (2013) 'The determinants of state spending on higher education: How capital project funding differs from general fund appropriations', *Journal of Higher Education*, 84(3): 329–357.

Ness, E.C., Tandberg, D.A. and McLendon, M.K. (2015) 'Interest groups and state policy for higher education: new conceptual understandings and future research directions', in M. B. Paulsen (ed.), *Higher education: Handbook of theory and research*, Vol. XXX, New York: Springer, pp. 151–186.

Newfield, C. (2016) *The great mistake: How we wrecked public universities and how we can fix them*, Baltimore: Johns Hopkins University Press.

Nicholson-Crotty, J. and Meier, K.J. (2003) 'Politics, structure and public policy: the case of higher education', *Educational Policy*, 17(1): 80–97.

Pascarella, E.T. and Terenzini, P.T. (2005) *How college affects students, Vol.2: A third decade of research*, San Francisco: Jossey-Bass.

Perna, L.W., Klein, M.W. and McLendon, M.K. (2014) Insights and implications for state policymakers, *Annals of the American Academy of Political and Social Science*, 655: 209–230.

Priest, D.M., Becker, W.E., Hossler, D. and St. John, E.P. (eds), (2002) *Incentive-based Budgeting Systems in Public Universities*, Northhampton, MA: Edward Elgar.

Pusser, B. (2008) 'The state, the market and the institutional estate: revisiting contemporary authority relations in higher education', in J.C. Smart (ed.), *Higher education: Handbook of theory and research* (Vol. 23), Dordrecht, Netherlands: Springer.

Reckhow, S. (2012) *Follow the money: How foundations dollars fuel public school politics*, New York: Oxford University Press.

Schmidtlein, F.A. and Berdahl, R.O. (2011) 'Autonomy and accountability: who controls academe?', in Altbach, P.G., Gumport, P.J. and Berdahl, R.O. (eds), *American higher education in the 21stCentury: Social, political, and economic challenges*, Baltimore, MD: Johns Hopkins University Press, pp. 69–87.

Schugurensky, D. (1999) 'Higher education restructuring in the era of globalization: Toward a heteronymous model?', in R. Arnove, and C. Torres (eds), *Comparative education: The dialectic of the global and the local*, Lanham, MD: Rowman and Littlefield, pp. 283–304.

Schumpeter, J. (1942) *Capitalism, socialism and democracy*, New York: Harper.

Shinn, Larry D. 2014 'Liberal Education vs. Professional education: the false choice.' *Trusteeship Magazine*, January/February, http://agb.org/trusteeship/2014/1/liberal-education-vs-professional-education-false-choice (accessed 30 November 2016).

Smith, A.A. (2015) Uniting to regulate for-profits, *Inside Higher Education*, Available online at https://insidehighered.com/news/2015/10/12/federal-agencies-join-forces-regulate-profit-colleges (accessed 2 September 2016).

Snyder, M. and Fox, B. (2016) *Driving better outcomes: Fiscal year 2016 state status and typology update*, Washington, DC: HCM Strategists.

Sponsler, B. (2010) 'Coveting more than thy neighbor: beyond geographically proximate explanations of postsecondary policy', *Higher Education in Review*, 7: 81–100.

Squire, P. (2000) Uncontested seats in state legislative elections, *Legislative Studies Quarterly*, 25(1): 131–146.

Squire, P. (2007) Measuring state legislative professionalism: The Squire Index revisited, *State Policy and Politics Quarterly*, 7(2): 211–227.

'Starving the beast: The battle to disrupt and reform America's public universities.' (2015) Video documentary by Steve Mims available online at https://kanopystreaming.com/product/starving-beast.

Tandberg, D.A. (2006) 'State-level higher education interest group alliances', *Higher Education in Review*, 3: 25–29.

Tandberg, D.A. (2010) 'Politics, interest groups and state funding of public higher education' *Research in Higher Education*, 51(5): 416–450.

Tandberg, D.A. (2013) 'The conditioning role of state higher education governance structures', *Journal of Higher Education*, 84(4): 506–543.

Tandberg, D.A. and Griffith, C. (2013) 'State support of higher education: Data, measures, findings, and directions for future research', in M.B. Paulsen (ed.), *Higher education: Handbook of theory and research*, Volume 28, New York, NY: Springer, pp. 613–685.

Tandberg, D.A. and Ness, E.C. (2011) 'State capital expenditures for higher education: "Where the politics really happens."', *Journal of Education Finance*, 36(4): 394–423.

Thelin, J. (2004) *A history of American higher education*, 2nd edn, Baltimore: Johns Hopkins University Press.

Thomason, A. (2016) Wisconsin regents approve post-tenure policies condemned by faculty, Chronicle of higher education. Available online at http://chronicle.com/blogs/ticker/wisconsin-regents-approve-post-tenure-policies-condemned-by-faculty/116042 (accessed 9 December 2016).

Toutkoushian, R. K., and Bellas, M. L. (2003) 'The effects of part-time employment and gender on faculty earnings and satisfaction: evidence from the NSOPF:93', *Journal of Higher Education*, 74(2): 172–195.

Toutkoushian, R.K., and Hollis, P. (1998) 'Using panel data to examine legislative demand for higher education', *Education Economics*, 6(2): 141–158.

Walker, J.L. (1969) 'The diffusion of innovations among the American states', *American Political Science Review*, 63(3): 880–899.

Wong, K.K. and Shen, F.X. (2002) 'Politics of state-led reform in education: market competition and electoral dynamics', *Education Policy*, 16(1): 161–192

Woodhouse, K. (2016) Mixed reviews for plan to change Tennessee higher education governance, Inside higher ed. Available online at https://insidehighered.com/news/2016/01/14/mixed-reviews-plan-changetennessee-higher-education-governance.

Zumeta, W. (1992) 'State policies and private higher education: policies, correlates and linkages', *Journal of Higher Education*, 63(4): 363–417.

Zumeta, W. (1996) 'Meeting the demand for higher education without breaking the bank: a framework for the design of state higher education policies for an era of increasing demand', *Journal of Higher Education*, 67(4): 367–425.

Zumeta, W. (2001) 'Public policy and accountability in higher education: Lessons from the past and present for the new Millennium', in D.E. Heller (ed.), *The states and public higher education: affordability, access, and accountability*, Baltimore, MD: Johns Hopkins University Press, pp. 155–197.

Zumeta, W. and Kinne, A. (2011) 'Accountability policies: New and old', in D.E. Heller (ed.), *The states and public higher education policy: Affordability, access and accountability* (2nd edn), Baltimore: Johns Hopkins University Press, pp.173–199.

4
The Australian hybrid: public and private higher education funding

ANDREW NORTON

Higher education never exists in a political vacuum. The boundaries between university and state authority, and the financial connections between universities and governments, differ over time and between nations. Although in every country higher education policy changes through the decades, distinct national patterns persist over time. In Australia, a mixed public and private funding model has usually dominated.

This chapter examines Australian higher education funding policy since World War II. It shows how longstanding policy institutions and political views shape current arrangements, and limit the likely range of future changes. In doing so, it draws on Julian Garritzmann's hypothesis about national differences in higher education finance systems. Garritzmann argues that in some countries enduring postwar social democratic governments established stable systems of zero or low higher education student charges. Conservative parties eventually adapted to voter expectations of free or cheap higher education. By contrast, in other countries long-term postwar conservative governments entrenched student charges, and social democratic party eventually accepted this political fact (Garritzmann, 2016).

Australia broadly fits into this second group. Conservative political dominance in the postwar decades created a relatively small state compared to other OECD countries, and consequent partial reliance on private funding of social services, including education. A social democratic government abolished public university tuition fees in 1974, but did not survive long enough to entrench its policy. The need to fund additional student places on limited taxation revenue led to student charges being reintroduced in the 1980s. Commercial education markets, especially for international students, proved to be highly successful. By 2015, direct government grants made up just over 40 percent of all university revenue, down from a peak of 90 percent during the free education period.

The Australian hybrid • 49

The history of Australian higher education funding

Early political history of Australian higher education

In Australia, higher education became but was not originally a matter of national politics. When six British colonies united to become states in the Commonwealth of Australia in 1901, the new national government could only legislate on matters specifically listed in its Constitution. Education was not mentioned, and so the six new states retained power over it within their borders. All states had universities by World War I, with five of the six relying partly on student fees for income; the University of Western Australia (UWA) on its own decision initially charged no tuition fees (Alexander, 1963: 16–17).

Given its limited constitutional responsibilities and powers, the national government – often called the Commonwealth government in Australia – had little influence on higher education until the 1940s. From 1941 the Labour Party, a left-leaning party founded by the trade unions, was in power. During and after World War II, Labour used the Commonwealth's defence power to finance education for war-related occupations and help returning servicemen attend university (Tracey, 2001). It wanted continued involvement in higher education after the war, and in 1946 held a successful referendum to amend the Constitution, authorising payments of 'benefits to students'. This gave general scholarship programs a secure legal basis, but at the time the new power was not thought to support direct grants to universities. These remained a state responsibility.Unfortunately for universities, legal and political developments during the war diminished the capacity of state governments to assist them financially. In 1942, the High Court upheld a Commonwealth government takeover of all income tax, which had previously been also imposed by state governments (Coper, 1988, Chapter 5). Combined with other constitutional limits on their taxation powers, the decision left state governments without the money to meet all their education, health, transport, policing and other responsibilities. Since that time, state governments have relied on Commonwealth government grants to supplement their own taxation revenue. This meant that whether or not the Commonwealth government directly invested in higher education, national political priorities would inevitably influence university finances. Without Commonwealth intervention, Australian higher education institutions would have needed high student fees to provide quality education.

The postwar expansion of higher education

In the 1949 national elections, Labor was defeated and did not win another election until 1972. During this period Australia was ruled by a Liberal-Country Party coalition. The Liberal Party was formed in the mid-1940s from a coalition of anti-Labor groups; despite its name it has been the main vehicle for conservative as well as Liberal politics. The Country Party was established to represent the interests of regional Australia; it has clear conservative politics. This coalition's dominant figure was Robert Menzies, prime minister from 1949 to 1966. He took a strong personal interest in higher education, commissioning several reviews that profoundly altered Australian higher education.

The first of these, the 1950 Mills review, prompted an innovation in higher education finance that sidestepped the limits of the 'benefits to students' power. To support higher education more directly, the Commonwealth government used a constitutional power to give the states conditional grants – in this case, that they pay money to named universities. In the Menzies era, this funding was primarily aimed at lifting the quality of Australia's universities. In 1950, Australia's universities were suffering the effects of economic depression and war. Quality was still a concern for the 1957 Murray review. It concluded that universities had poor facilities and teaching, and were ill-equipped to produce the number of graduates Australia would need (Murray et al., 1957). The Murray report led to a large increase in Commonwealth government funding to universities, which by 1965 was eight times as high as it had been in 1957 (Martin et al., 1964: 100).[1]

The Murray committee thought that some 'suitably qualified' school leavers could not attend university due to cost. But the idea of abolishing student fees was not mentioned in their report. The Menzies government's funding formula encouraged universities to charge fees, as Commonwealth grants were linked to state grant and fee income (Murray et al., 1957: 24); the higher these were the more the Commonwealth paid. This eventually prompted the UWA to introduce tuition fees. Rather than ending fee charging, the committee recommended expanding existing scholarship programs (Murray et al., 1957: 64–67). The number of students receiving Commonwealth scholarships nearly doubled between 1957 and 1965 (Commonwealth Scholarships Board, 1971: 35).

The 1964 Martin report similarly did not recommend regulating fee charging, but nor did it see fees as a major solution to higher education funding needs. The Martin report observed in a matter-of-fact way that rapid enrolment growth meant that income from fees and donations could no longer sustain universities, and that they must instead rely more on grants from government (Martin et al., 1964: 84).

Although Menzies himself and the reports he commissioned, valued a broad Liberal education, the policy imperatives were to meet rising student demand and labour market need for more skilled workers. Between 1949 and 1972, the number of students increased from less than 32,000 to more than 182,000 (Department of Education and Training, 2014). Public expenditure increased rapidly, as Figure 1 shows.

Educational opportunity was a significant consideration, long a part of university practice and a goal of the Commonwealth scholarships (Commonwealth Scholarships Board, 1971; Forsyth, 2014: 10–13). Most students received at least some financial assistance from outside their family, mainly from their university and Commonwealth and state governments (ABS, various years-a). The fees charged were low compared to average per student university income. In 1972, average annual recurrent university grants per equivalent full-time student were $17,200 in $A2015 (AUC, 1972: 109). By contrast, in 1971 fees ranged between $2,200 and $6,000 a year with an average of $4,300 (all A$2015) (National Archives, 1981: 22–23). Despite substantial public subsidies, the system was however some way from the free education model in other countries.

Universities rather than the government still set per student fees, which had increased significantly over time for those who paid them (Tescher and Bain, 1972). While shrinking as a share of all university income, total student fee revenue was increasing (Figure 1). The number of Commonwealth scholarships allocated fell well short of demand (Commonwealth Scholarships Board, 1974: 21). Scholarships were allocated based on academic merit, a system that favoured students from affluent families. A means-tested living allowance was available for scholarship holders, but there was no government income support for other students.

The Menzies-era hybrid model of financing universities fitted with the government's broad approach across other issues. Although government spending increased during the long postwar Liberal government, Australia did not become a European-style comprehensive welfare state (Roskam, 2001).

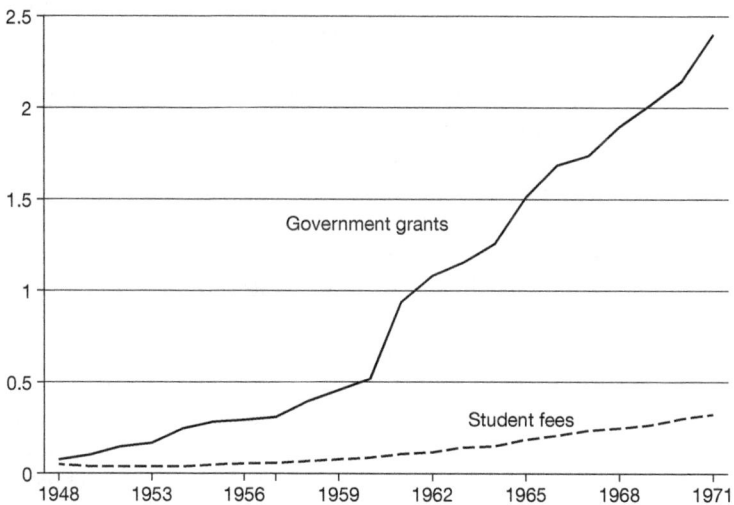

Figure 4.1 Student fee and government grant income for Australian universities, 1948–1971 ($2015 billion)

Notes: Government grants includes state and Commonwealth funding. Other revenue sources omitted. These were similar in scale to student fees in the 1960s.

Source: (ABS, various years-a)

Most government personal financial assistance was aimed at poverty relief, not preserving previous living standards on losing a job, becoming ill or retiring. The private sector retained a significant role in social service delivery. Despite nearly a century in which private schools received no government financial assistance, their enrolment share never fell below 20 percent of all students. Private schools received government support from the 1960s (Buckingham, 2010: 2). In the early 1970s, 80 percent of the population had private health insurance and more than a third of total health spending was private (Duckett and Willcox, 2015: 70–83). When the Liberals finally lost office in 1972, government revenues were 21 percent of GDP, compared to around a third of GDP in most European welfare states (OECD, 2016).

The free education era

After 23 years in opposition, Labour returned to power in late 1972. It was led by Gough Whitlam, who had a long-standing belief that, as he told parliament in 1953, education from kindergarten to postgraduate should be 'without cost to the individual' (Whitlam, 1985: 293). In the 1969 election, Whitlam became the first leader of a major political party to commit to free tertiary education (Stokes and Edmonds, 1990: 11).

One obstacle to Whitlam's policy was that his government neither charged university fees nor had any direct constitutional power to regulate them, for universities located in one of the six states. Universities could refuse any direction from the Commonwealth, if they were also willing to forego the Commonwealth's money, provided via conditional grants to state governments. But the growth in Commonwealth funding since the 1940s gave Whitlam substantial leverage, further increased by his willingness to relieve state governments of their higher education funding responsibilities. No university declined Commonwealth assistance, and tertiary education was free to students from 1974. About 90 percent of university revenue now came from the Commonwealth government (Norton and Cakitaki, 2016: 54).

For many students at the time, university was already free because scholarships paid their fees. But for students who did pay fees themselves, Whitlam argued that 'they were a very large percentage of parents' or students' income (McAllister and Moore, 1991: 106). The 1971 average fee of $4,300 compared to an average wage of $43,500 a year at the time (all A$2015) (ABS, 1971).

The Whitlam government also reformed student income support. The living allowances attached to competitive scholarships of the Liberal era were replaced with means-tested student income support (ABS, 1974: 662). This was consistent with the goals of a social democratic government, as it meant that all admitted students were eligible for assistance based on financial need, and not just those with the highest prior academic achievement.

In only the second year of free education the Whitlam government lost office. From 1975 to 1983, the Liberal Party, led by Malcolm Fraser, was back in office.

In 1972, Fraser had criticized Labor's free tertiary education policy on the grounds that it would lead to a 'wharf labourer paying taxes to subsidise a lawyer's education' (Fraser and Simons, 2010: 241). Within months of the Liberals resuming office they proposed fees for postgraduate and second degree students, although this was eventually abandoned for political reasons (National Archives, 1976).

In 1979, Fraser's Cabinet (the key executive decision making body in Australian government) considered a general reintroduction of university fees, at a suggested rate of about 20 percent of costs (National Archives, 1979). The Cabinet submission did not propose returning to the pre-1974 system in which fees supplemented government grants. Instead, the context was the financial problems afflicting Australian governments since the mid-1970s. By charging fees, the government could save money. Like Fraser in 1972, the submission suggested that it was 'inequitable' that general taxpayers subsidize students who go on to 'command above-average incomes'. The government did not proceed with the policy at that point, but in 1981 introduced a bill to charge up to $3,700 for second degrees ($A2015) (National Archives, 1981). It was rejected by the Senate, the upper house of Parliament in which the Liberals did not have a majority.

Student charges begin to return

The first cracks in the free education policy came with international rather than domestic students. From 1980, the Fraser government introduced charges for overseas students. In this case, the principal rationale was not to reduce government spending. International students, who mainly came from South-East Asia, were seen as part of Australia's foreign policy. Expenditure was controlled through quotas on student numbers, and the new charge, although well below tuition costs, would allow the quota to be increased (National Archives, 1979; Meadows, 2011).

Policy on international students was revisited by the Hawke Labor government, which replaced the Fraser government in 1983. From 1986 universities could charge international students fees for places over and above the quota for subsidized places. A minimum fee was set to avoid cross-subsidy from government grants to fee-paying students, but no maximum price.

The opening up of international student markets was supported, from the trade ministry, by John Dawkins, who became education minister in 1987. Dawkins is a central figure in increasing student funding of Australian higher education. Within the government, he had with finance minister Peter Walsh earlier pushed for fees to be reintroduced (Macintyre et al., 2013: 12). They were part of a strand of Labor thinking that saw higher education subsidies as regressive, favouring the present or future wealthy rather than Labour's constituency. The Cabinet memorandum on reintroducing fees argued this point, asserting that the 'substantial private returns' on education justified a charge, if fee exemptions or loans could provide access to people on low incomes (National Archives, 1985). In the end, however, the government pursued only a small 'administration charge' from 1987 (National Archives, 1986).

The Labor government also began creating a fee-paying postgraduate coursework market from 1988. Initially, they let universities charge fees for courses aimed at already-employed people upgrading their skills (DEET, 1993: 93). Restrictions were progressively removed over the next 6 years, so that by 1994 initial professional entry teaching and nursing qualifications remained in the public funding system, but other domestic postgraduate non-research courses were largely in a deregulated market (Anderson *et al.*, 1998: 111–112). As with international students, universities could decide on postgraduate coursework numbers and prices.

Income contingent loans

In the 1970s and 1980s, policymakers repeatedly tried to end or curtail free higher education, but with only limited success by the late 1980s. Most domestic students paid only a token amount for their education. But in 1988, Dawkins succeeded where he and his predecessors had previously failed and legislated the Higher Education Contribution Scheme (HECS), imposing a flat price for coursework students and creating the world's first national income contingent loan scheme (Chapman and Nicholls, 2013). From 1989, students paid $3,600 for a year's tuition, which they could borrow and repay when their income reached a threshold of $44,300 (all in A$2015), a little below the average wage at the time.

The broader higher education policy context was familiar – demand for higher education was growing. School completion rates increased significantly during the 1980s, pushing up the number of unsuccessful applications for university entry (Norton, 2016: 186). Until the mid-1970s Commonwealth governments responded to greater demand with more public funding, supplemented until 1974 with state government funding and student fees. But now the Commonwealth government was fully responsible for higher education student funding and facing significant budget problems. In real terms, total higher education funding was flat between 1975 and 1986 before the administration charge financed slightly increased outlays (DEET, 1993: 71). There was little prospect of substantial additional public funding to finance more student places.

For student demand to be met another revenue source had to be found. A student charge with an income contingent loan was the solution, at least for people in the Dawkins strand of Labor thinking. The HECS system avoided upfront charges that might make higher education impossible for some students, high fees that might prove a financial deterrent, or loan repayments that could take a large share of a graduate's income. HECS also dealt with Dawkins' objections to free higher education. A report Dawkins commissioned to justify reintroducing student charges repeated the critique: higher education subsidies were inequitable because students tended to come from privileged backgrounds, and because graduates enjoy significant private benefits, including better jobs, lower unemployment and relatively high lifetime income. The taxpayers who did not directly benefit from higher education should not have to finance its growth (Wran, 1988: ix–xi).

Although HECS had fewer policy problems than alternative methods of charging students, its successful enactment was not a foregone conclusion. Whitlam's free higher education policy had achieved iconic status in some sections of the community (Norton, 2008). Dawkins faced substantial opposition within the Labour Party and outside the government, led by higher education staff and student unions (Chapman and Nicholls, 2013; Macintyre et al., 2013). That HECS was implemented owes much to the political skill of Dawkins and a talented team of advisers, many of whom went on to significant careers in Australian higher education policy.

The Liberal Party was not initially in favour of HECS. The problem was not students paying for their education, but rather a 'graduate tax' in which the financial relationship was between students and the government, rather than between students and the universities. But by 1991, they had accepted income contingent loans (Norton, 2013a: 286–289). Since, then the major political parties have differed on many higher education policy details, but with bipartisan support for income-contingent loan supported student charges for domestic undergraduates.

Student charges increase under a Liberal government

In 1996, after 13 years in opposition, the Liberals returned to power, with John Howard as prime minister. As with the Fraser Liberal government 20 years earlier, their higher education policy was initially driven by their budgetary problems. The most radical change was the introduction from 1997 of 'differential HECS' – HECS charges based on discipline, rather than the flat rate introduced by Labour. The three different rates, all higher than the previous flat amount, were based on a mix of cost and lifetime earnings factors (Vanstone, 1996: 10). Medicine and law were allocated the highest charge, equivalent to $8,900 a year (A$2015), and humanities and nursing were in the lowest category with a charge of $5,300 a year. The increased rates allowed corresponding reductions in government funding.

Other policy changes were also significant. As the imperative in 1996 was to save money, previously planned increases in student places were rescinded. To limit effects on undergraduate numbers, cuts were focused on postgraduate coursework places, where universities could substitute unsubsidized fee-paying students. Universities were also allowed to offer unsubsidized fee-paying places to undergraduates, once they had filled their government allocation of HECS students. Income contingent loans were not available for these students.

By 1998, higher education policy was an awkward mix of Dawkins' reforms and budget-driven Liberal policies. In 1999 the then education minister, David Kemp, put a radical alternative to Cabinet. It proposed abolishing controls on student numbers, providing subsidies to all domestic undergraduates whether at public or private institutions, letting student fees be set in the market and creating a loan scheme that covered all students (Kemp, 2001). But Kemp's submission was leaked to Labour, and after a brief controversy it was abandoned by the government (Norton, 2013a: 290–293).[2]

The most important late 1990s policy change was making it easier for former international students to migrate to Australia, triggering rapid growth in enrolments and fee revenue for universities (Norton, 2013a: 293–294). Rising demand from Asia, the relaxation of migration rules, and policy-driven stagnation in domestic undergraduate income combined to give universities an opportunity and a need to promote international education.

In the early 2000s, the Liberals returned to higher education policy. Kemp rescued part of his 1999 package and introduced income-contingent loans for unsubsidized fee-paying domestic postgraduate students from 2002. Their full-time equivalent enrolments increased by a third in 3 years (Norton, 2016: 190).

In 2005, the domestic undergraduate student financing system was reformed again by another Liberal minister, Brendan Nelson. With the government's budget in surplus, public expenditure went up by a cumulative 7.5 percent per student place over 3 years, with universities implementing governance and workplace reforms in exchange. HECS student charges set by and paid to the government were replaced with student contributions set by and paid to universities, up to a maximum legislated by the government. For most disciplines, the maximum was 25 percent higher than previous differential HECS rates. HECS loans were replaced with HECS-HELP loans. With no public funding cut to justify, the fee increase did not need the private benefit argument used by Labor in the late 1980s and the Liberals in the mid-1990s. Instead, the government claimed that their policy would promote flexibility and diversity as universities could set their own student contributions between $0 and the maximum amount (Nelson, 2003: 20).

Contrary to the government's expectations, soon all universities charged the maximum student contribution amount. Nelson's system of pricing government-supported places did not produce the price variability he wanted, but it has lasted. With some discipline-level tinkering it is still used in 2017. A 2014 attempt to cut per student public subsidies and deregulate student contributions was rejected by the Senate (Coaldrake and Stedman, 2016, Chapter 9). It is now 20 years since per student public subsidies were last reduced, and 12 years since the last general real increase in student contributions.

The hybrid system of public and private funding for public universities can be seen in Figure 2. For a time from the mid-1990s to early 2000s, private funding largely replaced lost public funding. From the mid-2000s, all revenue sources grew in most years; some good timing meant that strong periods from

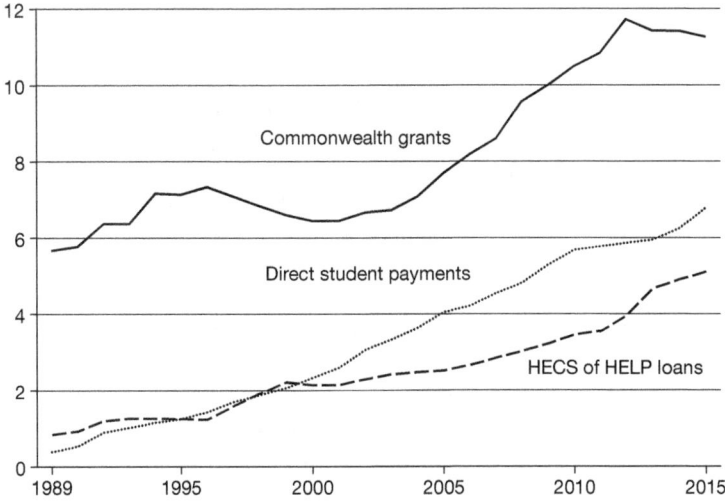

Figure 4.2 Revenue sources for public universities, 1989–2015 ($2015 billion)
Note: Includes University of Notre Dame since 1998. Other revenue sources not shown.
Source: (Department of Education and Training various years)

one revenue source have compensated for weak results from another. In the last decade substantial increases in both public and private funding supported an exceptional period of strong growth in student enrolments and research activity (Norton and Cakitaki, 2016: 20–24, 39–40, 52–53).

Private higher education providers

In Australia, public higher education was established first and has always dominated the sector. The early private higher education sector was small and sometimes partly co-opted into the public sector. Many private colleges were religious, including theological colleges (Murray *et al.*, 1957, Vol. 2). Several Catholic teacher training colleges were brought into the public funding system in the early 1970s (Beazley, 1977) – becoming the Australian Catholic University in 1991, with the same funding entitlements as government-founded universities.

In the late 1980s, two very different private universities were established. Bond University was a project of the businessman Alan Bond, whose companies stood to profit from the increased value of real estate around the university (Orr, 1991). It offered small classes and a stronger teaching emphasis than the public universities. The University of Notre Dame was designed to meet the staffing needs of Catholic schools and hospitals in Western Australia (Tannock, 2014). Its purposes were similar to those of the Australian Catholic University in the eastern states, but its later founding left it formally outside the public university system, although it now receives significant government funding.

Initially, however, the two private universities relied entirely on private funding. With a few exceptions, this was also the case for non-university private higher education providers, which nevertheless expanded in the 1990s. By 1999, nearly eighty private higher education institutions were operating. They awarded their own degrees for courses accredited by a state government regulator (accreditation is now the role of the national Tertiary Education Quality and Standards Agency, known as TEQSA). Most private education providers were small in 1999, enrolling about 31,000 students between them, or approximately 4 percent of all Australian higher education enrolments (Watson, 2000).

In 1998, a Liberal government-sponsored review recommended a phased eligibility of the private higher education sector for public financial support, starting with income contingent loans with tuition subsidies to follow (West et al., 1998). This idea went to Cabinet the following year, but was lost with David Kemp's broader reform package. Two further reviews, in 2008 and 2014, recommended extending general public subsidy eligibility to private higher education (Bradley et al., 2008; Kemp and Norton, 2014).[3] The 2014 review's recommendation was accepted by the Liberal government, but the Senate rejected the necessary legislation.

Tuition subsidies for private education providers remain as they have been since the 1990s. Based on ministerial discretion, they can be allocated government supported student places in 'national priority' areas, receiving for each student the same discipline-based tuition subsidy and regulated student contribution amount as the public universities. Only five private providers receive such places, with the vast majority granted to the University of Notre Dame. By contrast, since 2012 public universities can enrol unlimited numbers of government-supported bachelor-degree students.

Private higher education providers can enrol unlimited numbers of students at fees they set in the market, while from 2009 Labor abolished the public university fee-deregulated undergraduate places introduced by the Liberals 12 years earlier. Private higher education provider fees vary significantly, but in 2015 averaged A$15,000 a year for domestic bachelor-degree students in non-university higher education providers, nearly 50 percent higher than the maximum student contribution amount for students receiving public tuition subsidies (Norton, 2015).

Although the tuition subsidy funding system strongly favours public universities, other government funding sources offer more equal treatment. Student income support eligibility is defined by enrolment in an accredited higher education course, making it neutral between public and private higher education for undergraduates.[4] Students in private higher education colleges have been included in the means-tested student income support system from its beginning in 1974. Since 2005, income contingent loans have been available to students in all higher education providers that meet objective criteria. Most private higher education providers now offer their students a government-financed income contingent loan called FEE-HELP (Norton and Cakitaki, 2016: 101–103). FEE-HELP and student income support have made it easier for the private higher education sector to grow.

As of July 2016, 109 privately founded education providers were registered with TEQSA. A majority are for-profit, but forty-eight are registered as having a charitable purpose in the public benefit through advancing education (Norton and Cakitaki, 2016: 12–13). Often included with the private education sector are state government vocational training institutes that have branched out into higher education and subsidiary colleges of public universities. Although owned by public sector institutions, their students generally receive no tuition subsidies and pay market-set fees.

Because of their historical price and other disadvantages, private higher education providers rarely compete directly with public universities in domestic undergraduate markets. Instead, they typically serve niche markets that public universities cannot or do not want to enter. Fourteen providers operate as pathway colleges, specialising in diploma-level qualifications with content equivalent to first year in a bachelor-degree. Successful students continue their studies in the second year of a public university bachelor-degree course. Public universities are constrained in this market by the limited number of government-supported places allocated to diploma-level courses. More than twenty private colleges have a religious affiliation, while all government-founded universities are secular. Nineteen private higher education providers specialize in health-related courses, with a large presence in alternative health, providing courses most public universities are reluctant to offer.

International and postgraduate student markets are more price competitive between public universities and other education providers, as most students pay market-set fees. In twenty-eight non-university higher education providers, international students make up two-thirds or more of enrolments. In some postgraduate areas, private higher education providers have advantages over public universities with courses in the same field. For example, professional associations for nurses and chartered accountants which also offer postgraduate qualifications have strong visibility and credibility in their target markets. These different market structures show in enrolment shares. Only 4 percent of domestic bachelor-degree students are enrolled outside the public universities, compared to nearly 9 percent of domestic postgraduates and 11.6 percent of international students (Department of Education and Training, 2016a).

In total, private higher education providers had over 100,000 students in 2015. Although this is more than triple their 1999 enrolments, their share of all students is still small at about 7 percent (Department of Education and Training, 2016a).

There is no trend data on the private higher education sector's finances. TEQSA statistics on non-university higher education providers indicate 2015 higher education income of about A$1.4 billion, or just under 6 percent of higher education revenue for all providers (TEQSA, 2016). Students of private universities and non-university higher education providers borrowed A$500 million through HELP in 2015, or 9 percent of all HELP tuition fee lending (Department of Education and Training, 2016a).

Thematic analysis of private funding of public universities

Full-fee students

For most of Australia's higher education history governments did not directly regulate public university fees. But before free higher education began in 1974 fees were low by current standards, kept down by state and Commonwealth grants. The idea that fees should cover all tuition costs and also deliver profits developed from the 1980s – leading to the terminology of 'full-fee students', who pay the full cost of their course or more, while fees for government-supported students are described as a 'contribution' to costs. Several factors seem to explain the rise of full-fee students.

Although Australia has funded international students as part of its foreign aid programme for more than 60 years, Australian public universities were and are primarily for a local 'public'. Making all university places fully government funded from 1974 created a direct trade-off between local and foreign students. With domestic university applicants missing out due to too few places, this was a political problem. The issue was resolved with the students outside the Australian public, people who could not vote in Australian elections, paying more from 1980 and market fees later in the decade. It is inconceivable that 320,000 international higher education students would have been enrolled in Australian public universities in 2015 if they were still government funded.

Like the government, public universities do not see international students as members of the Australian public whose interests they were created to serve. Instead, international students are enrolled to make profits universities can spend on other purposes, especially research. To achieve this goal, international students are often charged very high fees (Norton and Cherastidtham, 2015b). Teaching surpluses financed at least 20 percent of all Australian university research expenditure in 2012 (Norton and Cherastidtham, 2015a). Financial reliance on international students has encouraged questionable practices in some universities, especially around recruitment and marking (ICAC, 2015) (NTEU, 2015: 21).

The domestic fee-paying postgraduate coursework market also developed in the context of a capped number of government-funded places. Higher education policy's equity focus meant that students entering university for the first time had priority, not people seeking additional qualifications. That was the logic behind the Fraser government unsuccessfully proposing fees for second degrees, the Hawke government's phasing in of postgraduate fee-paying places, and the Howard government's decision to focus its cuts on government-funded postgraduate coursework places. Full-fee places allowed enrolments to

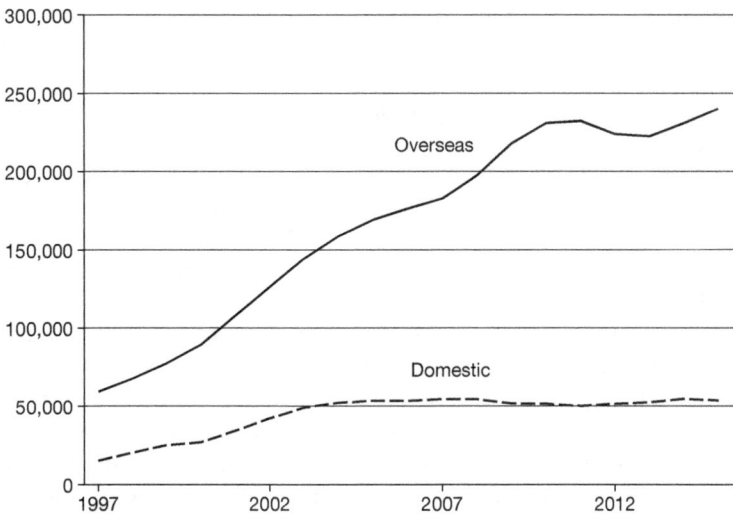

Figure 4.3 Full-fee paying students in Australian public universities (full-time equivalent), 1997–2015

Sources: (DETYA, 2000; Department of Education and Training, 2017)

expand in line with demand, while not compromising opportunities for an undergraduate education. The introduction of income contingent loans for postgraduate coursework in 2002 eased access issues created by upfront fees. The fees charged to domestic postgraduate students are typically significantly lower than those paid by international students for the same course, and sometimes also below what universities are paid for a government-supported student (Norton and Cherastidtham, 2015b). Despite high fees in some courses, universities still pursue aspects of their local public missions in domestic fee-paying markets.

Unlike the domestic government-subsidized undergraduate market until 2012, full-fee markets were usually unregulated in the number of student places; they are now entirely uncapped. International student enrolments increased in every year since deregulation until 2012; they are now back in a growth phase. Domestic full-fee enrolments are less robust; although postgraduate numbers are up by more than a quarter on a full-time equivalent basis since 2008, this has been offset by a decline in undergraduates since full-fee places were phased out from 2009 (Figure 3).

Charges paid by government-supported students

The largest group of higher education students in Australia remains domestic undergraduates in government-supported places. The government pays a tuition subsidy on their behalf to their higher education provider, while students pay a student contribution up to a legislated maximum (Norton and Cakitaki, 2016: 57). On average, students are charged 42 percent of the total funding rate, but the proportion varies depending on subjects taken, from less than 30 percent in agriculture to more than 80 percent in law and business. These differences occur because student charges vary with expected future financial benefit while overall funding rates vary principally with historical estimates of teaching costs. Additional subsidies are paid via the HECS-HELP loan scheme, due to bad debt and low interest rates (Norton and Cakitaki, 2016: 47–48). About 90 percent of eligible undergraduates take out a loan to pay for their student contribution.

Australia's tuition charges are high compared to other OECD countries, a point often made locally, including by government-commissioned higher education funding reviews (Bradley *et al.*, 2008: 141), (Lomax-Smith *et al.*, 2011: 98). Significant sentiment remains for free or cheaper higher education. In a 2015 poll, 63 percent of respondents thought government should pay more for university education, while 23 percent thought students should pay more (The Australia Institute, 2015). University staff hold these views more strongly than the general community. A 2015 survey found 58 percent agreement with the proposition that 'university education should be free for all Australians', while only 24 percent agreed that because students derive a private benefit from their education they should pay at least half its cost (NTEU, 2015: 13).

Despite these views, charging for higher education is not anomalous in Australia's political context. Australia fits within the broad patterns of higher education finance identified in Julian Garritzmann's international survey (Garritzmann, 2016). Its conservative government for 23 years of the post-World War II period left Australia with a relatively small state and extensive private provision and funding of social services. The strong personal interest in higher education of Liberal Party Prime Minister Robert Menzies, in office from 1949 to 1966, probably led to more public funding than would have occurred under another leader. But neither his government nor the policy reviews it commissioned questioned universities being allowed to charge fees.

No subsequent Liberal government – from 1975 to 1983, from 1996 to 2007, and from 2013 to the present – has believed in free higher education or made it cheaper. All three have sought to reintroduce or increase student charges. This is not an isolated stance on higher education: it is part of a broader preference for minimising taxation, charging for social services where possible, and using non-government organizations in social policy (Norton, 2004). As the Liberal Party has been the governing or major opposition party since the mid-1940s, this worldview meant that a Labor policy of free or cheap higher education was always going to be unstable.

Free or cheap higher education is a better ideological match with the Labor Party, in power whenever the Liberals are not. In the 1970s, Whitlam's belief in free higher education was part of a broader worldview supporting a move away from the Menzies-era limited and targeted welfare state to more universal benefits (Carney and Hanks, 1994: 42–43). But there were always people within Labor who did not support free higher education. This owed something to Labor being founded by the labour movement rather than as a social democratic party. Francis Castles has long argued that Australia and New Zealand developed distinctive welfare regimes, based from the early twentieth century on using the wage fixing system to maintain living standards (Castles, 2010). State welfare expenditure focused on filling gaps, not providing universal benefits.

Commonwealth Labor governments after Whitlam – from 1983 to 1996 and 2007 to 2013 – were more cautious in their public spending. They never developed social service and welfare programmes, or taxation levels, on the scale seen in European welfare states. Government support remained targeted on low-income households more than in most other OECD countries. With this focus on needs, criticisms of higher education subsidies as favouring the wealthy rather than the poor resonated with Labor as well as the Liberals. Labor's history helps explain why it did not firmly commit to free higher education earlier than the late 1960s, and retreated from it in the 1980s.

John Dawkins in the late 1980s understood that free higher education in a fiscally-constrained country leads to relatively elite education – expenditure is controlled by limiting student numbers, which via academic merit based student selection directs most spending to relatively affluent families. The supply of student places has been the main constraint on higher education participation in Australia. In all years for which we have records, demand has exceeded supply (Norton, 2016: 186). Free education in the 1970s did not increase lifetime higher education attainment rates, because with a large baby boom cohort reaching university age there were too few student places to meet additional demand (Norton and Cherastidtham, 2014: 67). Private funding of student places to increase their number was, in the Australian context, the most feasible way to increase higher education opportunity and attainment.

While the post-Dawkins funding system has had varying levels of responsiveness to student demand, Figure 4 shows that Australia and other higher-fee countries have good higher education attainment rates for adults aged 25–34, partly because private revenue lets them finance more student places. Australia's attainment rate should improve significantly in coming years, as the Labor government's 2012 lifting of all funding constraints on bachelor-degree student numbers has increased late teenage participation rates (Norton and Cakitaki, 2016: 22).

Figure 4.4 shows that there is no one way to achieve high attainment rates. Zero-fee Nordic countries do very well. But higher education funding systems integrate with a broader political, social and economic context. In the Nordic countries, postwar politics established large welfare states with significant tax bases and public support, including for free higher education (Garritzmann, 2016; OECD, 2016). For Australia, the long period of Liberal Party rule after World War II, its subsequent periods in office, the brevity of the Whitlam government and the character of later Labor governments all counted against

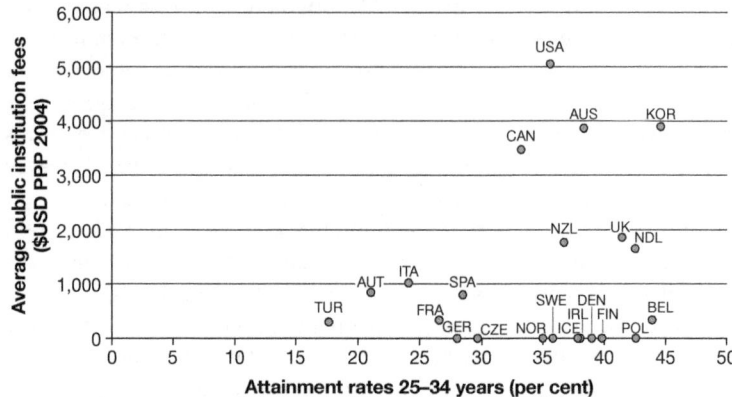

Figure 4.4 OECD higher education attainment by student fees

Notes: The fees data is lagged to reflect the time when people aged 25–34 are likely to have studied. When a range of fees is reported, the mid-point is used.

Sources: (OECD, 2015), table A1.3a; (OECD, 2007), table B5.1a

a political context in which free higher education could become an established policy. The Australian welfare state generally expects people to pay for or contribute to social services when they can, and taxation is correspondingly a lower share of GDP than in other OECD countries. Student charges with income contingent loans and means-tested student income support are consistent with this overall approach.

The future of private higher education funding in Australia

Within the constraints of its political system, Australia will continue to debate public and private provision and funding of higher education. The level of public subsidy, how flexible student contributions for government-supported students should be, and whether the private higher education sector should receive more public funding are all on-going issues.

Level of public subsidy

The last significant cut in per student public funding occurred in 1997, with a compensating increase in per student private funding. Although continued per student funding stability is possible and perhaps likely, the main trigger for seeking cuts – a large Commonwealth government budget deficit – is present. After a period of budget surpluses, every year since 2008–2009 has resulted in a deficit, (Australian Government, 2016). Both major political parties want to restore the Commonwealth's finances. As in 1997, there is a Liberal government with no ideological commitment to cheap higher education. On Budget night

2016, the current minister signalled his intention to pursue further savings by issuing a discussion paper with various options for reducing public expenditure (Department of Education and Training, 2016b).[5]

Somewhat paradoxically, given the usual political association between markets and small government, market mechanisms in Australian higher education have made it more difficult to limit public spending. Lifting controls on the number of government-supported student places was a major reason for the rapid public spending increase between 2008 and 2012 shown in Figure 2. Universities rushed to fill unmet demand, and advertized to attract more students. Under the previous system, the government typically limited the supply of student places when its own finances were strained. Under the current system, enrolment growth was strong until 2015, when it moderated of its own accord. In the main bachelor-degree market, current legislation allows the government to freeze but not reduce spending (Norton, 2013b: 25–26). Without easy ways of controlling bachelor-degree student numbers, there is more pressure to use per student funding rates to control public spending.

Given the clear signals provided in 2016, the May 2017 Budget will almost certainly propose reducing public funding per student and increasing the maximum student contribution. But the government's 2016 discussion paper did not raise radical options, such as abolishing student subsidies entirely or in some disciplines. Instead, it stated that as higher education produced both public and private benefits, it should be financed jointly by taxpayers and students (Department of Education and Training, 2016b: 16–17). Versions of this argument have been made since the 1980s (Wran, 1988; Vanstone, 1996; Lomax-Smith *et al.*, 2011). In practice, these considerations justify policy rather than set its detail. Calculations of public benefits have never been used to set funding rates, and estimates of private benefits for only one of the three major changes to student charges since 1988, differential HECS in 1997.

Politically, Australian governments do not subsidize higher education to achieve specific public benefits, but because these payments are embedded in a wider web of taxes and benefits that shape public expectations of government. When the tax base cannot support the benefits, as in recent years, subsidy levels are re-examined, but only in an extreme budget crisis would abolition be considered. Proposed expenditure reductions would be proportionate to the size of the overall fiscal savings target.

Whether any cuts would be approved by the Senate is not clear at the time of writing. Between them, the Labor Party, the Australian Greensand small populist parties have a Senate majority. The government has lost numerous Budget savings Senate votes since it took office in 2013. Much would turn on the Labor Party's strategic judgment. They do not want to reduce higher education spending, but unless they cooperate with the Liberals on improving the government's finances, Labor's next term in office will be dominated by budget issues. Perhaps recognizing this problem, in 2016 Labor supported converting some student income support payments to a loan, and reducing the income threshold for repaying HELP debt. Labor's current policy is to retain an uncapped number of bachelor-degree places partly financed by student contributions (Plibersek, 2016). As with HECS in 1989, that may reflect a judgment that with limited public funds it is far better to offer a larger number of student places at a lower government funding rate than a smaller number of places at a higher rate.

If reduced public funding per student offset with higher student contributions eventuates, Australian higher education will become more privately funded. That would not reflect any significant shift in higher education policy goals on either side of politics. Private funding has always been supported on the Liberal side and long been accepted on the Labor side. What changes is the government's financial capacity to support a higher education system large enough to meet student demand.

Deregulated domestic undergraduate fees

Deregulated fees differ from student contribution increases that compensate for reduced public funding, because they allow overall funding levels to be set by universities in the market. Deregulated fees for international students, postgraduates and undergraduates outside the public universities are established features of Australian higher education. But they are very controversial for undergraduates in public universities, and will not happen in the foreseeable future.

For Labor, deregulated fees are quite different from increased student contributions. Deregulation contains the potential for very large fee increases – for many years, they have warned of '$100,000 degrees'. For market and mission reasons, most universities would not charge, and most domestic students would not pay, this much for a 3-year bachelor-degree. But experience in the existing deregulated markets suggests that total funding rates per student would vary significantly between universities (Norton and Cherastidtham, 2015b). For social democrats, these revenue differences could lead to a 'two tier' education system that exacerbates broader inequalities in society (Marginson, 2016, Chapter 9). By contrast, the current student contribution system integrates with a maximum overall funding rate that is fixed and equal between universities.

In its 2016 discussion paper, the Liberal government did not return to the 2014 plan for fee deregulation, but did suggest allowing higher fees for 'flagship courses' – 'high quality, innovative' courses offered to a limited number of students (Department of Education and Training, 2016b: 13–14). Reaction to the flagship idea was largely negative in submissions received on the discussion paper. Among other objections, the scheme looked complex and bureaucratic (Universities Australia, 2016). There are also fiscal reasons for caution. In another example of the paradox of markets in higher education increasing public expenditure, less regulation of fees in a system where student numbers are not controlled makes it harder to control the HELP loan scheme's costs. The more money the government lends through HELP, the greater its cost in bad debt and interest subsidies. If the government proceeds with the flagship proposal, it will almost certainly be rejected by Labor and the Senate.

Private higher education providers

Students at private higher education providers have had student income support since 1974 and HELP loans since 2005, but do not yet have general access to tuition subsidies. There are no principles-based eligibility rules for tuition subsidies; just a list of entitled institutions. Higher education providers that were publicly funded in the 1980s are on the list, while other providers are not. A distinction based so heavily on historical quirks probably will not survive over the long run, but could do so in the medium term.

Despite the current Liberal government attempting to make undergraduates in private higher education eligible for tuition subsidies in 2014, they are unlikely to try again soon. They want to reduce higher education spending, rather than subsidize additional students. They have recently reformed a vocational education student loan scheme to curb malpractice by for-profit providers. The private higher education sector, with tougher regulation and market conditions, has had few scandals. But the reputation of for-profit education more generally has been badly damaged. Labor is unlikely to support for-profit providers becoming eligible for tuition subsidies even if the Liberals propose it.

If tuition subsidies are extended to private higher education providers their students could benefit from reduced fees and HELP debt, but the market would not be transformed anytime soon. Many private higher education providers would stay in the unsubsidized deregulated fee market if public funding comes with maximum student contribution amounts, as it almost certainly would. This is because their current fees exceed Commonwealth student funding rates (Norton, 2015). They would lose their distinctive character by adopting cheaper public university teaching methods, and in the case of commercial providers their profits would be reduced. Almost all private higher education providers would start from niche markets with finite prospects for expansion. While some private providers enjoy strong reputations in their industry or profession, none have the prestige of established universities. Making private higher education providers more price competitive would remedy only one of their market weaknesses.

Existing deregulated markets

Whether or not government policy on student subsidies or fees changes in coming years, prospects are favourable for existing deregulated markets. Onshore commencing international student numbers rose 13 percent in 2016 compared to 2015 (Department of Education and Training, 2016c). These students will provide increased fee revenue in coming years as they move through their degrees. Political developments unfavourable to international students in the United Kingdom and the United States may help Australian universities gain international student market share. Domestic fee-paying postgraduate numbers for 2016 are not yet available, but broad trends favour expansion. The rapid growth in bachelor-degree completions in recent years creates a larger pool of potential postgraduate students. Student demand for postgraduate qualifications is likely to be encouraged by employment trends. Between 2010 and 2016, more than half the growth in managerial and professional employment went to people with postgraduate qualifications (ABS various years-b).

Conclusion

Enrolment trends mean that, whether government policy changes or not, private funding will play a greater role in Australian higher education. Fee-paying markets have stronger growth potential than the subsidized domestic undergraduate market. This means that direct government grants as a share of public university revenue, which have been around 40 percent in recent years, will decline (Department of Education and Training, various years). The drop will be larger if government funding is reduced.

Despite these trends, the hybrid public-private model of funding looks secure for domestic undergraduates. There is no suggestion of eliminating tuition subsidies entirely, and certainly no parliamentary majority in favour of it. Despite the popularity of free or cheaper higher education in opinion polls, the Liberal Party opposes it, the Labour Party has other priorities, and no other party has any chance of forming government. The political conditions do not exist for a fundamental transformation in either direction of Australia's mixed public-private higher education funding model.

Notes

1 After adjusting for inflation.
2 I was his adviser on higher education policy at the time.
3 I was a co-reviewer in the second of these reports.
4 For a more detailed overview of the funding system, see (Norton and Cakitaki, 2016), Chapters 5 and 6.
5 I served on an expert panel providing the minister with advice on higher education policy options.

References

ABS. (1971) *Average weekly earnings, March quarter 1971 (reference 6.18)*, Canberra: Australian Bureau of Statistics.
ABS. (1974) *Year Book Australia, 1974. Cat. 1301.0*, Canberra: Australian Bureau of Statistics.
ABS. (various years-a) *Year Book Australia, Cat. 1301.0*, Canberra: Australian Bureau of Statistics.

ABS. (various years-b) *Education and work, Cat. 6227.0*, Australian Bureau of Statistics.
Alexander, F. (1963) *Campus at Crawley: A narrative and critical appreciation of the first fifty years of the University of Western Australia*, Melbourne: FW Cheshire.
Anderson, D., Johnson, R. and Milligan, B. (1998) *Access to postgraduate courses: Opportunities and obstacles*, Australian Government Publishing Service.
AUC. (1972) *Fifth report of the Australian Universities Commission, May 1972*, Canberra: Australian Universities Commission.
Australian Government. (2016) *Budget 2016–17: Budget strategy and outlook budget paper No. 1*, The Commonwealth of Australia.
Beazley, K. (1977) 'The Labour Party in opposition and government', in I. Birch and D. Smart (eds), *The Commonwealth Government and Education 1964–1976: Political initiatives and developments*, Drummond Publishing.
Bradley, D., Noonan, P., Nugent, H. and Scales, B. (2008) *Review of Australian higher education: Final report*, Canberra: Department of Education, Employment and Workplace Relations.
Buckingham, J. (2010) *The rise of religious schools*, Sydney: The Centre for Independent Studies.
Carney, T. and Hanks, P. (1994) *Social security in Australia*, Melbourne: Oxford University Press.
Castles, F. (2010) 'The English-speaking countries', in F. Castles, S. Leibfried, J. Lewis, H. Obinger and C. Pierson (eds), *The Oxford handbook of the welfare state*, Oxford University Press.
Chapman, B. and Nicholls, J. (2013) 'HECS', in G. Croucher, S. Marginson, A. Norton, J. Wells (eds), *The Dawkins Revolution 25 Years on*, Melbourne University Press, pp. 108–125.
Coaldrake, P. and Stedman L. (2016) *Raising the stakes: Gambling with the future of universities* (2nd edition), University of Queensland Press.
Commonwealth Scholarships Board. (1971) *Commonwealth scholarships board annual report 1970*, Canberra: Australian Government.
Commonwealth Scholarships Board. (1974) *Commonwealth scholarships board annual report 1973*, Canberra: Australian Government Publishing Service.
Coper, M. (1988) *Encounters with the Australian Constitution*, Sydney: CCH Australia.
DEET. (1993) *National report on Australia's higher education sector*, Canberra: Department of Employment, Education and Training.
Department of Education and Training. (2014) *Time series data 1949–2000*, Department of Education and Training.
Department of Education and Training. (2016a) *Students: Selected higher education statistics 2015*, Department of Education and Training.
Department of Education and Training. (2016b) *Driving innovation, fairness and excellence in Australian higher education*.
Department of Education and Training. (2016c) *International student data 2016 – 2016 pivot tables*, Department of Education and Training.
Department of Education and Training. (2017) *uCube – Higher education statistics*, Department of Education and Training.
Department of Education and Training. (various years) *Finance: Selected higher education statistics*, Department of Education and Training.
DETYA. (2000) *Selected higher education student statistics, 1999*, Department of Education, Training and Youth Affairs.
Duckett, S. and Willcox, S. (2015) *The Australian health care system*, Melbourne: Oxford University Press.
Forsyth, H. (2014) *A history of the modern Australian university*, Sydney: New South Publishing.
Fraser, M. and Simons, M. (2010) *Malcolm Fraser: The political memoirs*, Melbourne: Melbourne University Press.
Garritzmann, J. (2016) *The political economy of higher education finance: The politics of tuition fees and subsidies in OECD countries, 1945–2015*, Palgrave Macmillan.
ICAC. (2015) *Learning the hard way: Managing corruption risks associated with international students at universities in NSW*, Independent Commission against Corruption.

Kemp, D. (2001) 'Appendix 4: leaked cabinet submission: proposals for reform in higher education', in Senate Standing Committee on Education and Employment (ed.), *Universities in crisis*, Senate of Australia.

Kemp, D. and Norton, A. (2014) *Review of the demand driven system: Final report*, Department of Education.

Lomax-Smith, J., Watson, L. and Webster, B. (2011) *Higher education base funding review, final report*, Department of Education, Employment and Workplace Relations.

Macintyre, S., Croucher, G., Davis, G. and Marginson, S. (2013) 'Making the unified national system', in G. Croucher, A. Norton, S. Marginson and J. Wells (eds), *The Dawkins revolution 25 years on*, Melbourne University Press, pp. 9–55.

Marginson, S. (2016) *Higher education and the common good*, Melbourne: Melbourne University Press.

Martin, L., Bayliss, N., Myer, K., Sunderland, S., Trendall, A., Verdon, J. and Wills, K. (1964) *Tertiary education in Australia: Report on the committee on the future of tertiary education in Australia, volume 1*, Melbourne: Australian Universities Commission.

McAllister, I. and Moore, R. (eds) (1991) *Party strategy and change: Australian political leaders' policy speeches since 1946*, Melbourne: Longman Cheshire.

Meadows, E. (2011) 'From aid to industry: a history of international education in Australia', in D. Davis and B. Mackintosh (eds)., *Making a difference: Australian international education* UNSW Press.

Murray, K., Clunies-Ross, I., Morris, C., Reid, A. and Richards, J. (1957) *Report of the Committee on Australian Universities*, Commonwealth of Australia.

National Archives. (1976) *Submission No 711: Re-introduction of tertiary education fees – Decision 1582*, October 1976, Canberra: National Archives of Australia.

National Archives. (1979) *Cabinet records: 1979 – Fraser government*, Canberra: National Archives of Australia.

National Archives. (1981) *Submission No 4880 – Limited reintroduction of tuition fees in universities and colleges of advanced education – Related to Decision No 15709*, Canberra: National Archives of Australia.

National Archives. (1985) *Cabinet Memorandum 2270 – Finance savings option – Reintroduction of fees in tertiary education – No Decision*, Canberra: National Archives of Australia.

National Archives. (1986) *Cabinet decision 8248/AER – Higher education administration charge – Without submission and decision 8113/ER (Amended)*, Canberra: National Archives of Australia.

Nelson, B. (2003) *Our universities: Backing Australia's future*, Canberra: Commonwealth of Australia.

Norton, A. (2004) 'Liberalism and the Liberal Party of Australia', in P. Boreham, G. Stokes and R. Hall (eds), *The politics of Australian society: Political issues for the new century*, second edition, Pearson Longman.

Norton, A. (2008) 'Another "free education" puzzle. ' Andrew Norton blog. Available online at http://andrewnorton.info/08/01/2008/another-free-education-puzzle/.8 January.

Norton, A. (2013a) 'The Coalition', in G. Croucher, S. Marginson, A. Norton and J. Wells (eds), *The Dawkins revolution 25 Years on*, Melbourne University Press.

Norton, A. (2013b) *Keep the caps off! Student access and choice in higher education*, Grattan Institute.

Norton, A. (2015) *Submission to the second inquiry into the provisions of the Higher Education and Research Reform Bill 2014*, Senate Education and Employment Legislation Committee.

Norton, A. (2016) 'Equity and markets', in A. Harvey, M. Brett and C. Burnheim (eds), *Student equity in Australian higher education: Twenty-five years of a fair chance for all*, Springer, pp. 183–206.

Norton, A. and Cakitaki, B. (2016) *Mapping Australian higher education 2016*, Grattan Institute.

Norton, A. and Cherastidtham, I. (2014) *Mapping Australian higher education, 2014–15*, Grattan Institute.

Norton, A. and Cherastidtham, I. (2015a) *The cash nexus: How teaching funds research in Australian universities*, Grattan Institute.

Norton, A. and Cherastidtham, I. (2015b) *University fees: What students pay in deregulated markets*, Grattan Institute.
NTEU. (2015) *State of uni survey 2015 report no.1: Overview report*, National Tertiary Education Union.
OECD. (2007) *Education at a glance, 2007*, Paris: Organization for Economic Co-operation and Development.
OECD. (2015) *Education at a glance, 2015*, Paris: Organization for Economic Co-operation and Development.
OECD. (2016) *OECD.Stat Revenue statistics – OECD countries: Comparative tables*, Paris: Organisation for Economic Co-operation and Development.
Orr, B. (1991) *Bond university, the beginning, 1985–1991: a personal view*, Canberra: Branxton Press.
Plibersek, T. (2016) 'Speech to the Australian Financial Review higher education conference.' Tanya Plibersek MP website http:// tanyaplibersek.com/speech_australian_financial_review_higher_education_conference_wednesday_16_november_2016.16 November
Roskam, J. (2001) 'Liberalism and social welfare', in J. Nethercote, (ed.), Liberalism and the Australian Federation: Federation Press, pp. 267–286.
Stokes, G. and Edmonds, A. (1990)'Dawkins and the Labour tradition: instrumentalism and centralism in federal ALP higher education policy 1942–88', *Politics*, 25(1): 6–20.
Tannock, P. (2014) *The founding and establishment of the University of Notre Dame Australia, 1986–2014*, University of Notre Dame Australia.
TEQSA. (2016) *Key metrics on Australia's higher education sector*, Tertiary Education Quality and Standards Agency.
Tescher, T. and Bain, A. (1972) *Commonwealth scholarships submission 1972*, Melbourne: Australian Union of Students.
The Australia Institute. (2015) *Polling brief – university deregulation*, The Australia Institute.
Tracey, H. (2001) *Education for all Australians: A history of the Commonwealth education agency 1945–2001*, Canberra: Department of Education, Training and Youth Affairs.
Universities Australia. (2016) *Submission in response to the government's options paper: Driving innovation, fairness and excellence in Australian higher education*, Canberra: Universities Australia.
Vanstone, A. (1996) *Higher education funding report for the 1997–99 triennium*, Canberra: Department of Employment, Education, Training and Youth Affairs.
Watson, L. (2000) *Survey of private providers in Australian higher education, 1999*, Department of Education, Training and Youth Affairs.
West, R., Banks, G., Baume, P., Chipman, L., Clark, D., Doherty, C. and Lee Dow, K. (1998) *Learning for life: Review of higher education financing and policy*, Department of Employment, Training and Youth Affairs.
Whitlam, G. (1985) *The Whitlam government 1972–1975*, Melbourne: Viking.
Wran, N. (1988) *Report of the committee on higher education funding*, Canberra: Department of Employment, Education and Training

5
The United Kingdom divided
Contested income-contingent student loans

GARETH WILLIAMS

Introduction

This chapter is mainly about the finance of the higher education system in England which, since 1992, has been financially and legally largely separate from much smaller systems in Scotland, Wales and Northern Ireland. For 4 decades after the end of the Second World War higher education in the whole United Kingdom was unambiguously treated as a trusted public service paid for by taxpayers and, subject to an unwritten 'compact' between the government, the University Grants Committee (UGC) and the universities which had almost total freedom over how the money was spent. This golden period, as it was seen in retrospect by many academics who lived through it, came to an end in the late 1980s and since then English higher education has been progressively privatized and become much more commercial in both policy and practice.

There were a few significant developments between 1945 and 1988, worth noting by way of introduction that provided the context for the radical changes after 1988. Until 1962, Local Education Authorities had the right, but not the duty, to offer grants to their qualified school leavers to pay their university fees and their cost of living while engaged in full time study. Unsurprisingly this led to wide differences across the country in opportunities to enter higher education. The Anderson Committee, set up to examine this issue reported in 1960. It claimed that:

> The country is ... committed ... to a large expansion in the places available in higher education, and it is the function of the awards system to ensure that those qualified to take advantage of these costly facilities are not deterred from doing so.
>
> (Anderson para 168)

The Committee recommended a national system of grants to cover fees and living expenses on a household means-tested basis, paid for by central government, available for all school leavers with the qualifications necessary for entry to higher education. This proposal was accepted by the then Conservative government and came into operation in 1962.

The Anderson Committee did briefly consider a loan scheme as at least a partial alternative to grants; (loans had been available from some local authorities before the war, my father had one that enabled him to undertake teacher training and it took him nearly 20 years to pay it off) but it came down emphatically against the idea :

> ... we have had no hesitation in rejecting loans as an integral part of the national awards system. The principle of using loans as a standard means of financing students has now been abandoned by public authorities in Great Britain, and our evidence disclosed no wish to see it revived. The obligations to repay, no matter how easy the terms, must represent an untimely burden at the outset of a career.
>
> (Anderson para 24)

The influential Robbins Committee on the future of higher education which reported 3 years later also considered the issue and was rather less dogmatic on the issue of student loans:

> We do not recommend immediate recourse to a system of financing students by loans. At a time when many parents are only just beginning to acquire the habit of contemplating higher education for such of their children, especially girls, as are capable of benefiting by it, we think it probable that it would have undesirable disincentive effects. But if, as time goes on, the habit is more firmly established, the arguments of justice in distribution and of the advantage of increasing individual responsibility may come to weigh more heavily and lead to some experiment in this direction.
>
> (Robbins para 647)

At the time, the concern was mostly over the living expenses of full time students. University and college fees were very low, the higher education institutions (HEIs) depended for most of their income on direct subsidy from public funds, in the form of quinquennial grants, i.e. grants that were fixed for 5 years in real terms.

This public service model of higher education, with various changes of detail along the way, mainly related to government attempts to restrain public expenditure because of problems elsewhere in the economy and partly about the level of university and college fees and the family contribution to these fees (which were abolished entirely in 1976), remained in operation until the passage of the 1988 Education Reform Act. Financial problems of the national economy led to sharp reductions in the public funds made available to higher education in the early 1980s and all government subsidies with respect to the cost of educating students from outside the European Union area was withdrawn in 1980. Universities began to treat foreign students as paying customers and took active steps to recruit as many as possible through the use of advertising and the employment of recruitment agents.

The 1988 Education Reform Act, marked the first formal step in transforming HEIs from being a planned public service to being a regulated, financially competitive set of activities. The UGC, which had protected the autonomy of universities was abolished and replaced by separate funding councils for England, Scotland and Wales, which were much more directly influenced by government policy. Financial grants to universities which had previously been based on UGC estimates of what they needed as institutions were henceforward to depend on the number and types of students recruited. Grants for teaching were explicitly separated from money for research which depended on the outcomes of the Research Assessment Exercise which had been established in 1986. The Act decreed that instead of universities and colleges receiving unconditional direct public subsidies as had been the case since the creation of the UGC in 1919, they were to be treated as suppliers of services under contract to the state and other purchasers of their services.

> I shall look to the (Universities Funding) Council to develop funding arrangements which recognise the general principle that the public funds allocated to universities are in exchange for the provision of teaching and research and are conditional on their delivery... I very much hope that it will seek ways of actively encouraging institutions to increase their private earnings so that the state's share of institutions' funding falls and the incentive to respond to the needs of students and employers is increased.
>
> (DES, 1988)

The Act was supplemented in 1992 by a Higher Education Act which transformed all the previously local authority controlled polytechnics into autonomous universities and, henceforth, all HEIs were to be financed and regulated by separate Higher Education Funding Councils for England, Scotland, Wales and Northern Ireland. From then on financial arrangements for the systems began to diverge along national lines.

From public service to regulated market

Despite many changes of detail, the provisions of 1988 and 1992 Acts of Parliament have remained the underlying basis of higher education policy in the United Kingdom ever since. The main features are the higher education systems of England, Scotland, Wales and Northern Ireland are separately financed and administered, all HEIs are partly funded and regulated by government dominated Higher Education Funding Councils in each part of the United Kingdom; public funding of HEI is provided on the basis of contractual arrangements for specific services rather than in the form of institutional subsidies and they are strongly encouraged to seek funds from student fees and other non-government sources.

It was the shift towards treating all HEIs as autonomous financial enterprises, funded as organizations selling teaching and research services that was the most far reaching and which has resulted in the almost complete marketization of the system by 2017. The costs of the teaching function of HEIs have been progressively shifted from the public purse on to students and their families. The shift from state finance of higher education as a public service to its almost complete commercialization has been the subject of much controversy.

One immediate effect of the 1988 Act was a rapid expansion in student numbers and a sharp fall in income from the government per student as HEIs all sought to increase their own income. In 1990, the Education (Student Loans) Act established a new system of financial support for students. It had three main components: means tested basic maintenance grant, a loan facility provided by the Government and additional 'access funds' for students facing particular financial difficulties. However, although public expenditure per UK student fell sharply, the rise in numbers was so rapid that the cost to public funds rose to levels that the government considered unsustainable and in 1994 limits were imposed on the number of students each higher education institution was permitted to recruit.

Once loans had been introduced, successive governments progressively increased the proportion of full time student maintenance costs met by loans rather than grants. In 1993, the government announced a reduction in student grant levels and an increase in their eligibility for repayable loans.

> ... the Government will continue to maintain the real value of the funds offered to students through the main rates of grant and loan and supplementary grants, which together will increase by 4% in cash. Reductions in the main rates of grant of 10% against their 1993/94 levels will be offset by increase in loan entitlements. Similar adjustment will be made over the next two years; on present estimates they will bring the grant and loan into broad balance in 1996/97. This shift from grant to loan represents an acceleration of the Government's existing plans.
> (DFE, 1993)

For the following 4 years, the grant component of student maintenance support gradually fell and the loan component increased correspondingly. However, the shift was causing very considerable controversy without reducing significantly the public sector cost of higher education which for a government committed to reducing public expenditure was difficult to justify.

An election was due in 1997 and partly in order to remove student fees, grants and loans from the election debate the government established a bipartisan National Committee of Inquiry into Higher Education, usually referred to as the Dearing Committee after Sir Ron Dearing, its chairman. The committee was asked to make recommendations on how the purposes, shape, structure, size and funding of higher education, including support for students, should develop over the next 20 years. Although the Dearing Committee covered a wide range of issues in the structure, organization, management and content of the newly achieved mass higher education in England, it was the recommendations for the funding of universities and colleges and the living costs of their students that received most political attention.

Changes to student support levels were identified as necessary both immediately and in the long term. The Committee recommended a substantial rise in fees to be covered by loans and that repayment of any loans incurred by students to cover fees or living costs should be repayable on income contingent terms after they had graduated. In practice, income contingency shifted much of the risk of default from the individual graduate back to the public purse

> Although the average graduate receives a good financial return from higher education, some will experience periods of unemployment, some will need to take career breaks, and others will have low paid jobs. If graduates are to be asked to make an increased contribution, they need the reassurance that they will not be faced with unreasonable payment burdens. This can be achieved by introducing payment mechanisms which relate the annual level of payment to a graduate's income: income contingent loans.
>
> (Dearing,1997 para 85)

The principles of the Dearing recommendations were accepted by the new Labour government in 1997 though it made several changes of detail. Essentially it aimed to lessen the financial burden on students from less affluent families and graduates in less well paid jobs. About a third of students from poorer families were exempted from paying fees and a further third paid less than the £1,000 per year fee set by the government. Public funds were still to pay three quarters of the total cost of teaching in higher education.

The period since 2000 has seen a rising share of the costs of higher education coming from student fees. In 2004, a new Higher Education Act allowed universities and colleges, if they wished to raise their fees for full time students to £3,000 per year from 2006 and permitted them to rise with inflation thereafter. Not surprisingly nearly all decided to raise fees by the full amount permitted.

The financial collapse of 2008 was the next blow to the system of funding higher education and in 2009, the government set up a panel under the chairmanship of Lord Browne of Madingley to conduct 'An independent review of higher education funding and student finance'. The panel reported in October 2010 by which time, the Labour government had been replaced by a Conservative dominated coalition. Browne's recommendations were very much in line with the market dominated ideology of the Conservative party, though during the 5 years of coalition government it was held in check somewhat by its Liberal-Democrat partners.

The Browne panel's central proposal was that most of the costs of higher education should be met by student fees and that students should incur debts to cover the cost of these fees repayable out of their higher incomes after they graduated. Individual universities and colleges would be allowed to charge whatever fees they considered necessary to cover their costs. The panel devoted much attention to the arrangements for the repayment of debts and the interest rate to be charged in order to protect those whose higher education did not lead to high incomes, but to retrieve as much as possible of the public funds that had been devoted to their studies. They also accepted the principle that no individual graduate should be required to repay more than she/he had borrowed. Another principle was that those universities able to charge very high fees should share some of the income with other universities and colleges though the payment of a levy on any fees charged above £6,000 per year. The panel also recommended that all full time students should be eligible for a personal loan of £3,750 towards their living costs while studying, and that students from poorer families should be eligible for a grant of up to £3,250 dependent on their family income.

The Report caused considerable controversy among all with a stake in higher education and also within the coalition government which came to power in 2010. The government accepted the underlying principle of the of the Browne Report that the teaching component of the income of HEIs should be paid by the individuals receiving it but it should be free for students during their studies: they should pay for it out of the higher incomes they could expect after they graduated thus removing much of the long term cost from the general taxpayer to the direct beneficiaries. However, there were many changes of detail arising in part out of compromises between the partners in the ruling coalition. The government rejected the idea that universities should set their own fees and imposed a £9,000 limit on the permitted annual fee with no transfer of resources from the richer institutions to the less affluent. This meant that the maximum amount students could borrow for fees was limited to £9,000 which was a 50 percent increase on the existing maximum. The money borrowed would be repaid by a levy on graduates' incomes after they rose above average earnings. This caused much embarrassment to the Liberal Democrats, junior members of the coalition, because they had promised before the election to reduce, not increase, the fees paid by students and, although technically students did not pay fees while studying, the debt they incurred was widely interpreted as a fee. There was much opposition in the streets but most HEIs raised their fees to the maximum permitted level and the new arrangements came into operation from 2012 onwards.

These are broadly the arrangements currently in operation in England. Wales is broadly similar but in Scotland a somewhat similar scheme was introduced and then abolished: Scottish domiciled students and other from EU countries other than England now pay no fees.

However, in 2016, the by now majority Conservative majority government introduced a new Higher Education Bill which if passed by Parliament will introduce further radical changes in shifting English higher education towards becoming a regulated market similar in structure to many other previously public services, such as gas and electricity, railways and communications. This is made clear by the proposal to abolish the Higher Education Funding Council, the Quality Assurance Agency and various other regulatory agencies and to amalgamate their activities into a single market regulator, the Office for Students (OfS) which would have 'competition, choice and the student's interest at its heart' (BIS, 2016: 19), and (be) funded primarily through provider (i.e university and college) registration fees. Apart from this overarching regulatory agency the three main proposals are:

1 to make it much easier for organizations, including profit seeking commercial enterprises to achieve the status of universities,
2 to create a Teaching Excellence Framework (TEF), and to make institutions' ability to charge higher fees largely dependent on its score in the TEF,
3 to create a similar overarching body for the regulation of research in HEIs UK Research and Innovation (UKRI).

If this Bill becomes law in anything like the form proposed the transformation of English higher education from a state funded public service to a regulated commercial sector will be completed.

Rationale of the finance of English higher education in 2016 and the immediate future

Over the 3 decades' considered in this chapter higher education policy in England has been driven by five separate, but ultimately linked, imperatives:

1 economic turmoil, especially in the mid-1970s and post-2008;
2 ideological changes in the dominant political climate;
3 expansion in student numbers;
4 concerns, at least rhetorical, about equity;
5 belief that in a globally competitive economy standards of living in a rich country could continue to improve only by remaining among the leaders of technological and organizational change in a knowledge society.

Economic turmoil

It is unrealistic to separate any consideration of higher education finance in a system of mass higher education from an awareness of the state of the economy generally. Universities and colleges make considerable claims on resources and if financed with public funds they are in competition with many other powerful claimants such as health, social security, other education, policing and national defence. In recent decades, there has also been considerable political pressure to reduce the taxation required to pay for such services. These tensions become more acute when the economy generally is not growing. Severe crises occurred in the mid-1970s, as a result of huge worldwide increases in the price of oil products and were largely responsible for the severe cuts in higher education expenditure in the early 1980s. More importantly the economic crises led to the election of a radical right wing government in 1979, which was in power for 18 years and radically changed the ideological climate surrounding higher education. An equally severe economic crisis occurred in 2008 and helped bring about further pressure on public expenditure on higher education, the effects of which are still being worked out, including another likely long period of radical right wing government.

Ideological drivers

The coming to power in 1979 of a Conservative government with a substantial parliamentary majority, committed to reducing taxation and hence public expenditure, the privatization of many public services and reducing the power of the trade unions marked a radical shift in the political and economic climate that had been dominant in the period since the end of the second world war.

Initially it was only the public expenditure reductions that affected higher education. The (then UK) system was able to continue much as it was only with some financial stringency. However, the reaction of universities to the cuts in income helped to build up government ideas of a more explicit higher education market in two main ways. One was that the autonomy of universities and the lifetime tenure of most of their academic staff made it extremely difficult to implement rational expenditure reductions through staff redundancies. The government considered that it needed to consider ways of making the system more responsive to public policy. The other was that universities responded to the imposition of full cost fees for students from overseas in 1980 by actively seeking to recruit more foreign students and within a few years their number had increased dramatically. This made it clear that given the right financial incentives universities were quite capable of behaving in commercially aggressive ways.

As indicated above, the 1988 Education Reform Act made it clear that the government saw universities as enterprises which responded to economic incentives but which like all market sectors would need regulation to protect the public interest. The Act was followed by big increases in student recruitment and by the mid-1990s the demands this was making on public expenditure became a major policy problem. Political opinion was veering towards the idea that individuals, most of whom received substantial financial benefits as a result of their higher education should bear at least part of the costs. The Dearing Committee formalized the idea and recommended that some of the costs should be borne by the individual beneficiaries. However, this raised a problem that has dogged debate about how to meet the costs of higher education ever since the idea was first mooted by economists in the 1960s. If fees are to be paid up front many families have insufficient resources to pay them and many able potential students are likely to be denied the opportunity of receiving higher education. Loans are the obvious answer which transfers the responsibility for payment to post graduation ability to repay the loan. However, although most graduates receive higher than average lifetime earnings not all do, either through bad luck or because they enter worthwhile occupations which are not highly paid. There is also a subsidiary issue of the interest rate to be charged on the loan. If it is very low students who do not need the money will be tempted to take the loan and reinvest it somewhere that earns a higher rate of return. If the interest rate is high, this will increase the number of graduates unable to repay their loan. Present day controversies on this issue, now that almost the whole teaching costs of higher education are met by students in the form of graduate repayments form the final section of this chapter.

The shift towards student fees being a significant source of university and college income has also increased competition between institutions which is also in keeping with a market oriented ideology. The May 2016, White Paper makes this quite explicit and proposes to take marketization a large step further.

> Competition between providers in any market incentivizes them to raise their game, offering consumers a greater choice of more innovative and better quality products and services at lower cost. Higher education is no exception.
> There is no compelling reason for incumbents to be protected from high quality competition. We want a globally competitive market that supports diversity, where anyone who demonstrates they have the potential to offer excellent teaching and clears our high quality bar can compete on a level playing field. If we place too much emphasis on whether a provider has a long established track record, this by definition will favour incumbents, and risks shutting out high quality and credible new institutions.
>
> (BIS, 2016: para 8)

If this Bill becomes law, there will be few restrictions other than teaching quality monitoring by the OfS on commercial and ideologically oriented organizations being able to award their own degrees.

Expansion in student numbers

Until 1988 the UK system of higher education was quite explicitly that envisaged by the Robbins Committee, essentially an elitist system catering for a growing number of students but meeting a narrow range of high academic standards. The 1988 and 1992 reforms encouraged much more rapid expansion and a growing pressure for higher education to encompass a much more diverse range of institutions, subjects, modes of study and students. By the beginning of the twenty-first century university education embodied a ranges of activities very much broader than had been the case 20 years earlier. (In some ways, this was merely an acceleration of a trend which had been apparent since the creation of the civic universities in the late nineteenth century. Histories of higher education show how economics, sociology, engineering and music among many others had to struggle to be recognized as legitimate university subjects.)

Marketization and expansion interacted. Increased numbers meant diversification and this made any kind of central planning virtually impossible. Diversity and differentiation could most effectively be accomplished by letting the market decide what was needed and putting the institutions in a position where they needed to respond to the market in order to survive.

Equity

As is implied in the earlier discussion of loans and their repayment, equity has remained a strong constraint on the privatization of higher education, at least rhetorically. Desire to shift the costs of higher education on to those that directly benefit from it has been tempered by a concern that this does not act as a serious disincentive to potential students from less affluent families or to those who do not expect high earnings after they graduate. This has been largely successful so far. Student numbers have continued to increase despite the rises in fees and various studies have shown little or no disincentive effects on participation by students from disadvantaged families once previous educational achievements are taken into account. (e.g. Haroun *et al.,* 2012)

Other dimensions and interpretations of equity are less clear cut and to a large extent it is dependent on which aspect of equity is being considered. It is indeed still the case that young people from affluent families are more likely to enter full time higher education after school but the gap has been narrowing showing that the system of fees and subsidized loans has not acted as a serious disincentive.

Other dimensions of equity are gender and ethnicity. In England, as in nearly all OECD countries women are now considerably more likely to enter higher education than men and recent studies have also shown that participation rates from most ethnic minority groups is higher than for the traditional white Anglo Saxon groups, especially young men. (e.g. Harrison, 2011; Brill, 2010)

There are also claims of discrepancies between ethnic, social and gender groups in attendance at what are considered the most desirable universities and studying the financially most rewarding subjects. However, it is difficult to relate these discrepancies to financial arrangements.

Knowledge society

An increasingly important driver of higher education policy during the past quarter century has been the concern that the country must stay in the forefront of technological and organizational progress in order to maintain both its influence in the global polity and the standard of living of its members. This conflicts in several ways with some of the other drivers such as the shift towards private finance of universities and colleges and some of the more extreme claims of equity.

As in sport, there is an intrinsic tension between providing resources for the most able to develop their talents to the full (and win gold medals in the Olympics and Nobel prizes in academia) and encouraging as many people as possible to develop their talents as best they can even though they will never become world champions.

The tension between the privatization of higher education provision and the need to ensure it makes the biggest possible contribution to economic and social development can be seen in the concern about the so-called STEM (Science, Technology, Engineering and Mathematics) subjects. It is widely believed that these are the areas of study that make the biggest contribution to the politically desirable aims of economic and social progress.

> In the modern global competition for economic success one of the vital elements is the development of people who generate, exploit and organize the knowledge base connected with the disciplines that fall under the acronym of STEM (Science, Technology, Engineering and Mathematics). It is, therefore, not surprising that successive governments, in the UK and elsewhere, have given much prominence to ensuring that the flow of graduates from STEM degrees into economic activity is appropriate and fit for purpose.
>
> (Wakeham 2016)

The problem is that most of these subjects are particularly expensive to teach and student numbers have not increased as rapidly as in many non-STEM subjects. Public subsidy has, therefore continued for much of the costs of these courses.

Postgraduate provision in STEM subjects is of particular concern. Students who have already incurred large debts for their undergraduate degree are becoming reluctant to incur further expenditure on higher degrees. Yet these are, for the most part of the qualifications that are considered to be most needed in an advanced knowledge economy. Some concern has been expressed also, that while some progress is being achieved in securing equitable access to undergraduate education this is not the case with postgraduate qualifications. It is people from more affluent households who are most able to take the risk of some years of further study. This has given rise to the problem that many postgraduate courses and research programmes are dependent on students from overseas for their continued existence and this conflicts with other government policies to limit even short term immigration into the country.

But it is research in universities which is thought to have the most direct implications for keeping ahead in the global knowledge society. Here also there have been developments and pressures similar to those in teaching. On the one hand universities have been encouraged to increase their research income from the private sector. On the other hand, because it is recognized that basic research findings have the essential characteristics of a public good (see Williams, 2015), it is therefore essential that it is publicly funded to a considerable extent. However, the ideological climate being that it is necessary for there to be competition between practitioners, research funding has been increasingly allocated through the Research Excellence Framework (REF) on a competitive basis and concentrated in those universities where peer and user review suggest it is likely to be most productive.

The net result of these pressures, assisted by media pressure for simple performance indicators is that the English higher education system now consists of a well-recognized hierarchy of universities and colleges and the financial arrangements tend to harden this hierarchy in both teaching and research despite desperate attempts by some universities to rise a few places in the 'league tables'.

Evaluation of present and proposed arrangements

As has been the case in all political changes in England for at least three centuries the developments in the past quarter century, though rapid, have been evolutionary rather than revolutionary. Despite the radically different ideological climate that emerged in the 1980s changes have taken the form of frequent incremental changes rather than complete upheavals. Fees were introduced at low levels in 1990 and supported by modest loans which partly replaced grants. The criteria for public funding of universities and colleges changed in 1988 but they continued to receive roughly similar amounts of public funds as previously. Indeed, where a particular institution would receive sharply reduced funding under the new formulae, transitional arrangements were put into operation to smooth the transition. Fees have gradually increased and grants for living expenses reduced: both being replaced by gradually increased loans. Repayment of loans is contingent on earnings after graduation the terms of which have become increasingly stringent in terms of the interest rate charged and the relative salaries at which repayments must be made.

Higher education providers have been encouraged to become more competitive in student recruitment and seeking research funds and to become more commercially minded generally. It has become easier for new institutions to achieve university status and will become considerably easier still if the 2017 Bill becomes law.

The upshot of all such incremental changes is a higher education system that, as Table 5.1 shows is almost unrecognisable in financial and regulatory arrangements from that of 3 decades ago. The May 2016 White Paper, envisages a further substantial rise in the percentage of current income coming from fees.

It may be worth noting that despite many efforts to generate endowment income, (nearly all universities now have at least one officer for this specific purpose it remains a very modest source of income for most institutions, though it has varied from a trivial amount in the early 1980s to 2.6 percent of total income in 1997 and fell to 0.9 percent in 2009 immediately after the global financial crash.

Current controversies

Since 2012, it has been government policy that most of the income for teaching by HEIs should come from fees paid by students and not from the direct public subsidy of the institutions. However, it is in many ways misleading to treat the fee component of institutional income as a direct cost to private households. As official documents have often pointed out:

> Higher education remains free at the point of use; the government lends money to students to enable them to pay universities the fee that they charge for tuition; once they have left university (whether or not they have graduated) former students repay their loans through the tax system by paying a 9 percent tax surcharge on income they earn above the

Table 5.1 Sources of income of UK higher education institutions 1982/3 to 2014/5

	1982/83	1988/9	1994/5	2004/5	2014/15
Grants from government funding agencies	68.8	59.0	43.7	38.4	15.9
Overseas student fees	3.1	5.6	4.5	7.7	12.7
Home and EU Tuition fees	9.9	7.6	18.1	16.3	34.2
Research grants and contracts	8.1	11.2	14.3	15.9	17.8
Other operating income	10.0	14.7	17.0	19.9	18.3
Endowment income	0.1	1.9	2.4	1.7	1.1

Sources: 1982/3 and 1988/9 Changing Patterns of Finance in Higher Education Chapter 2 (Gareth Williams 1992) 1994/5–2014/5 Higher Education Finance Statistics: Briefing Paper Number 5440 April 2016 (House of Commons Library) threshold level set by the government; and once they have repaid their loans, repayments cease.

(Thompson and Bekhradnia, 2013)

The system has evolved, certainly not been designed, to satisfy six overriding criteria:

1 efficiency is enhanced if institutions receive their income in the form of payment for services provided rather than direct subsidy;
2 those who derive most of the direct benefits should meet most of the costs;
3 nobody should be deprived of higher education because of inadequate household income;
4 nobody whose subsequent income does not reach adequate levels (originally set at average adult annual income) should be required to make loan repayments in any year in which this is the case;
5 nobody should repay more than the amount of the loan originally borrowed (plus an appropriate interest rate on any outstanding loan);
6 reduction of the immediate accounting cost to public funds. Although the upfront costs come from public funds, the fact that they are accounted as a debt owed to the state by the borrowers means that, according to current accounting conventions, they are not considered as part of the current account public income-expenditure deficit the reduction of which has been a cornerstone of government policy, especially since 2010.

As has been shown above the principle of universities and colleges receiving their income in the form of payment for services rendered was established in the 1988 Education Reform Act. However, initially the greater part of university and college income continued to come from central government though the newly established Funding Councils. The main concern at that time in accordance with the general political climate that had been in the ascendancy for nearly a decade was to encourage HEIs to become more financially efficient by being paid for the services they delivered rather than receiving a subsidy as intrinsically worthwhile organizations. It is possible to see the change as resulting from a loss of trust by the government in the sector's willingness to act in the public interest. There had, indeed, throughout the 1980s been some tension between the desire of many universities to maintain their traditional ideas of academic excellence, by restricting entry only to students who had already demonstrated high academic potential, and government wishes to expand student numbers along with most other OECD countries in the belief that this was a sure path to economic and social progress.

The early aim of increasing efficiency through payment for services rendered was certainly achieved in that expenditure per student fell sharply between 1989 and the mid-1990s. OECD figures show that average expenditure per student in current prices fell from the equivalent of $9,801 in 1990 to $7,225 in 1995. (OECD, 1998) Since this was achieved while there was a rise from 16 percent to 29 percent rise in the percentage of the age group entering higher education (DFES) and there was no significant increase in the number failing to complete their courses it was not unreasonable to claim an increase in efficiency.

However, the HEIs were becoming very concerned about their financial position and the dominant ideology of government was reducing public expenditure. The Dearing Committee recommended that students should meet some of the costs, but they should be able to borrow money to pay the tuition fees and repay the money borrowed at favourable rates of interest out of their subsequent higher incomes. This has broadly remained in place since it was put into operation by the newly elected Labour government in 1998. However, there have been many changes of detail and continuous political and academic debate over several issues:

- whether it is appropriate for fees to be charged;
- what proportion of costs should be paid by fees;
- on what criteria loans should be available;
- whether loans should be available to meet living costs as well as fees;
- at what income levels should former students begin to repay their loans;
- what interest rates should be charged;
- at what point should unrepaid loans be written off;
- how much public expenditure is actually saved.

At the beginning of 2017, universities and colleges that are recognized as providing higher education by HEFCE are allowed to charge fees up to £9,250 per annum for all subjects. These fees are paid directly to a student's HEI and the student incurs a corresponding debt, repayable on an income contingent basis after entering employment. This is probably more than cost covering for some subjects but far from cost covering for most STEM subjects that the government considers important for the economy. Public funds remain available to top up university income for these subjects and it is likely that in many institutions surpluses from the non-STEM subjects help to underpin STEM. Grants from HEFCE continued to account for nearly 16 percent of HEI income in 2014/15: much of which was for STEM subjects.

In addition, some students are still eligible for a grant to help with living expenses while studying. These range from £3,387 for students from households whose income is less than £25,000 per year (roughly the average annual income of those in full time employment) to zero when family income exceeds £42,620. The 2017 Bill proposes that all these grants should be replaced by loans. All students are eligible for an additional loan to help with living expenses of up to £8,000 a year depending on where they are living while studying. Thus on a conventional 3 year course it is possible for a new graduate to have a debt of over £50,000 and most will have a debt of at least £27,000.

There is much debate about how much these arrangements help to reduce public expenditure. In the short run, they increase the cost of higher education because HEI and their students have access to more public funds than previously. However, as McGettigan points out these do not appear as part of the public sector deficit, which is politically convenient.

> The headline public sector finance statistics for the deficit and debt treat student loans unlike other items. Classed as financial transactions; annual loan issuance and any repayments are excluded from the expenditure and receipts that determine the current measure of deficit.
> (McGettigan, 2015)

However, in the long term the proportion of the loans that is finally repaid does affect the current public income expenditure in future time periods. The amount the government can hope to recover from graduates *depends on the size of their loans, the repayment terms, their earnings, inflation and average earnings over the repayment period, and the discount rate.* (Thompson and Bekhradnia, 2013) The amount that is expected to not be repaid out of each year's lending does need to appear in the public sector accounts: this is known as the Resource Accounting and Budgeting (RAB) charge. Recent estimates have put the RAB at 45 percent of loans made (McGettigan 2015) implying that approaching half the public money spent on loans will never be repaid!

One consequence of such estimates is that the government has begun to seek ways of selling chunks of student loans to private investors. This would reduce the cost to the current budget in the short to medium run but would also mean the government received lower value for the repayments that graduates were able to make. Obviously the private investors would expect to make some profit from the deal.

More long term are proposals contained in the May 2016 White Paper which aim to reduce the RAB in several ways:

- by encouraging HEIs to be more price competitive and thus reduce cost of degrees by awarding university status and degree awarding powers to more institutions, including commercial institutions;
- by abolishing maintenance grants and replacing them with repayable loans;
- by increasing the interest rate on student loans;
- by reducing the effective level of earnings at which repayment of loans is required;
- by increasing the period over which loans are repayable before they are written off.

All legitimate markets require some regulation and during the course of the evolution of this fully marketized system there have emerged a number of regulatory agencies concerned with financial allocations, financial probity, teaching quality, equity in student admissions, student complaints and staff administration. The 2016 White Paper proposes to abolish all of these and replace them with an OfS. The OfS will have very considerable powers over the sector including the power previous held by the Privy Council, the monarch's supreme advisory body, to determine which institutions should have university status.

The OfS will also administer a new TEF in which the teaching arrangements and quality of HEIs will be monitored and which will largely determine how much fees individual universities will be allowed to charge. A substantial input into the TEF will be student satisfaction scores in the national Student Survey.

University research is to be completely separated from teaching as far as finance is concerned. The teaching function will be the responsibility of the Department for Education (DfE) while research will be administered by the Department for Business, Energy and Industrial Strategy (BEIS). Analogous to the OfS a new organization the UKRI will have complete responsibility for government funding and regulation of research; bringing under one body the previous research activities of five specialist research councils. It is likely that research funds will be allocated on an even more competitive basis than previously.

The English higher education system will have become in effect fully privatized but, like other privatized public utilities, subject to close central monitoring and regulation. Unsurprisingly many of these proposals are considered extremely controversial and it is not completely clear at the time of writing exactly how they will appear in practice. But the political climate is such that it appears likely there will be many years of Conservative government so it will not be surprising if something close to what has been described in these paragraphs is fully in operation in England by 2020. It certainly no longer makes sense to think of higher education in England as being a public service.

References

Anderson Report on *Grants to Students*, Cmnd 1051, 1959/60.
BIS. (2016) *Success as a knowledge economy: Teaching excellence, social mobility and student choice* Department for Business, Innovation and Skills.
Brill, C. (2010) *Equality in higher education: Statistical report 2010*, London: Equality Challenge Unit.
Dearing, (1997) *Higher education in the learning society* (summary report) pp.85.
DES. (1988) *Letter from the Secretary of State for Education and Science to the Chairman of the Universities Funding Council*, London: DES.
DFE. (1993) *Department for Education: Press Release*, 30 November 1993
Haroon, H., Crawford, C., Dearden, L., Goodman, A.and Vignoles, A. (2012) 'Widening participation in higher education: analysis using linked administrative data', *Journal of the Royal Statistical Society*, Series a.

Harrison, N. (2011) 'Have the changes introduced by the 2004 higher education act made higher education admissions in England wider and fairer?, *Journal of Education Policy*, *26*(3).

John, T. and Bahram, B. (2011) *The government's proposals for higher education funding and student finance – An analysis of the higher education white paper*,Higher Education Policy Institute.

John, T. and Bahram, B. (2013) *The government's proposals for higher education funding and student finance – an update*,Higher Education Policy Institute.

McGettigan, A. (2015) *The Accounting and budgeting of student loans*, HEPI: Oxford

OECD. (1998) *Education at a Glance*, Paris: OECD.

Robbins, L. (1963) *Committee on higher education: Report of the committee appointed by the Prime Minister*, Cmnd 2154: HMSO.

Wakeham. (2016) *Wakeham review of STEM degree provision and graduate employability*, Higher Education Funding Council for England.

Williams, G. (2015) 'Reflections on the Debate' in Filippakou and Williams (eds), *Higher education as a public good*, Lang: Peter.

6

The robust privateness and publicness of higher education
Expansion through privatization in Poland

MAREK KWIEK

Introduction: delayed massification

Privatization of higher education is closely linked to its expansion: when systems expand, there appears a fundamental question of how to fund them from the public purse. The growth of higher education in Poland under the communist regime (1945–1989), and especially in the 1970s and 1980s, was frozen: enrolments were stable and higher education was largely inaccessible.

Privatization following the 1989 regime change had two crucial dimensions: ideological (accompanying massive privatizations in the economy in general) and financial (financial austerity affecting all public sector services). The financial dimension of privatization was more important, and it was accompanied by a general lack of interest in social policies from policy-makers in the midst of large-scale economic reforms.

The two main types of privatization are *external* privatization (the booming private sector) and *internal* privatization (fee-paying courses in the nominally free public sector). 'Education can be privatized if students enroll at private schools or if higher education is privately funded' (Belfield andLevin, 2002: 19); Poland provided examples of increasing private provision and increasing private funding in both sectors. Belfield and Levin (2002) argued that 'the first factor to explain privatization in education is simple: many parents want it' (p. 29). Polish students (and their parents) clearly wanted higher education; consequently, as elsewhere in Central Europe, 'private higher education provide[d] stark solutions to the dilemma of how to keep expanding access while not expanding public budgets' (Levy, 2008: 13).

European transition countries in the 1990s were experimenting with the privatization of various segments of the welfare state, including both cash benefits (such as old-age pensions) and benefits in kind (such as health care and higher education).(Barr, 2004: 89–92). The traditional welfare state was 'overburdened' (Spulber, 1997), operating under increasing financial pressures, and the privatization of higher education was part and parcel of privatization of other public services (Feigenbaum *et al.*, 1998: 36–58; Kwiek, 2016a).

The demand-absorbing growth of private higher education made post-communist European countries different from Western Europe. 'The resources to finance mass, high-quality higher education from taxation' were not available there (Barr, 2005: 243). What happened was 'a non-elite response to the failure of the public sector to meet the growing demand for higher education': 'a public failure' meant avoiding tasks, both on the part of the state and public academic institutions, as described regarding private higher education expansion in Latin America in the 1970s (Levy, 1986a: 59). Higher education growth in Poland was achieved through the growth of demand-absorbing privates, accompanied by the delayed growth of publics. The massification occurred with a delay compared with Western European systems, and it took place in a double context of public underfunding of old public institutions combined with the emergence of new private institutions opening their doors to hundreds of thousands of new students, mostly from non-traditional socio-economic backgrounds (Kwiek, 2013; Pinheiro and Antonowicz, 2015).

The growth of ('independent' in the OECD classification) private higher education raised important equity, affordability and access issues: access for whom, access to what and access on what financial conditions. It did not mean 'better' or 'different' higher education; it meant most of all 'more' higher education (see Geiger, 1986). This expansion was made possible by powerful processes of external and internal privatization, dual phenomena that opened higher education to market forces from which Polish higher education had been isolated until 1989.

From numerus clausus policies (1945–1989) to open door policies (1990 and beyond)

Higher education in Poland under communism was traditionally research-focused, its 'distinctive mark' being its 'predominance of research and the teaching of research methods' (Szczepanski, 1974: 4). From 1970 to 1990, the number of students was strictly controlled and fluctuated between 300,000 and 470,000. The strict *numerus clausus* policy limiting student numbers was the rule. While Western European systems were already experiencing the processes of massification in the 1970s and 1980s, higher education in Poland was as elitist in 1990 as it was in decades past (Sieminska and Walczak, 2012). One of the major reasons for the phenomenal growth of private higher education was the heavily restricted access to public higher education before 1989, combined with new private sector employment opportunities in the changing economy. Increasing salaries in the emergent private sector pushed ever more young people into higher education. However, consistent with Geiger's findings, private higher education was forced to operate 'around the periphery of the state system' (1986: 107). Following 1989, the *numerus clausus* policy was maintained only in the public sector. In the emergent private sector, the 'open door' policy ruled.

Changes following 1989

In the face of massive social, political and economic transformations of an unprecedented scale, Polish universities were changing by accident, evolution and intention (Goodin, 1996: 39), with emphasis on the first two models: accident and evolution. Intentional changes in higher education policy were rare, but there was a set of overarching principles guiding transformations in the university sector: institutional democracy, institutional autonomy and academic freedom, all regained after the period of communism. Beyond general guiding principles, no further elaborate institutional design followed. The state seemed to have had no clear ideas about how to deal with disintegrating higher education institutions, characterized by radically decreasing academic salaries, brain drain and a collapsing system of research funding (Kwiek, 2012a). The Polish case is consistent with Levy's general observation on the private sector's roles: 'private higher education's roles emerge mostly unanticipated, not following a broad preconception or systemic design. For the most part, central policy does not create, design, or even anticipate emerging private sector roles' (Levy, 2002).

The first new private institution was opened in 1990, eleven opened in 1992, nineteen opened in both 1993 and 1994, twenty-five opened in 1995 and so on. The number of privates was systematically growing. Within the first decade of expansion through privatization, there emerged 195 new privates (195 in 2000) and by the end of the next decade, their number exceeded 300 (330 in 2009; see Figure 6.1).

There is only one comparator country in Western Europe with parallel privatization experiences: Portugal, with its huge expansion of the private

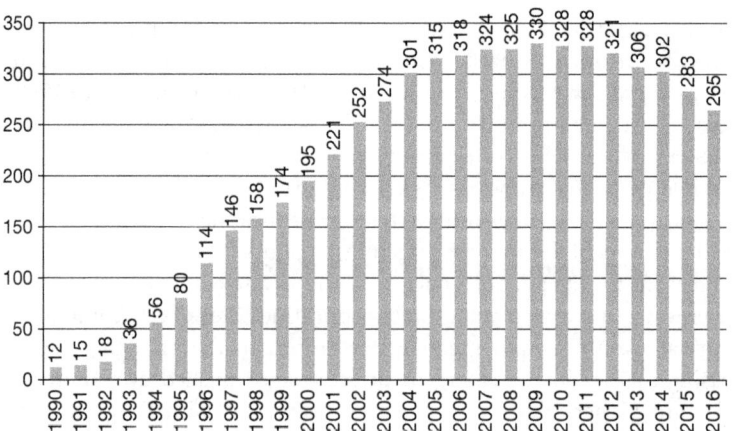

Figure 6.1 The number of private higher education institutions in Poland, 1990–2016.

Source: Own calculations based on GUS 2016 and its previous editions.

sector in the 1980s and its gradual decline since the mid-2000s (Neave and Amaral, 2012). The level of enrolments in the private sector in Poland, contrary to Portugal, depended exclusively on demand. In Portugal, students applied to enter higher education through a national competition, and in the application process, they applied for study programs and institutions, presenting their order of preference. In Portugal and Poland, the picture (after the democratic revolution of 1974 and after 1989, respectively) was similar: 'the main objective of many candidates was to enter a higher education institution, at any price and in any available study programme. . . . The private sector was allowed to develop almost without any control and without due attention being paid either to quality or to labour market needs' (Correia et al., 2002: 468–469). Portuguese privates were designed 'for short-term profit making rather than as sound academic and financial projects' (Teixeira and Amaral, 2001: 370). As in Poland in the 1990s, 'private institutions could do what they liked: and this they certainly did' (Teixeira and Amaral, 2001: 390–391; Teixeira, 2012). The assessment of private higher education in Portugal fits the Polish case perfectly and follows global assessments of a demand-absorbing private subsector: private institutions 'focused predominantly on teaching, have undertaken little, or no, research and appear to be of lower quality than the older institutions' (Teixeira and Amaral, 2001: 359). A major difference in Poland was the dominating financial austerity in public universities and impoverishing academic salaries in the 1990s.

The issue of fueling public funding to the private sector (Salerno, 2004) to let it survive more easily in adverse demographic conditions — which hit both sectors a decade ago — seems to have never been raised in Portugal. While Portuguese debates focused on changing institutional strategies, Polish debates focused on changing the national funding architecture, either through introducing universal fees in both sectors or through subsidizing the private sector. The catchword in the Polish debates was the 'healthy competition' between publics and privates.

Expansion through privatization

Internal versus external privatization

Privatization in higher education has different meanings (Fryar, 2012; Johnstone, 2007; Priest and St. John, 2006; Gómez and Ordorika, 2012). Here I use a distinction between internal and external privatization and define these concepts in terms of funding and provision (Kwiek, 2016a). From the perspective of funding, internal privatization occurs in public sector institutions (with ever more private funding over time) and external privatization occurs in private sector institutions (with ever more private sector institutions and private sector funding from fees in the system over time). From the perspective of provision, internal privatization refers to fee-paying students in public sector institutions and external privatization refers to fee-paying students in private sector institutions — and changes over time.

In 1990, immediately after the fall of communism, the Act on Higher Education allowed the existence of private higher education institutions. A 'mushrooming' period followed. Until 2002 when the State Accreditation Commission (PKA) started its evaluations, the licensing of private institutions and their liberal overseeing was done by the Ministry. Accreditation by PKA, started in 2002, became the main instrument in national educational policy to gain public control over the private higher education sector in order to increase the quality of private (and public) higher education and to restrain mushrooming of private higher education. Between 1990 and 2002 when this law was amended and PKA was formed, the state was largely unable to control the private higher education system (Kwiek, 2012b).

From 1990 to 2001, the legal control and supervision mechanisms at the state's disposal were weak (the relevant formulation in the act and in lower-level regulations were general and often ambiguous), the Ministry was not staffed enough and, technically speaking, its physical access to and its power to impose decisions on private higher education institutions were very limited. The existing representative body of the academic community, RGSW (The Main Council for Higher Education) was unable — both technically and legally, as well as in terms of infrastructure, staff and resources — to provide support to the Ministry in controlling and supervising the private sector. No other institutions were legally able to assess the quality of education offered in the sector (or any other dimension of its functioning). The state in the 1990–2001 period was highly liberal with respect to the new sector (Pinheiro and Antonowicz, 2015). The conditions to enter the Polish higher education market for privates were liberal, and the scale of the emergence of the private sector was unexpected. In particular, the state was unable to effectively control private sector growth and the quality of teaching privates offered.

The private sector exerted powerful influence on the functioning of the public sector, which was also growing substantially, especially through its fee-based part-time tracks. This influence was partly positive as a result of the new cross-sectoral competition — but mostly negative as a result of private institutions using almost exclusively public sector academics and the almost universal 'moonlighting' of public sector academics working full-time in both sectors, with an emergent hot issue of 'multiple employment' (Antonowicz, 2016). The growth of the private sector led to a powerful decline in research activities conducted by academics and generally-reported neglect of their teaching duties in their original, main workplaces (i.e. public universities; see Kwiek, 2012a on the deinstitutionalization of the research mission in Polish universities).

The naivety of policymakers in the 1990s was linked to several larger assumptions: most of all, a widespread assumption that 'the market knows best' and that market mechanisms (rather than state-imposed regulations) would better serve higher education. The laissez-faire attitude of the state regarding private sector growth was a side-effect of the general political feeling that the market was better than the state and less state regulation was better than more state regulation. The overall attitude of the private sector was that the state should leave it alone, apart from rudimentary licensing requirements as laid down in the 1990 law and rudimentary, mostly voluntary supervision. In the period of early Polish capitalism, the emergence of private higher education institutions was viewed as the triumph of the individualistic thinking over statist thinking from the pre-1989 period. A powerful argument of the private sector in the early 1990s against state interference was that the sector was fully fee-based.

The growth of the higher education sector in the 1990s — fuelled by internal and external privatization — was mostly financed by students; public funding was not substantially increased until the next decade.

The public-private 'distinctiveness'

The terms 'public' and 'private' still have well-defined senses in the Polish context and Poland usefully illustrates the concept of 'private-public distinctiveness'. Levy makes a clear distinction between the private and the public assuming that 'the private-public distinction matters' (1986b: 293), against dominating global (both American, see Geiger, 2007; Altbach *et al.*, 2010; Sanyal and Johnstone, 2011; and European, see Enders and Jongbloed, 2007) trends of seeing the two concepts as increasingly blurred. In financing, the public sector in Poland is 'truly public' and the private sector is 'truly private' (as Levy referred to his Latin American cases, 1986b: 293; see a panorama of private sectors in seventeen countries/regions globally in Shah and Nair, 2016; Altbach and Levy, 2005; and Teixeira *et al.*, 2017). My preferred approach to privatization (and de-privatization in the final section) is related to this strong public-private distinction and makes use of two dimensions: funding (percentage of public and percentage of private funding over time) and provision (percentage of enrolments in the public and private sectors over time, as well as the percentage of fee-paying and non-fee-paying students over time). Funding and provision are the two major dimensions of the privatization agenda (Kwiek, 2016a).

A popular argument used in Polish debates about public funding for the private sector is that the major policy distinction should no longer be between public and private institutions but between good and bad ones. The blurring of the public-private distinction seems to serve the goal of making the channelling of public funding into the private sector more publicly acceptable. However, policy debates about the private–public mix of financing in Poland in the context of the possible decline of the private sector in the next decade are neither historically nor geographically unique. Levy (1986a: 206–207) identified debates about the very growth of private institutions, followed by debates about whether new private sectors should receive public funds and finally debates about tuition in the public sector. The same policy issues were raised in Poland.

The difference between the two sectors in Poland is not becoming blurred from the double perspective of funding and provision: public funding for the private sector is marginal (in 2015 it was 3.2 percent in research funding and 1.7 percent in state subsidies for teaching); private sector institutions have private founders and owners (individuals, associations, or companies). Private funding through fees in the public sector is still substantial but decreasing in the last decade and expected to further decrease for demographic reasons, reaching 8.47 percent of public universities' operating budgets, or about 460 million USD in 2015. Management and governance modes in the two sectors are different and clearly defined: while public institutions are still following traditional collegial models, private institutions are following business-like, managerial models (Kwiek, 2015a; Kwiek, 2015b). In terms of who makes decisions in educational institutions, who owns them and who pays for educational (and research) services, the blurring of the public–/private distinction is not evident in the Polish system.

Demand-absorbing private sector growth

Consistent with findings in global private higher education literature, the largest growth in Poland occurred through non-elite demand-absorbing types of institutions (Levy, 2009; Geiger, 1986). As elsewhere in rapidly expanding systems, students were 'not choosing their institutions over other institutions as much as choosing them over nothing' (Levy, 2009: 18). The demand-absorbing private subsector was both the largest private subsector and the fastest growing one. Consistent with Geiger's findings (1986, : 107) about 'peripheral private sectors' (as opposed to 'parallel public and private sectors'), the traditionally university component of higher education was monopolized by public institutions and the traditionally vocational component by private institutions. 'Market segmentation' rather than 'open competition' with the dominant public sector was the general characteristic (Geiger, 1986: 158). However, there is a potential for the development of a very limited number of semi-elite institutions (a maximum of 10–20). Elite private institutions are an almost fully American phenomenon, but semi-elite institutions in several countries can compete with second-tier public institutions.

Declining private provision

External privatization lasted for about a decade and a half and stopped for mostly demographic reasons, in terms of the number of private institutions (see Figure 6.1) and private sector enrolments (between 2006 and 2015, enrolments fell by 50 percent; see Figure 6.2), as well as first-year students and graduates in the private sector (Table 6.1).

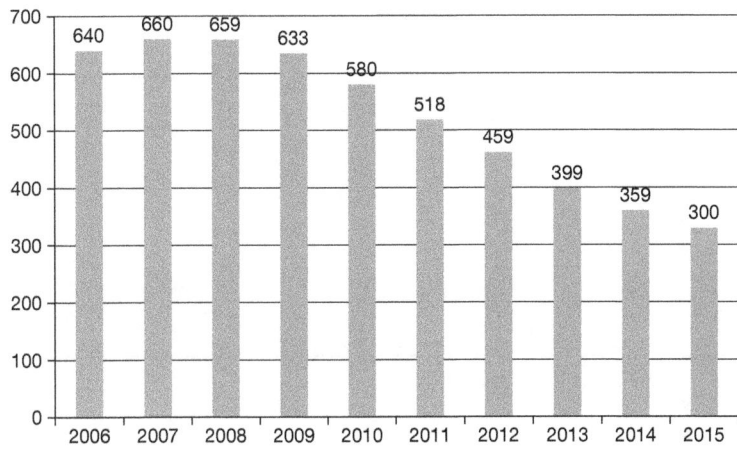

Figure 6.2 Enrolments in private higher education, 2006–2015, in thousands.

Source: Own calculations based on GUS 2016 and its previous editions.

Table 6.1 First-year students and graduates, private sector, change from 2006–2015 (2006 = 100%).

Year	First-year students	Change in number, in percent (2006 = 100%)	Graduates	Change in number, in percent (2006 = 100%)
2006	189,845	100.00	130,844	100.00
2007	194,466	102.40	144,639	102.40
2008	188,789	99.40	154,846	99.40
2009	160,525	84.60	157,563	84.60
2010	132,309	69.70	169,039	69.70
2011	114,897	60.50	171,822	60.50
2012	99,903	52.60	158,554	52.60
2013	86,930	45.80	140,971	45.80
2014	81,000	42.70	122,650	42.70
2015	78,424	41.30	106,146	41.30

Source: Own calculations based on GUS 2016 and its previous editions.

Not only has the private sector as a whole been shrinking, but individual private institutions have also been drastically reducing in size. Over a seven-year period of contraction (2007–2014) for which data are available, the number of private institutions enrolling fewer than 500 students increased from 88 to 144, or from about a quarter (27.9 percent) to about half of all privates

Table 6.2 The distribution of private higher education institutions in Poland by enrolments, 2014 (in percent).

Enrolments	Number of institutions	Percentage of institutions (%)
under 500	144	49.66
500–1,000	54	18.62
1,001–2,000	52	17.93
2,001–3,000	12	4.14
3,001 and more	28	9.3
Total	290	100

Source: Own calculations based on MNISW 2015.

(49.7 percent); in a similar vein, the number of institutions enrolling fewer than 1,000 students increased from about half (49.8 percent) to more than two thirds (68.3 percent; Table 6.2). From both a business perspective and from a perspective of teaching quality, if half of the sector is comprised of institutions with fewer than 500 students, the sector is not sustainable in the future. Falling demographics have powerfully hit the private sector, throwing its future into question. The average institutional size has been decreasing, both for semi-elites and demand-absorbing types. Among the top twenty biggest private institutions in 2007, the first five institutions enrolled 87,559 students and the last five 32,412, compared with 64,235 and 19,076 students in 2014.

Standard survival strategies for the private sector under demographic pressures have been discussed in several national contexts (Portugal: Teixeira and Amaral, 2007; USA: Levine, 1990; Japan and Korea: Kinmonth, 2005; Yonezawa and Kim, 2008; the OECD area: Vincent-Lancrin, 2008). However, the introduction of universal fees in the public sector has not played a fundamental role (played any role, for that matter) in any of those contexts. The Polish case is exceptional, and policy choices made can be studied in the future in all those systems in which the private sector has emerged in a period of educational expansion and its future became unclear in a period of demographically-driven contraction. Lessons learnt may have more than regional relevance.

The standard supply-side (private providers) solution could be high quality education that matches education and labour market needs and achieves high social recognition. However, the policy of non-interference and loose governmental control of the 1990s and 2000s contributed to the very low competitiveness of the private sector vis-à-vis the public sector. A handful of exceptions (semi-elites) do not make a big difference but need to be noted. As the introduction of fees in the public sector does not seem a viable policy option, mergers, acquisitions and closures seem a necessity.

Public and private funding

Public funding: public support going (almost exclusively) to the public sector

Following Levy's typology of public-/private mixes in higher education systems, it is analytically useful to view Poland as fitting the fourth pattern (dual, distinctive higher education sectors: smaller sector funded privately, larger sector funded publicly; Levy, 1986a: 199). Private-public blends require a number of important questions: single sector or dual; if single sector, statist or public-autonomous; if dual sectors, homogenized or distinctive; if distinctive, minority private or majority private? (Levy, 1986a: 198). The fourth pattern of financial policy identified by Levy fits Poland best: there exist dual and distinctive sectors (public and private), where the private sector has more than 10 percent but less than 50 percent of total enrolments and relies mostly on private finance, and the public sector relies mostly on public finance.

Consistent with the pure types of 'public' and 'private' sectors in Poland, privates have been almost exclusively self-financed. Policy proposals made in the early 2010s (during the last wave of reforms) could have marked the beginning of an evolution (Kwiek, 2016c). They seemed to indicate willingness to change policy patterns in financing higher education under a general theme of the 'convergence of the two sectors' (Woznicki, 2013). However, this evolution did not start, with a few small exceptions: public funding was channelled to private higher education for doctoral-level education and for state-subsidized loans. The private sector was also given the right to apply for highly competitive research grants from a newly-created National Research Council (the NCN). However, slowly, the inflow of public funding has been noticeable, becoming a marginal source of income (Table 6.3). Similarly, research funds were channelled to the private sector: about 26 million USD out of 813.5 million USD in 2015, or 3.2 percent. Table 6.3 shows the structure of the total operating budget of the Polish private sector in the last decade; the share of research income has been gradually increasing, reaching 4.4 percent in 2015

Table 6.3 Operating income of higher education institutions in Poland in 2015 by sector, in million PLN. 1 USD = 4 PLN.

	Total operating budget	Teaching income	Income from fees	Research income
Total	23,455	18,320	3,472	3,254
Public	21,109	16,308	1,826	3,150
Private	2,346	2,011	1,646	103

Source: Own calculations based on GUS 2016 and its previous editions.

(accompanied by 85.7 percent of income coming from fees, and the rest coming from 'other operating activities', see Table 6.4).

The Polish case confirms a general observation that 'it is difficult, though far from impossible, for private universities to sustain themselves fully over long periods on private funds' (Levy, 1986a: 205). Speaking of the growth of the private sector generally, the twentieth-century norm is state funding of public universities and, overwhelmingly, private sources of funding for private institutions (Levy, 2009; Altbach and Levy, 2005). Poland closely follows this global funding pattern.

The concentration of public competitive research funding (apart from that of public subsidies) in the public sector in Poland can also be shown through the distribution of research funds available from the National Research Council (NCN). In its first 6 years of operation (2011–2016), the NCN disbursed 3.33 billion PLN (or 833 million USD), of which about 1.5 percent (50 million PLN or 12.5 million USD) went to the private sector. The top five public institutions garnered 46.12 percent and the top five private institutions 1.46 percent (see Table 6.5). The domination of the public sector institutions and its research teams is almost total — the public sector is where research is based.

Table 6.4 Income from research by sector, 2006–2015, in million PLN. 1 USD = 4 PLN.

	Total (million PLN)	Public sector (million PLN)	Private sector (million PLN)	Percentage of res. income in the public sector (%)	Percentage of res. income in the private sector (%)	Percentage of res. income in the total operating budget of the public sector (%)	Percentage of res. income in the total operating budget of the private sector (%)
2006	1,533	1,450	33	97.8	2.2	11.6	1.4
2007	1,933	1,896	37	98.1	1.9	13.6	1.4
2008	2,092	2,057	35	98.3	1.7	14.1	1.3
2009	2,331	2,277	54	97.7	2.3	14.8	1.8
2010	2,693	2,607	86	96.8	3.2	15.9	2.8
2011	2,865	2,764	101	96.5	3.5	16.2	3.2
2012	2,864	2,760	104	96.4	3.6	15.9	3.6
2013	2,876	2,768	108	96.2	3.8	15.0	4.0
2014	3,065	2,955	110	96.4	3.6	14.9	4.3
2015	3,254	3,150	103	96.8	3.2	14.9	4.4

Source: Own calculations based on GUS 2016 and its previous editions.

Table 6.5 The concentration of research funding in Poland by sector: the share of individual project-based competitive research funding awarded by the National Research Council (NCN) in its first 6 years of operation (2011–2016) for the first five public (Top 5 Public) and the first five private (Top 5 Private) institutions, in million PLN. 1 USD = 4 PLN.

Institution	Amount (mln PLN)	Percentage
Top 5 Public		
Uniwersytet Jagiellonski (Kraków)	498,839	14.98
Uniwersytet Warszawski (Warszawa)	493,696	14.82
Uniwersytet im. Adama Mickiewicza (Poznan)	222,613	6.68
Uniwersytet Wrocławski (Wrocław)	167,238	5.02
Akademia Górniczo-Hutnicza im. Stanisława Staszica (Kraków)	154,028	4.62
Top 5 Private		
SWPS Uniwersytet Humanistycznospołeczny (Warszawa)	32.44	0.97
Akademia Leona Kozminskiego (Warszawa)	7.96	0.24
Wyzsza Szkoła Informatyki i Zarzadzania (Rzeszów)	3.67	0.11
Polsko-Japonska Akademia Technik Komputerowych (Warszawa)	2.69	0.08
Wyzsza Szkoła Finansów i Zarzadzania (Warszawa)	2.13	0.06

Source: Own calculations based on NCN 2017.

Private funding comes predominantly from fees (part-time students in the public sector, all students in the private sector). Under declining demographics combined with no longer expanding but still stable tax-based full-time studies in the public sector, the role of fees in the public sector has been declining as the number of fee-paying students has decreased by half (52.3 percent) in the last decade, against global trends (Heller and Callender, 2013; see Figure 6.3). The public-private dynamics in enrolments have changed radically. Additionally, within a decade (2006–2015), the share of fee-paying students in the system as a whole has decreased by half, from 59 percent to 40 percent (Figure 6.4), with a heavily declining provision-related indicator of privatization: the number of fee-paying students in the system has gone down from 1.137 million to 0.567 million.

Fee-paying students bring in fees to both sectors. However, their role in the public sector is decreasing, following an enrolment trend of fewer part-time students enrolled every year. Consequently, major funding indicators of privatization — a share of total income from fees in the system as a whole and

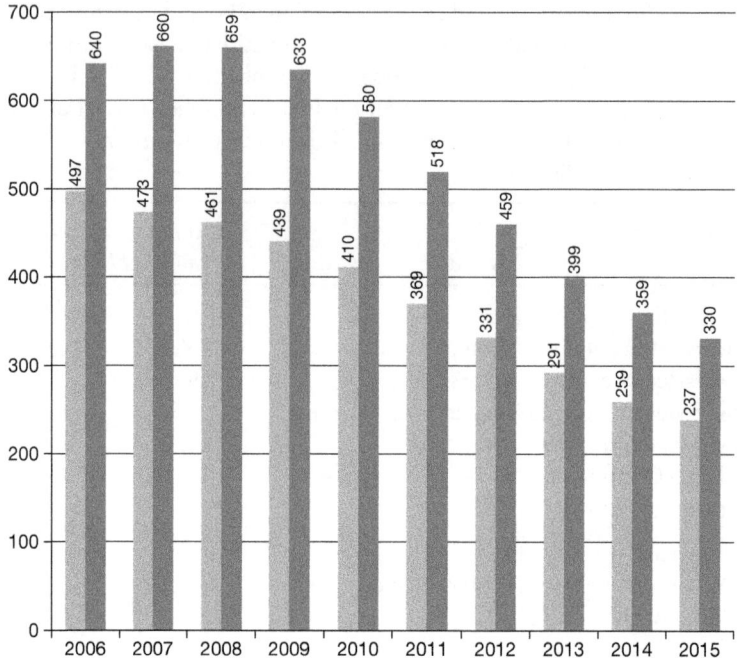

Figure 6.3 The number of fee-paying students in the public sector (grey) and enrolments in private higher education (black) in Poland, 2006–2015 (in thousands)

Source: Own calculations based on GUS 2016 and its previous editions.

a share of income from fees from part-time students in the public sector — have been decreasing for a decade now (from 27.5 percent to 14.7 percent, and from 16.2 percent to 8.6 percent, respectively, in 2006–2015; see Figure 6.5). Revenues from fees have been declining in both sectors, but more intensively in the private sector. In 2013, income from fees in the public sector was higher than income from fees in the private sector, the gap increasing every year. The total in 2015 was 3.47 billion PLN, with 1.83 billion garnered by the public sector and 1.65 billion garnered by the private sector, with the total operating budget for both sectors reaching 23.57 billion PLN.

The private sector: self-declared autonomy and demands for public funding

For the first 15 years (1990–2005), the private sector was booming: regulations were very relaxed and entry conditions and operating requirements were light. The business side of private institutions was phenomenal; the academic side was often non-acceptable, but the state and its agencies were unwilling to

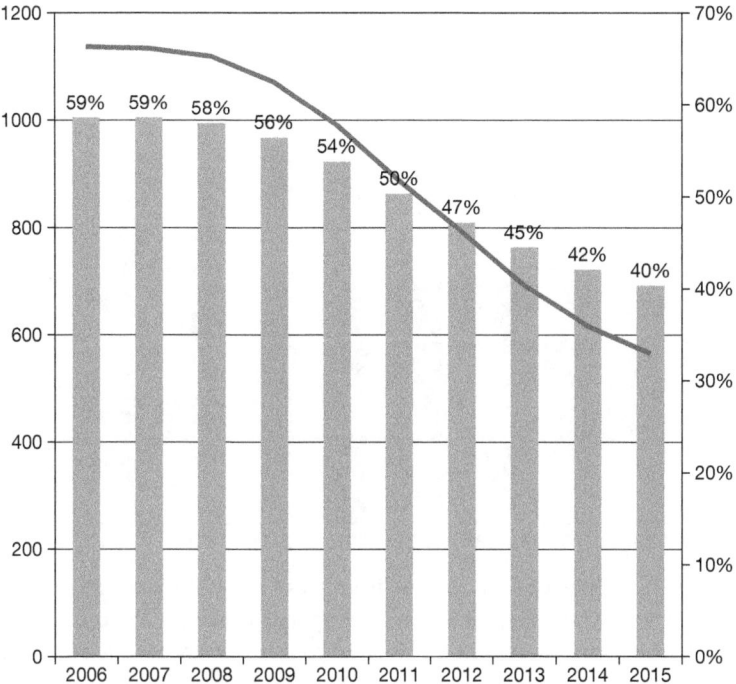

Figure 6.4 The number (dark grey line, in thousands) and the share of fee-paying students in public and private sectors combined in Poland, 2006–2015 (in percent)

intervene in the sectors' academic activities (Antonowicz *et al.*, 2017). However, further external privatization was threatened by two parallel processes, a combination of declining demographics and internal privatization (the public sector offering part-time studies in fee-based tracks). On top of that, public sector finally became better financed and has been able to offer ever more tax-based vacancies. Around 2010, there were numerous debates whether the private sector should be publicly financed — but no public funding followed. The private sector was left on its own, with ever fewer students every year, and no prospects for any other funding than fees. The whole system began to contract about 2006; the era of expansion was followed by the era of contraction.

From the very beginning, the private sector demanded full autonomy from the state and its regulations, with a set of relatively simplistic arguments: higher education provision should be governed by market rules of supply and demand and should be treated as a business activity in a highly competitive arena. The introduction of 'fair competition', 'free competition', or 'healthy competition' between public and private institutions was the major demand. Public funding

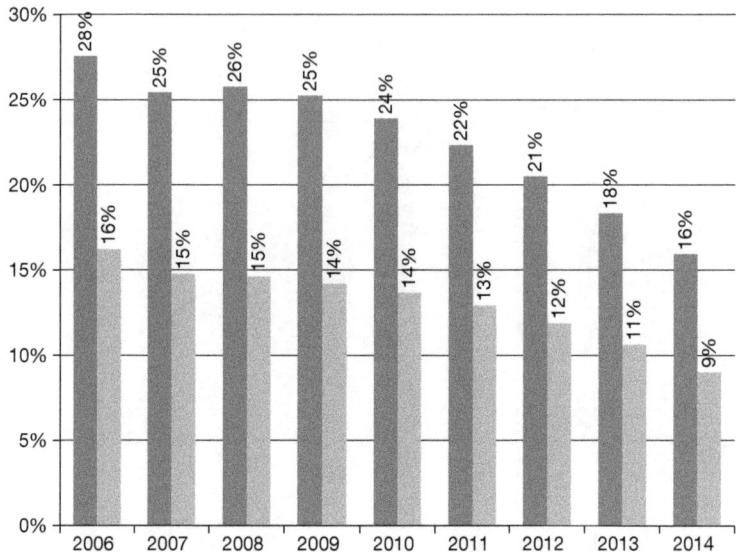

Figure 6.5 Share of total income from fees (= private funding, public and private sectors combined) in total operating budget in both sectors (dark grey); and share of total income from fees in the public sector in operating budget of the public sector (light grey), 2006–2015

Source: Own calculations based on GUS 2016 and its previous editions.

should be channelled to both sectors; otherwise, the competition would be 'unfair'. A popular idea expressed by private sector rectors was that

> the future of Polish higher education depends primarily on the political decisions regarding methods of funding; will the current monopolistic access to funds by state universities remain, coupled with the absurd Constitutional statement regarding the right to a free education in a situation of continued budgetary cutbacks? State universities retain their monopoly on public funding and fair competition is non-existent. . . . Private institutions focus on the welfare of students and of the Polish state and demand access to public funds.
>
> (Pawłowski, 2000: 73)

The social legitimacy issue emerged as key: being profit-oriented (in practical terms), the sector was unable to achieve the status of a respectable partner in a national higher education arena. Lack of social respect led to lack of social legitimacy — and consequently, the lack of future chances for larger access to public funding. Demands became dramatic, and arguments presented became irrational. For instance, private sector rectors strongly opposed increased financing of public institutions, which was ridiculous in the context of the chronic underfunding of Polish universities:

> the state budget, by financing our competitors, current functioning and development of the state higher education sector, by breaking all the rules of free competition, is sealing our future fate.
>
> (Malec, 2010: 59)

State financing of public universities and their research was viewed as the major obstacle in the private sector's survival, leading to a dramatic question: 'are we not needed?' (Malec, 2010: 59).

Rectors of private institutions argued dramatically in their open letter to the Ministry that the 'totalitarian monopoly of public higher education institutions' should be stopped and students in the public sector should be paying fees:

> the state must not conserve archaic models of higher education, teaching and research from the former regime because the state is not the only employer and the owner of economy any more. The society is free and the economy is a private market economy. . . . The functioning of research and higher education must, after 20 years of the existence of the new regime in Poland finally take into account the laws of the market economy.
>
> (SRZUN, 200: 1)

Polish higher education was viewed as a 'caricature of the education market, with traits of an organized robbery of the state budget' – and 'a totalitarian monopoly' of the public sector was diagnosed. Consequently, the rules of 'fair and efficient competition' — leading to 'competitive access to public funding' based on 'pure competition' — were strongly requested (Pomianek, 2010: 2).

However, the comprehensive answer from the state in the 2009–2011 wave of reforms was simple: if the private sector wanted public subsidies, its institutions needed to enter a newly-created national research assessment exercise (termed 'parameterization') encompassing all public sector faculties (Kwiek, 2016c; Kwiek, 2016b). The condition was for each institution to be involved in research, to use its own academic staff, and to support the academic careers of one own's young academics. The private sector, being primarily demand-absorbing, teaching-focused and using academics from the public sector, was unable to meet these conditions.

To reduce costs, the private sector employs limited numbers of full-time (in the so-termed 'first place of work') academic faculty and very few full professors. In 2014 (the latest data available), out of 290 private institutions, almost eight in ten had fewer than fifty academics, and four in ten had fewer than twenty academics. Forty-seven institutions had fewer than ten academics. On top of that, full professors are a very rare species: almost half of private institutions employ fewer than five full professors, and two thirds of them employ fewer than ten (Table 6.6). To put the data in the right context (GUS, 2015: 164): in 2014, the public sector employed 80,177 full-time academics, including 5,865 full professors (and an average university faculty employs about twenty full professors). Additionally, the number of doctoral students and doctoral and Habilitation degrees awarded in the private sector — another dimension of research activities — is marginal: in 2014, there were 675 doctoral students (out of 43,399, or 1.6 percent), 98 doctoral degrees awarded (out of 5,712, or 1.7 percent), and merely 21 Habilitation degrees (out of 2,847, or 0.7 percent). There is a high concentration in these areas: a Warsaw-based SWPS Uniwersytet Humanistycznospołeczny (SWPS University of Social Sciences and Humanities), with five branch campuses across Poland, has almost half (47.6 percent) of doctoral students in the private sector and awarded three in ten (30.6 percent) of doctoral and four in ten (42.9 percent) of Habilitation degrees in 2014. All these research-related data are understandable in the context of a dominantly demand-absorbing type of sector — but these statistics illustrate that it is impossible for private sector institutions to meet the above research conditions to gain larger access to public funding.

Again, consistent with global findings, the Polish private sector is not exceptional. As elsewhere, private institutions play mostly equitable roles and rarely elite roles: 'they rarely assume or claim to assume academic elite roles complete with doctoral education, basic research, large laboratories or libraries, or mostly full-time academic staffs' (Levy, 2002: 5). The question relevant for Poland is under what type of rationale the current private higher education decline could be reversed or diminished in scale, once equity roles are no longer dominant: with declining demographics, the public sector is increasingly taking over equity roles—as it is able to cater to ever greater shares of age cohorts.

Table 6.6 Full professors and academic faculty employed full-time (in the "first place of work") in the private sector, 2014.

Full professors per institution (range)	Number of institutions	Percentage of institutions (%)	Academic faculty per institution (range)	Number of institutions	Percentage of institutions (%)
1	37	14.9	01–09	47	16.2
02–04	97	39.0	10–19	79	27.2
05–09	57	22.9	20–49	102	35.2
10–49	57	22.9	50–99	40	13.8
50–99	1	0.4	100–299	19	6.6
100 and more	0	0	300 and more	3	1.0

Source: Own calculations based on MNISW 2015. Percentages do not add up to 100% due to rounding.

A farewell to privatization: a note about the future

Poland is not unique in having its higher education system contracting—and in having its private sector contracting. In parts of post-communist Europe (Poland, Romania, Bulgaria and Estonia), global assumptions about the ever-growing demand for higher education and the constant growth in enrolments (Altbach *et al.*, 2010) — combined with assumptions about the increasing pressure to privatize higher education mostly for financial reasons (Priest, St. John and Boon, 2006; Johnstone, 2006; Sanyal and Johnstone, 2011) — seem not to hold. On the contrary, new public-private dynamics in these countries tend to suggest opposite processes. In the context of educational contraction, privatization processes are in reverse and college-age cohorts are declining. Consequently, the pressure to privatize public higher education (internal privatization) and to expand private higher education (external privatization) is lower than ever before.

The provision aspect of de-privatization includes a decreasing number of private higher education institutions, decreasing enrolments in the private sector, the decreasing number (and share) of fee-paying students in both sectors combined, the decreasing number (and share) of fee-paying students in the public sector, the increasing share of enrolments in the public sector and the increasing share of tax-based (tuition-free) students in the public sector. The funding aspects of de-privatization in Poland include the decreasing income from fees in the public sector and in the private sector, the decreasing share of total income from fees (in public and private sectors combined) in the total operating budgets of both sectors, the decreasing share of private income in the public sector in the operating budget of the public sector, and the increasing share of public income as a proportion of the operating budget of the public sector. Processes of de-privatization in Poland are likely to continue; however, unexpected political decisions introducing universal fees can always be taken.

Conclusions

In discussing privatization in higher education, the Polish case study is important for two reasons. First, Poland has been the European country with the biggest private sector enrolments. Expansion through privatization in 1990–2005 was a successful experiment of increasing participation through a demand-absorbing private subsector, using private rather than public funding. Second, Poland shows the powerful role of changing demographics and stable politics in the changing public-private dynamics in higher education. Once the champion of privatization, Poland — through a combination of demographic and political factors — became a radically de-privatizing system in which expansion and privatization were replaced by contraction and de-privatization. Between 2009 and 2015, the number of private providers shrank from 330 to 265; private sector enrolments in 2006–2015 fell by half, from 660,000 to

330,000 students; and the role of fees in the public sector and in the national system declined significantly, with the number of fee-paying students in both sectors declining by half, from 1.14 million (2006) to 0.56 million (2015). The demographic factor was predictable — but political willingness to support the public sector expansion was not. In a zero-sum game in which students are either publicly financed or privately financed, privatization processes in higher education have been slowing down for a decade now and de-privatization processes are expected to intensify. Expansion through privatization emerges as being highly sensitive to demographics and public funding; when the student population is contracting and the state is willing and able to keep financing the shrinking public sector, the private sector is doomed. Rare as it is today, de-privatization and contraction of higher education is an interesting trend in otherwise globally privatizing and expanding higher education.[1]

Notes

1 Acknowledgments: The author gratefully acknowledges the support of the National Research Council (NCN) through its MAESTRO grant DEC-2011/02/A/HS6/00183 (2012–2017).

References

Altbach, P.G., Reisberg, L. and Rumbley, L.E (2010) *Trends in global higher education: Tracking an academic revolution*, Paris: UNESCO Publishing.
Altbach, P.G. and Levy, D.C. (eds) (2005) *Private higher education. A global revolution*, Rotterdam: Sense.
Antonowicz, D. (2016) 'Digital players in an analogue world: Higher education in Poland in the post-massification era', in B. Jongbloed and H. Vossensteyn (eds), *Access and expansion post-massification, opportunities and barriers to further growth in higher education participation*, London: Routledge, pp. 63–81.
Antonowicz, D., Kwiek, M. and Westerheijden, D. (2017) 'The government response to the private sector expansion in Poland'. in H. de Boer *et al.* (eds), *Policy analysis of structural reforms in higher education*, New York: Palgrave, pp. 119–138.
Barr, N. (2004) *Economics of the welfare state* (4th edn), Oxford: Oxford University Press.
Barr, N. (ed.) (2005) *Labor markets and social policy in central and Eastern Europe: The accession and beyond*, Oxford: Oxford University Press.
Belfield, C.R. and H.M. Levin. (2002) *Education privatization: Causes, consequences and planning implications*, Paris: UNESCO.
Białecki, I. and Dabrowa-Szefler, M. (2009) 'Polish higher education in transition: between Policy making and autonomy', in D. Palfreyman and D. T. Tapper (eds),*Structuring mass higher education: The role of elite institutions*, London: Routledge.
Correia, F., Amaral, A. and Magalhães, A. (2002) 'Public and private higher education in Portugal: unintended effects of deregulation', *European Journal of Education*, 37(4): 457–472. http://onlinelibrary.wiley.com/advanced/search/results?searchRowCriteria%5B0%5D.fieldName=author&start=1&resultsPerPage=20&searchRowCriteria%5B0%5D.queryString=%22Alberto%20Amaral%22
Enders, J. and B. Jongbloed (eds), (2007) '*Public-private dynamics in higher education*', expectations, developments and outcomes, Bielefeld: Transcript.
Feigenbaum, H., Jeffrey, H. and Hamnett, c. (1998) *Shrinking the State: The political underpinnings of privatization*, Cambridge: Cambridge University Press.

Fryar, A.H. (2012) 'What do we mean by privatization in higher education'?. in, J.C. Smart and M.B. Paulsen (eds), *Higher Education: Handbook of theory and research, Volume 27*, Dordrecht: Springer,pp. 521–547.

Geiger, R.L. (2007) 'The publickness of private higher education', in, J. Enders and B. Jongbloed (eds), *Public-private dynamics in higher education: Expectations, developments and outcomes*, Bielefeld: transcript, pp. 139–155.

Geiger, R. L. (1986) *Private sectors in higher education: Structure, function and change in eight countries*, Ann Arbor: The University of Michigan Press.

Goodin, Robert E. (1996b) 'Institutions and their design'. in, R.E. Goodin (ed.), *The theory of institutional design*. Cambridge: Cambridge University Press,pp 1–53.

Gómez, R.R.and Ordorika, I. (2012) 'The chameleon's agenda: entrepreneurial adaptation of private higher education in Mexico', in B. Pusser, K. Kempner, S. Marginson and I. Ordorika (eds), *Universities and the public sphere*, New York: Routledge,pp. 219–242.

GUS. (2016) *Higher education institutions and their finances in 2015*, Warsaw: GUS (Central Statistical Office) (and previous editions).

Heller, D.E. and Callender, C. (eds), (2013) '*Student financing of higher education', A comparative perspective*, Routledge: New York.

Johnstone, D.B. (2006) *Financing higher education, Cost-sharing in international perspective*, Boston: CIHE.

Johnstone, D. B. and Marcucci, P. (2010) *Financing higher education worldwide: Who pays? Who should pay?*, Baltimore: The Johns Hopkins University Press.

Johnstone, D.B. (2007) 'Privatization in and of higher education. Paper presented at the International Comparative Higher Education Finance and Accessibility Project'. Available online atwww.gse.buffalo.edu.

Kinmonth, E.H. (2005) 'From selection to seduction: the impact of demographic change on private higher education in Japan', in J.S. Eades, R. Goodman, Y. Hada (eds), *The 'Big Bang' in Japanese higher education: The 2004 reforms and the dynamics of change*, Melbourne: Trans Pacific Press.

Kwiek, M. (2012a) 'Changing higher education policies: from the deinstitutionalization to the reinstitutionalization of the research mission in polish universities', *Science and Public Policy*, 39: 641–654.

Kwiek, M. (2012b) 'Universities, regional development and economic competitiveness: the polish case, in: R. Pinheiro, P. Benneworth and G.A. Jones (eds), *Universities and regional development. A critical assessment of tensions and contradictions*, New York: Routledge.pp 69–85.

Kwiek, M. (2013) 'From system expansion to system contraction: access to higher education in Poland', *Comparative Education Review*, 57(3), (Fall): 553–576.

Kwiek, M. (2015a) 'The unfading power of collegiality? University governance in Poland in a European comparative and quantitative perspective', *International Journal of Educational Development*, 43:77–89.

Kwiek, M. (2015b) 'Academic generations and academic work: patterns of attitudes, behaviors and research productivity of polish academics after 1989', *Studies in Higher Education*, 40(8):1354–1376.

Kwiek, M. (2016a) De-privatization in Higher Education: A Conceptual Approach. *Higher education*. DOI 10.1007/s10734–016–0047–3 (published on-line 18 August 2016), pp. 1–21.

Kwiek, M. (2016b) 'From growth to decline? Demand-absorbing private higher education when demand is over', in M. Shah and S. Nair (eds), *A global perspective of private higher education*, New York: Elsevier. pp. 53–80

Kwiek, M. (2016c) 'Constructing universities as organizations. University reforms in Poland in the light of institutional theory, in E. Samier (ed.), *Ideologies in educational administration and leadership*, New York: Routledge, pp. 193–216.

Levine, A. (1990) *Shaping higher education future: Demographic realities and opportunities, 1990–2000*, San Francisco: Jossey-Bass Publishers.

Levy, D.C. (1986a) "Private' and 'public': Analysis amid ambiguity in higher education, in D.C. Levy (ed.), *Private education. studies in choice and public policy*, Oxford: Oxford University Press.
Levy, D.C. (1986b) *Higher education and the state in Latin America. Private challenges to public dominance*, Chicago: The University of Chicago Press.
Levy, D.C. (2002) Unanticipated development: Perspectives on private higher Eeucation's emerging roles. *PROPHE Working Paper Series no. 1*.
Levy, D.C. (2008) 'Private higher education's global Surge: emulating U.S. patterns'?, in *Privatization in higher education*, Haifa: Neaman Press, pp. 32–52.
Levy, D.C. (2009) 'Growth and typology', in: Svava Bjarnason *et al.* (eds), *A new dynamic: private higher education*, Paris: UNESCO.
Levy, D.C. (2010) 'An international exploration of decline in private higher education,, *International Higher Education*, (61)Fall 2010:10–12.
Levy, D.C (2011) 'Public policy for private higher education: a global analysis', *Journal of Comparative Policy Analysis*, *13*(4): 383–396.
Levy, D.C. (2013) 'The *decline* of private higher education', *Higher Education Policy*, *26*: 25–42.
Malec, J. (ed.) (2010) *Perspektywy uczelni niepublicznych w strategiach rozwoju szkolnictwa wyzszego*, Kraków: KAAFM.
MNISW (2015) *Szkolnictwo wyzsze 2014. Dane podstawowe*, Warsaw: Ministry of Science and Higher Education.
NCN (2017) Statistics of the National Research Council. Available online at www.ncn.gov.pl (accessed 23 April 2017).
Neave, G.and Amaral, A. (eds), (2012) *Higher education in Portugal 1974–2009: A nation, a generation*, Dordrecht: Springer.
OECD. (2016) *Education at a glance. OECD indicators*, Paris: OECD.
Pinheiro, R. and D. Antonowicz (2015) 'Opening the gates of oping with the flow? governing access to higher education in Northern and Central Europe', *Higher Education*, *70*(3): 299–313.
Pomianek, T. (2010) 'Konieczne zmiany w systemie szkolnictwa wyzszego i nauki'. *PAUza Akademicka*, 79 April 29: 2–3.
Priest, D.M. and St. John, E.P. (eds), (2006) *Privatization and public universities*, Bloomington: Indiana University Press.
Salerno, C. (2004) 'Public money and private providers: funding channels and national patterns in four countries', *Higher Education*, *48*:101–130.
Sanyal, B.C. and Johnstone D.B. (2011) 'International trends in the public and private financing of higher education', *Prospects*, *41*: 157–175.
Shah, M. and Nair, C.S. (eds), (2016) *A global perspective on private higher education*, Cambridge, MA: Elsevier.
Sieminska, R. and Walczak D. (2012) 'Polish higher education: from state toward market, from elite to mass education', *Advances in Education in Diverse Communities: Research, Policy and Praxis*, *7*: 197–224.
Slantcheva, S. and Levy D.C. (eds), (2007) *Private higher education in post-communist Europe. in search of legitimacy*. New York: Palgrave.
Spulber, N. (1997) *Redefining the state: Privatization and welfare reform in industrial and transitional economies*. Cambridge, England: CUP.
Szczepanski, J. (1974) *Higher education in Eastern Europe*, New York: International Council for Educational Development.
SRZUN (2009) Open Letter to Minister Barbara Kudrycka, 29 May 2009.
Teixeira, P., Kim, S., Landoni, P. and Gilani, Z. (eds) (2017) *Rethinking the public-private mix in higher education*, Rotterdam: Sense.
Teixeira, P.N. (2012) 'The changing public–private mix in higher education: Analysing portugal's apparent exceptionalism', in G. Neave and A. Amaral (eds), *Higher education in Portugal 1974–2009: A nation, a generation*, Dordrecht: Springer.

Teixeira, P. and Amaral, A. (2007) 'Waiting for the tide to change? Strategies for survival of portuguese HEIs', *Higher Education Quarterly*, 61(2).

Teixeira, P. and Amaral, A. (2001) 'Private higher education and diversity: an exploratory survey', *Higher Education Quarterly*, 55(4).

Vincent-Lancrin, S. (2008) 'What is the impact of demography on higher education systems? A forward-looking approach for OECD Countries', in *OECD, Higher Education to 2030, Volume 1. Demography*. Paris: OECD.

Woznicki, J. (ed.), (2013) *Financing andderegulation in higher education*, Warsaw: Institute of Knowledge Society.

Yonezawa, A. and Kim, T. (2008) 'The future of higher education in the context of a shrinking student population: policy challenges for Japan and Korea', in *OECD, Higher Education to 2030, Volume 1. Demography*. Paris: OECD.

7
Germany
Resistance to fee-paying

BARBARA M. KEHM

Introduction

In this chapter, the highly controversial debates about tuition fees in German higher education are described and analysed. It presents a brief history of the different phases of these debates, commencing after the Second World War and culminating in the reform of German federalism in 2006, which led to the introduction of tuition fees in seven out of the sixteen German states. The remaining sections are more analytical: providing an account of the principles shaping the funding of higher education in Germany, and an insight into the current debates generated by some of the stakeholders; while the conclusion offers a perspective on future possible developments.

Before beginning with the history of the tuition fee debate in German higher education, a few basic principles of the German system will be provided, so that readers can better understand the characteristics of the system.

The first principle is that the sixteen German states are responsible for all educational matters (including higher education) and culture. This principle was introduced after the Second World War in order to prevent too much centralization and concentration of power in the Federal Government. In fact, a federal ministry for (higher) education did not exist until 1969 when the general responsibilities of the Federal Government in the funding and promotion of research were extended to also include educational planning. Although with several changes of name and portfolio, the current Federal Ministry for Education and Research came into being in 1998.

The second principle is that the German higher education is essentially a public system and publicly funded. The Basic Constitutional Law establishes education, including higher education, as a civil right and a public good and thus a public responsibility. This is based on the broadly shared ideas of the welfare state and a socially responsible market economy which were gradually established after 1945. This consensus is eroding to some extent due to the spread of neo-liberal ideas of the market economy, which include the view of higher education as a private rather than a public good. But higher education studies are free in Germany and this does not only apply to domestic students but also to international (European as well as non-European) students. It also applies to all three degree levels: Bachelor's, Master's and the doctorate.

The third principle is that the German system of higher education is known as being essentially a binary system consisting of universities (121) and universities of applied sciences (UASs) (220). The latter offer a smaller range of mainly Bachelor's degree programmes of a professional and applied nature including public administration, and do not have the right to award doctoral degrees. However, the system is somewhat more diversified than that. In addition to universities and UASs, there are also fifty-eight higher education institutions of fine arts and music. The (public) university sector as such can also be divided into: full universities offering the broadest range of subjects, technical universities focusing on engineering and technical subjects but also offering some programmes in the social sciences, a distance learning university and two universities for the military forces.

An alternative classification of the system would be to divide it into state or public higher educations (238) and non-state but state recognized higher education institutions (161). The latter are private but not-for-profit institutions (121) and include faith- or church-related higher education institutions (40) (Hochschulrektorenkon-ferenz, 2015). Despite the fact that the number of private higher education institutions (HEIs) seems relatively high, they enrol just around 7.5 percent of the overall number of students which was 2.7 million in 2015. Students at private HEIs pay tuition fees while students at state or public HEIs do not.

Brief overview of the early history of tuition fees and state support for students

Until 1970, German universities levied tuition fees of around 150 German Marks per semester. These fees were abolished after students from Hamburg University successfully organized a boycott. The late 1960s and early 1970s were the time of the student movement which also had a social agenda and supported policies of widening participation for students from lower socio-economic backgrounds.

In 1971, under a social-democratic coalition government, federal state assistance for students at secondary schools and higher education institutions was introduced (German acronym: BAFöG). Eligibility for BAFöG was needs-based and determined by parental income. Originally, the BAFöG was a non-repayable grant which changed to a combination of grant and loan in the late 1970s, and from the 1980s onwards to a repayable loan set at zero interest. German re-unification in 1990 led to another change in the BAFöG because East-German students were used to receiving state financial assistance, and many more students were eligible for BAFöG than in West-Germany. The financial assistance was then changed to half grant and half repayable loan. At the highest level current (2017) BAFöG support for eligible students is 735 Euros per month.

Apart from the issue of tuition fees, there has been a student contribution every semester since the late 1960s which has to be paid upon first enrolment and at re-enrolment every semester. This contribution has always been seen as clearly distinct from tuition fees. It has increased somewhat over the years but varies between currently 100 and 350 Euros per semester. HEIs are free to determine its level. It includes a contribution to assist student self-governance (German acronym: Asta) which exists at every HEI, a contribution to the German National Association for Student Affairs (German acronym: DSW) which offers state-subsidized student halls of residence, runs cafeterias and dining halls at higher education institutions and is responsible for the provision of a variety of support and advice services for students (financial, legal, emergency, mental health, etc.). In some cases, the semester contribution also covers reduced tickets for the use of public transport. In recent years, higher education institutions in nine out of sixteen states have added an administrative fee (ranging from 50 to 150 Euros per semester) to the students' semester contribution in order to cover the costs of enrolment and re-enrolment procedures.

The reform of federalism and the issue of tuition fees

Ever since the first wave of higher education expansion (in the mid- to late 1960s) and the first post-World War Two social-democratic coalition government in 1969, there was a general consensus in Germany that education should not be merely a consumer good but was to be regarded as a human right, and thus it was the responsibility of government to fund it. This view had underlying implications for issues of social justice and equity. But it was also supported by more neo-liberal ideas of the need to exhaust the existing pool of talent to produce highly qualified graduates for the booming economy.

With higher education expansion during the 1960s and early 1970s, the federal government had increasingly supported the states in the funding of their higher education institutions. This was due to the fact that some of the poorer states were no longer able to fully fund their higher education institutions. The federal government had always been active in funding research through competitive grants provided by the national research council and through financing a comparatively large sector of research institutions outside universities (e.g. Max-Planck Institutes and Institutes of the Fraunhofer Society). The federal government was also responsible for providing state assistance to students in the form of loans and grants. Higher education expansion led to the involvement of the Federal Government in (higher) educational planning and funding the construction of new buildings and large-scale research facilities. In addition, access and degrees became centrally regulated (Kehm, 1999: 25ff).

The increasing involvement of the Federal Ministry for Education and Research led to the enactment of the first Framework Law for Higher Education in 1976. Many state governments saw this as an unwanted interference into their responsibilities but had to acknowledge the right of the Federal Government to pass framework laws and they also needed the money which flowed into the higher education sector from the Federal Government. The Framework Law for Higher Education included a prohibition of tuition fees.

This move of the Federal Ministry into higher education affairs, which the states once deemed to be their exclusive responsibility, was an issue that had festered for many years. Finally in 2003, a commission of representatives of the states and the Federal Government was established whose remit it was to prepare the grounds for a major reform of German federalism. The main aim of the states was to strengthen their own competences *vis-à-vis* the Federal Government. A year later, the Commission failed because it could not achieve a consensus on the question of how to rearrange educational policy.

After general elections in the fall of 2005 and the formation of a major coalition government (it was a coalition between the two largest political parties, the Conservatives and the Social Democrats), the coalition negotiations included a restart of the move to reform federalism. Legislation related to the distribution of legislative competences between the Federal Government and the states and the participation of the states in the legislative activities of the Federal Government was drafted. Then in September 2006, a new law regulating German federalism came into force.

The implications of the reform of federalism for higher education were essentially fourfold:

First, the Federal Government lost its competence to issue framework laws. Consequently, the Framework Law for Higher Education was no longer valid. It was never officially abolished but silently and unceremoniously put in its grave.

Second, the Federal Government retained competences to regulate access to higher education (for reasons of equity throughout the country) and monitor degrees as well as a continued involvement in educational planning.

Third, the previous task of funding new buildings in the higher education sector which was a joint task of the Federal Government and the states moved into the exclusive competence of the states.

Fourth, the previous principle of a unified remuneration of civil servants (all professors in the German higher education system are civil servants) was given up and the states could determine their salaries and pay scales in the future.

In 2004, in order to demonstrate their dissatisfaction with the level of Federal Government involvement in higher education matters and most probably knowing or at least speculating that the envisaged reform of federalism was coming soon, those states that had a government led by the Conservative Party brought action against the Framework Law of Higher Education to the Constitutional Court arguing that the prohibition of tuition fees contained in it was an illegitimate intervention into the legislative competences of the states. In January 2005, the Constitutional Court decided in favour of the states.

As a result of this, seven conservative led West-German states introduced tuition fees at somewhat varying levels but capped at 500 Euros per semester (i.e. 1,000 Euros per year). The East-German states – regardless whether led by the Conservative Party or by other parties – had decided from the start that they would not introduce tuition fees because most of their higher education institutions had the capacity to accept more students and they hoped that more students from tuition fee states in the West would decide to come to the East to study there. West-German states who decided not to introduce tuition fees were typically led by Social Democratic (coalition) governments, a party which stands more explicitly for social justice, equity and education as a human right. The Conservatives agreed that (school) education was a human right and should be free for all, i.e. exclusively funded by the state(s), but were divided over the question whether this principle should be applied to higher education as well. A majority of Conservatives had adopted the neo-liberal argument in terms of higher education, namely that higher education beyond being a public good also led to private benefits and that students should therefore at least contribute to the costs of it. And although this was referred to as tuition fees in the general discourse, the official designation was 'study contribution'. Of course, students protested but the potential flows of students from states with tuition fees to states without them were closely monitored and were much lower than anticipated (Kehm, 2014).

The change in political, and at least parts of the public, opinion from being opponents to proponents of tuition fees was based on a rather complex configuration of stakeholder views. In his analysis of the German debate about tuition fees, Krause (2008) states that the change in attitude started in 2001 and lists five main aspects for this change (cf. summary of arguments by Lieb, 2008: 65).

First, the financial situation of the states in 2002/03 was precarious while at the same time student numbers had increased to more than 2 million. Politicians started to promote the need for more individual responsibility.

Second, the fear of politicians to lose votes or having to face serious student protests had diminished.

Third, the fact that the Constitutional Court had given in to the claim of the conservative-led states that the prohibition of tuition fees in the Framework Law constituted an unacceptable interference of the Federal Government into state affairs, opened the public discourse for the proponents of fees. And while the Constitutional Court's decision was a matter of federalism, mass media could interpret the decision as implying the rightfulness and legitimacy of tuition fees.

Fourth, a well-known German think tank, the Centre for Higher Education Development (German acronym: CHE) played an important role in the background. The CHE is jointly financed by the German Rectors' Conference and the Bertelsmann Foundation (an offspring of an influential media company) and its task is to propose and promote solutions to problems in higher education. The CHE is known for its neo-liberal stance. Its role in the debate about tuition fees was to link the arguments of the fee proponents, provide them with a scholarly or analytical perspective, and to influence public opinion.

Fifth, the political debate about a crisis of public spending under pressures of globalization and demographic change led to a policy of austerity and created a climate in which citizens were asked to take on more personal responsibility and to accept more competition. Resistance to this logic could then be interpreted as the protection of vested rights by special interest groups that had become marginalized.

However, over time, whenever state elections (every 4 years) resulted in a change of government from Conservative-led to a majority for another, more left leaning party (e.g. Social Democrats, the Green Party and the Left Party), tuition fees were abolished again in those states that had introduced them. For example, the state of Hesse had tuition fees for only 1 year. Lower Saxony (until 2014/15) and Bavaria (until 2013/14) were the last states to abolish tuition fees. Interestingly, in Bavaria it was not a change of government which led to the change. The conservative Bavarian government anticipated that the general pre-election mood was such that the insistence on continuously levying tuition fees would cost it votes. Instead the Conservatives allowed a referendum in Bavaria which resulted in a majority of voters rejecting tuition fees. Thus, a promise was made by the Conservatives to abolish fees if they were re-elected.

The abolition of tuition fees was handled in different ways by each state. However, some exceptions in terms of the no fees policy can be noted which were introduced widely. First, fees would be levied from students embarking on a second course of studies. This does not mean moving from a bachelor's to a master's degree programme in the same field but starting a whole new course of studies in a different subject. Second, fees will be levied for a course of studies offered as continuing professional education or being arranged in such a way that students can continue to be gainfully employed and study in their spare time. Third, fees will also be levied on students who have studied between four and six semesters longer than the prescribed regular study time of a programme (typically 3 years for a Bachelor's degree and 2 years for a Master's degree). Fourth, two German states will introduce tuition fees for international non-EU students in the near future. Baden-Württemberg will levy fees at a level of 1,500 Euros per semester for international (non-EU) students from the winter semester 2017/18 onwards. Saxony will also introduce tuition fees for non-EU international students but allows its higher education institutions to determine the fee level themselves.

After fees were abolished, the universities, i.e. the rectors and presidents, started to protest. They felt that they had been underfunded for a long time that the additional income generated through tuition fees was absolutely necessary if they were to continue offering high quality education and training, and that the loss of this income led to serious budgetary deficits compromising the quality of teaching and learning. They began to negotiate with the respective state ministries about additional funding which would compensate them for the loss of income from tuition fees. In the end, all sixteen German states – even those which had never introduced tuition fees – agreed to provide more funding to their universities to improve the quality of teaching and learning. These extra funds are called QSL-money, an acronym referring to the German *Mittel zur Qualitätssicherung von Studium und Lehre* (funds to assure the quality of teaching and learning). The interesting issue about these extra funds is that the internal institutional allocation of them, or at least a sizeable portion of them (50 percent and more), is co-determined by students. The state ministries had formulated this as a condition when they decided to provide these extra funds. Thus, a central commission was formed at each higher education institution involving students as majority stakeholders to decide about applications for the funding of projects and activities coming from departments and student groups and demonstrating that they have the potential to improve the quality of teaching and learning. The remaining portion of the money (50 percent or less) was usually distributed to the departments which decided themselves how to spend it but they had to prove that the money was used to improve the quality of teaching and learning.

The political question: fees and stakeholders

'The level of tuition fees charged by tertiary educational institutions is one of the most hotly debated public policy issues in education today, both in civil society and among policy makers, with many countries implementing reforms in the last few years' (OECD, 2016: 236). This quote from the latest publication of OECD's *Education at a Glance* also holds true for Germany, except that the debates do not focus on the level of fees but on the question whether or not to charge fees at all.

From what has been described so far, it should be clear that the question of tuition fees is not only highly politicized in Germany but opponents and proponents of fees can be found within and across almost all stakeholder groups. The debates about the introduction of tuition fees had been going on for a number of years before fees were finally introduced. But two of the main stakeholders in this issue, both in favour of fees, had been blocking a concrete decision for some time. For reasons mentioned already above the Conservatives were proponents of fees, but they also hoped to save costs in their state budgets if the higher education institution could get access to a sizeable sum of additional income through fees. The majority of university rectors and presidents – regardless of political colour – were in favour of fees as well because they felt that they had been underfunded for years and fees would provide a very welcome additional source of income helping to mitigate underfunding. Their position was publicly represented by the German Rectors' Conference. However, the rectors and presidents argued that they would only support the introduction of fees if the whole sum of student contributions for each higher education institution would be given to them without any reduction in the basic budget provided by the state. But this was not the intention of the state governments – they were looking for savings. Thus both stakeholders in favour of fees blocked any decisive outcome for several years.

The overwhelming majority of students was, and still is, clearly against tuition fees. In 2009, there were strikes, demonstrations and protests of students, pupils and apprentices all over the country against the Bologna Reforms, tuition fees and generally against the so-called economization of education. In November of the same year, a 'Global Week of Action for Free Education' was organized.

Employers of higher education graduates tend to be on the conservative and neo-liberal spectrum of political beliefs and generally support the idea of introducing tuition fees.

The German political parties differ in their views of tuition fees:

- The Conservative Parties (CDU and CSU) endorse tuition fees by a majority
- The Social Democratic Party (SPD) rejects tuition fees for the first degree
- The Liberal Democratic Party (FDP) is split but a majority endorses tuition fees
- The Left Party (Die Linke) rejects tuition fees
- The Green Party (Die Grünen) rejects tuition fees for the first degree
- The Free Voters Party (Freie Wähler) rejects tuition fees for the first degree.

With regard to this overview two issues need to be pointed out. First, tuition fees would probably get the support from those parties rejecting them for students only studying for their first degree or those who continue to go onto a master's degree directly after graduation. Eligibility for doctoral programmes requires a Master's degree. Second, some of the parties mentioned are more or less regional. For example, the Left Party has its voters pre-dominantly in the East-German states, while the smaller of the two conservative parties, namely the CSU, is active only in Bavaria. Thus, the tuition fee debate also depends heavily on the outcome of state elections and – in most cases – the resulting coalition governments.

Principles governing the public funding of higher education in Germany

The income of public German HEIs (in total almost 50 billion Euros in 2012) is composed of basic funds provided by the states; administrative income, e.g. from services or publications (altogether 16 billion Euros in 2012); and third-party research funding which amounted to 6.7 billion Euros in 2012 (Hochschulrektoren-konferenz, 2015). Expenditures of HEIs are classified according to three large categories: salaries of personnel, new investments (e.g. buildings or IT infrastructure) and running costs (e.g. for offices, classrooms and library).

The basic budget of German higher education institutions consists of funds provided by the respective state ministry. The budget for each HEI is determined first by the number of graduates successfully completing their studies within the prescribed period of study (i.e. typically 3 years for a Bachelor's degree and 2 years for a Master's degree with some exceptions in medical subjects). For students graduating beyond the prescribed deadline, the budget will be reduced but not cut completely. Second, the amount of third-party research funding each higher education institution has been able to attract will also determine part of the basic budget. The proportion will differ for universities and UASs. Thus, grant capture and graduates constitute the two most important indicators according to which the basic budget for each HEI is calculated. In 2012, the basic budget of all higher education institutions in Germany together was 22.1 billion Euros. The proportion of GDP provided for higher education was 1 percent in 2013 (Hochschulrektorenkonferenz, 2015).

In addition, the states provide the so-called QSL-money to compensate for the loss of income from tuition fees. This money is earmarked for projects and activities to improve the quality of teaching and learning. Furthermore, there are special performance agreements between the state(s) and the higher education institutions which are called 'higher education pacts'. Typically these pacts last 4 to 5 years and are then extended. The Federal Ministry for Education and Research and the state ministries responsible for higher education sign an administrative agreement to provide jointly additional funding in order to reach specified goals. The 'Higher Education Pact' (since 2007) provides funding for more than 600,000 additional study places and is currently in its third phase.

A second pact is called the 'Quality Pact for Teaching' (operational since 2011) which differs from the QSL-money. On a competitive basis, it funds project applications from HEIs to improve the quality of learning and teaching.

Finally, there is the 'Pact for Research and Innovation' (operational since 2005) which provides an annual budget increase of 3 percent for the extra-university research institutes and the national research council. The research council budget does not go directly to the universities but is spent on a competitive basis for successful grant applications.

Current debates and conclusions

The German controversies about the issue of tuition fees can be based on two contrasting arguments which are not exclusively German but can be found globally among proponents and opponents of tuition fees. The main argument of the proponents of fees is a neo-liberal, economic one: as individual returns and benefits of a higher education degree are high (especially in terms of later income), it is only fair that students should contribute to the cost of their study. The main argument of the opponents of fees is based on social justice and equity issues: students from families with a lower socio-economic background tend to be more debt and risk averse than students from middle-class families. Therefore, tuition fees will deter them from going into higher education which constitutes a problem for equity, social justice and equal opportunities. Essentially the issue boils down to the question whether higher education is a private (at least in part) or a public good. The 'private good' argument is based on economic perspectives, the 'public good' argument more on political perspectives. A good summary of the ongoing debates about this issue can be found in Marginson (2016).

There is one more particularly German influence on German policy regarding tuition fees for higher education. Andreas Schleicher, an avid advocate of fees, is head of OECD's Directorate for Education and special advisor on educational issues to the Secretary General of OECD. In addition, he is the coordinator of the PISA and PIACC international comparative studies. Schleicher's argument in favour of tuition fees in Germany is composed of three main elements (Schleicher, 2015):

- In international comparisons, participation in higher education in Germany is relatively low and strongly dependent on the socio-economic background of prospective student. As more young people from privileged economic backgrounds go into higher education than young people from lower socio-economic backgrounds, this constitutes a social justice problem because families with lower incomes through their taxes help to finance the study opportunities of young people from families with higher incomes.
- Limited public funding leads to access restrictions which have a negative influence on the participation rates of young people from lower socio-economic backgrounds.
- The tuition fee model with the most positive effects on equity and social justice is that of state-financed loans for all students which later have to be paid back once a certain level of income is achieved. If income is below a defined minimum threshold no repayment of the study loan will be required.

Schleicher's arguments are based on the tuition fee model of Australia and England which – combined with stipends or grants – he claims constitutes a socially just system of funding. Of course there are a number of counter-arguments, and in Germany the arguments continue to oscillate.

But despite the fact that competition for funding as well as accountability have increased in German higher education, there is still a general consensus that it is a public system and should be funded by the state(s). The abolition of tuition fees even by conservative state governments reflects this consensus. In fact, the current Federal Minister for Education and Research, a member of the Conservative Party, issued a major increase in the level of needs-based state financial assistance to students at the beginning of her term of office in 2014.

However, there are also considerable differences in the system of funding according to institutional and regional factors. First of all, the winners of the German 'excellence initiative' – a competitive funding programme of the Federal Ministry and the states designed to support a group of universities to acquire world-class status – have received and continue to receive considerable amounts of additional funding in the hope that they will be able to achieve better positions on the global ranking scales. Second, higher education institutions in the poorer states (most of them located in East-Germany) receive less money and their academic staff is paid lower salaries, while higher education institutions in the richer states (typically in the South of Germany) are much better funded. This indicates an ongoing shift away from a traditionally horizontally diversified system towards a more vertically stratified one (Kehm and Pasternack, 2009).

Finally, the debate about tuition fees – though dead at the moment – can easily be revived in the future. It has not disappeared from the agenda once and for all. Government policies continue to be in favour of tuition fees, as are most representatives of institutional leadership, though for different reasons. Employers of graduates support the idea of tuition fees. However, there is currently a lack of general public support, but should this change – and influential advisory bodies and think tanks are working towards such a change – the idea could be introduced again. And with two states planning to introduce tuition fees for non-EU international students in the near future, we can observe the beginning of the erosion of the consensus at the margins, which might eventually break the dam of anti-fee public opinion.

References

Hochschulrektorenkonferenz. (2015) Hochschulen in Zahlen 2015. Available online at URL: www.hrk.de

Kehm, B. M. (1999) 'Higher education in Germany', *Developments, Problems and Perspectives*, UNESCO-CEPES: Bucarest and HoF Wittenberg: Wittenberg.

Kehm, B. M. (2014) 'How Germany managed to abolish university tuition fees', *In The Conversation*, 9 October 2014. Available online at URL: https://theconversation.com/drafts/32529/edit

Kehm, B. M. and Pasternack, P. (2009) 'The German excellence initiative and its role in restructuring the national higher education landscape', in D. Palfreyman and T. Tapper (eds), *Structuring mass higher education: The role of elite institutions*, New York, Abingdon: Routledge, pp. 113–127.

Krause, N. (2008) *Die Debatte um Studiengebühren: Die systematische Rekonstruktion eines rapiden Meinungswandels*, Berlin: Springer VS.

Lieb, W. (2008) *Die Debatte um Studiengebühren: Die systematische Rekonstruktion eines rapiden Meinungswandels*. Available online at URL: http://nachdenkseiten.de/?p=3243&output=pdf

Marginson, S. (2016) *Public/private in higher education: A synthesis of economic and political approaches*, London: CGHE Working Paper 1.

OECD. (2016) *Education at a glance 2016*, Paris: OECD.

Schleicher, A. (2015) Studiengebühren oder Studium aus öffentlichen Mitteln? Was sich aus dem internationalen Vergleich über gerechte und effiziente Hochschulfinanzierung lernen lässt. Available online at URL: http://bpb.de/gesellschaft/kultur/zukunft-bildung/200978/studiengebuehren

8
Is higher education in Latin America a public good? Issues of funding, expansion, stratification and inequity

ALMA MALDONADO-MALDONADO AND
JOSÉ HUMBERTO GONZÁLEZ REYES

Higher education in Latin American has expanded rapidly in the last 15 years; the net gross enrolment has grown from 20 percent in 2000 to 43 percent in 2013. The size of the current higher education system stands at 20 million students, 10,000 institutions and 60,000 programs (Ferreyra, et al., 2017: 2). At the same time, although growth varies by country, most private higher education sectors in Latin American countries experienced at least at a 7 percent growth during these 13 years. (Ferreyra, et al. 2017: 12). In this context, the debate on whether higher education is considered a public good or a private is relevant since the enrolment keeps increasing but the resources are not always sufficient to fund it adequately, especially in the public sector. Balán and Trombetta (1996, 388) noticed 2 decades ago that the discussion over the budget became 'the principal focus of debate on higher education policies' in the region.

In June 2008, the Latin American and the Caribbean Regional Higher Education Conference stated: 'Higher education is a social public good, a universal human right and an obligation of the State"'. The Conference also considered that higher education must play a strategic role in the region's sustainable development process (OEI, 2017). This was the declaration they agreed to present at the World Conference of Higher Education organised by UNESCO held in Paris in 2009. During this conference, the Latin American delegation wanted to ensure their position was established in the final declaration, and threatened to walk out without signing if higher education was not explicitly defined as a public good in that document (Maldonado and Verger, 2010). For Latin American delegates, the inclusion of higher education as a public good would have been regarded as a triumph, as they believed it would protect public funding for higher education in their countries and others in the region, especially in the face of the world economic crisis that was unfolding. For other countries, such as the United States, adding this clause would be impossible because their higher education system involves a public sector, non-profit private sector and for-profit private sector. Therefore, the declaration as such did not go forward, but the situation reflects the dominant way that higher education has been perceived in the region. After a process of negotiation, the final declaration stated: 'Higher Education as a public good is the responsibility of all stakeholders, especially governments' (UNESCO, 2009). This story reflects in many ways the tensions between the public and the private sector in the region and more importantly the debate on the financing of higher education in general.

Currently, two issue seem to converge in the Latin American region: 1) a rhetorical emphasis on the importance of higher education with a lack of supportive data from those who defend public universities and 2) a political position that emphasizes the individual benefits of higher education in order to reduce the pressure on the government to allocate more economic resources to this sector. This rhetoric includes the acceptance that higher education fully contributes to the development of Latin American societies because it educates their citizens, increases social mobility and represents the best space to allow critical thinking and social debates; it develops Latin American culture and helps to disseminate it to society; it produces scientific and technological innovation; and it enhances their democratic systems. While these are all great possible contributions of higher education, they are not backed with supportive evidence. At the same time, most Latin American governments would agree on paper that these are important contributions by higher education, but the public financing provided conveys something different.

Therefore the dilemmas of Latin American higher education discussed in this paper are: its growth (which is closely related to demographic growth in the region); its insufficient funding of public (and mostly free) institutions; its increase of private institutions but with less quality within or less control over the education offered; its lack of accreditation mechanisms and quality insurance controls; and its limited access for those with the lowest quintiles or deciles of income. Specifically, this chapter first discusses higher education funding in the region (including the science and technology funding, and the financing of the main Latin American universities); it then presents a general view of the growth of the private sector (and especially the for-profit institutions) in the region; third, it discusses the stratification of the higher education systems in Latin America; fourth it includes an analysis on how the stratification of the higher education systems affects inequity and whether higher education can be defined as a public good, before presenting some concluding remarks.

Higher education and Latin America

There are many ways to look at funding in higher education. It can be understood in terms of public expenditure, when the State provides a part or most of the funding. As an indicator, expenditure can be measured in terms of gross domestic product (GDP), but could also be analysed in terms of absolute numbers (in this case cost per student), not just percentages or proportions. According to UNESCO (2012), Latin American and Caribbean countries have raised their average public spending on education from 4.5 percent of GDP in 2000 to 5.2 percent in 2010, which compares to the United States' investment of 5.6 percent of its GDP on education. Translated into cost per student, in the United States the average amount spent per student is $27,924 dollars, in Germany $16,825, in Mexico $7,568, in Brazil $13,540 and in Chile $7,880 dollars per student (OECD, 2016). The size of the higher education system should be always taken into consideration with this data: the US has 19.5 million students, Germany 2.9 million, Brazil 8.1 million, Mexico 3.5 million and Argentina 2.8 million (UNESCO, 2017).

In Latin America, private investment on education represented 2.1 percent of GDP in 2010, which is higher than the OECD average of 0.9 percent. This data is disconcerting considering that Latin American countries have higher levels of poverty and inequality, which means that students from poor families and students themselves are often paying for their own education.

Despite differential growth throughout Latin American countries, public spending on education has been on the rise, at least between 2000 and 2013 when Ecuador's considerable 337 percent growth in spending overshadowed other countries such as Peru, where growth was below one percent (Graph 1).

On the other hand, although Ecuador had the highest increase in education spending as a percentage of GDP, Cuba still led the region in 2013 with 12 percent of GDP destined for education, which is far greater than other major Latin American economies such as Brazil, Argentina and Mexico.

If the percentage of GDP invested is analysed in each level of education in Latin American countries, primary schools receive the most funding, followed by secondary schools, while tertiary education is allocated the lowest

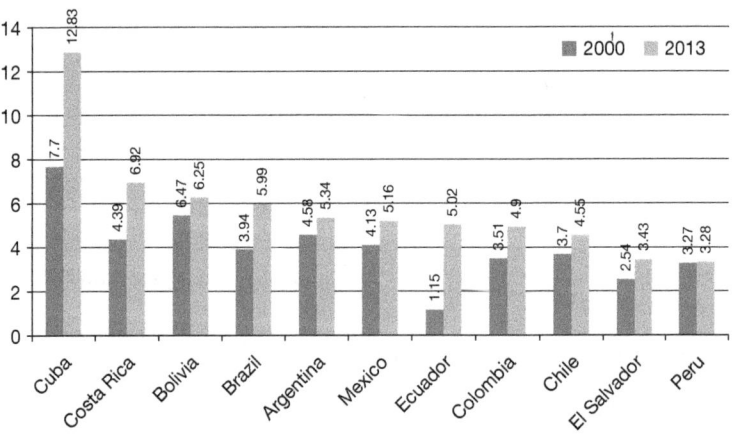

Figure 8.1 Percentage of GDP invested in education (all levels) in selected Latin American countries. 2000–2013

Source: UNESCO (2017). *Unesco Institute for Statistics*. Retrieved 3 January 2017 from http://data.uis.unesco.org/Index.aspx. Graph elaborated by the authors.

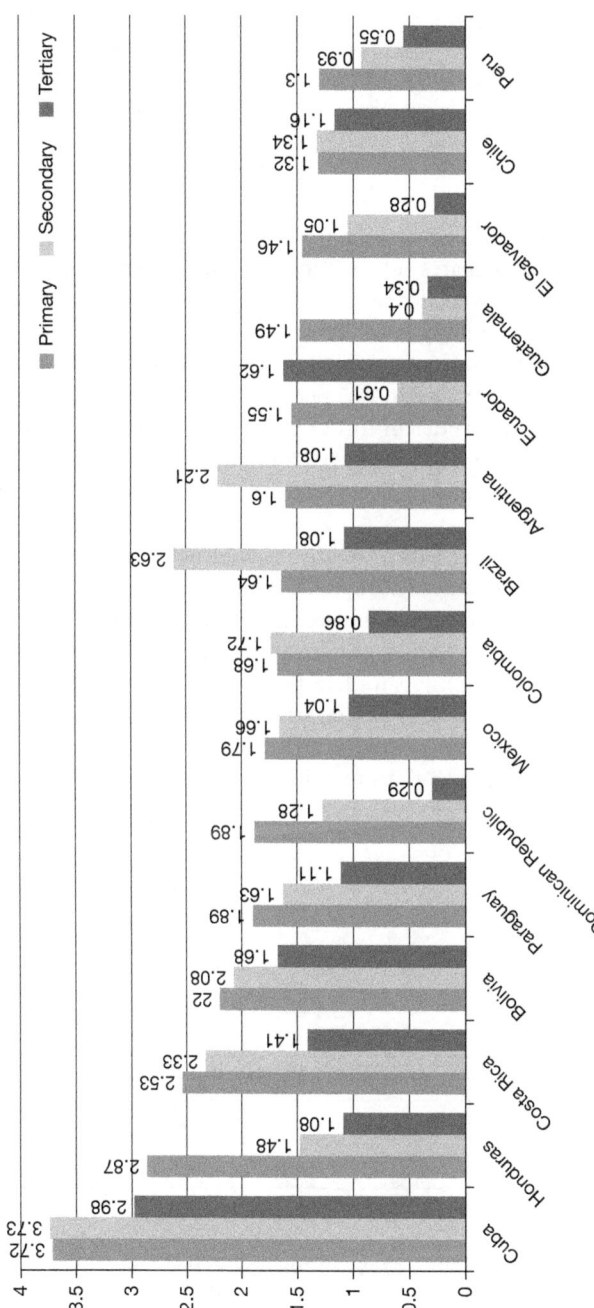

Figure 8.2 Government spending as a percentage of GDP per level of education in selected Latin American countries

Source: UNESCO (2017). *Unesco Institute for Statistics*. Retrieved 20 February 2016 from http://data.uis.unesco.org/Index.aspx. Graph elaborated by the authors.

amount of funding. According to available data, Cuba has the highest all around school investment in the region. Meanwhile, Peru trails in the region for primary school funding, Guatemala has the lowest secondary school spending and El Salvador is behind all other Latin American countries for tertiary education funding (Graph 2).

Science and technology funding

Higher education and science and technology development feed off each other. Higher education prepares future scientists and students who in turn develop science and create knowledge that makes higher education relevant, which is why the data on funding is so important. In terms of percentages of GDP, Latin American countries have raised their average science and technology spending from 0.53 percent in 2000 to 0.67 percent in 2013. During this period, Brazil became the highest spender in this area, increasing funding from 0.99 percent in 2000, to 1.23 percent of GDP in 2013. In other words, Brazil's science and technology spending has grown 24 percent and surpassed regional averages (Graph 3).

However, when contrasting Latin American investments with those made by the United States (2.81 percent in 2012) or the United Kingdom (1.63 percent in 2013) or other developed countries, the overall funding is still very low. Some of the countries have even bigger percentages in science and technology such as Israel (4.21 percent in 2013); Japan (4.15 percent in 2013); or Korea (4.15 percent in 2013) (Maldonado, 2017: 61). The same can be said for private science and technology funding which is very limited in Latin America where most research is publicly funded. On the other hand, in the case of Brazil, it is important to note that the country is currently experiencing a financial crisis

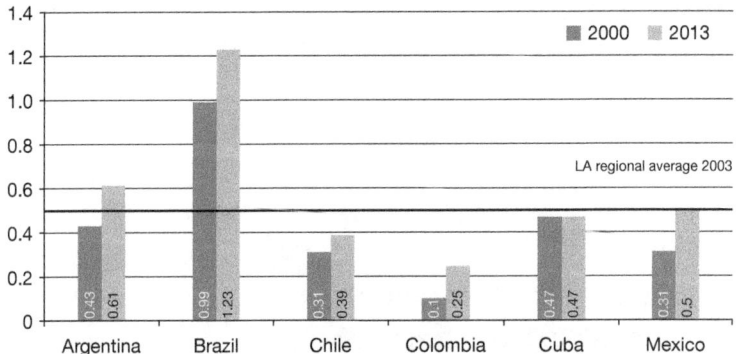

Figure 8.3 Science and technology spending as a percentage of GDP in selected Latin American countries 2000–2013

Source: UNESCO (2017). *Unesco Institute for Statistics*. Retrieved 20 February 2016 from http://data.uis.unesco.org/Index.aspx. Graph elaborated by authors.

and has reduced its expenditure on science and technology. A recent example was the cancellation of the programme 'Science Without Borders' which started with an initial budget of 1.2 billion dollars and was later dissolved (Sá, 2016).

Funding for Latin America's main universities

In 2015, the National Autonomous University of Mexico (UNAM) had the highest budget in the region with 2.5 billion dollars (Table 8.1).

However, official figures do not always tell the full story. Many institutions may not record all funding in their financial reports. Second, funds received by universities should be contrasted with student body size, faculty size and the diversity of academic programmes and activities offered. Third, student fees, scholarships, selection procedures and services offered must also be taken into account. The full extent of education costs at this level is complicated and difficult to grasp not only in Latin America, but is true generally.

In her recent book, *Paying the Price*, Sara Goldrick-Rab (2016) explains the problems that higher education students in the United States must overcome to make ends meet, even when receiving some degree of government support. Students face the complexities of academic demands, paying for fees and living expenses while juggling support programmes while some may barely have the funds to feed themselves. Similar studies are yet to be conducted in Latin America, where fees are much lower, but signs point to comparable difficulties for students who may make great sacrifices to stay in school, especially underperforming students from low socio-economic backgrounds who are left with no option but to pay for their education at low-quality private universities if rejected by the heavily subsidised prestigious public universities.

Table 8.1 Funding for Latin America's Main Universities, 2015

University	Country	Budget 2015 (USD)
University of São Paulo	Brazil	1,676,959,328
University of Chile	Chile	981,692,372
University of Buenos Aires	Argentina	777,527,876
National Autonomous University of Mexico	Mexico	2,520,406,298

Please note: 2015 budgets in US dollars were converted according to local January 2015 rates.
Source: USP: Coordenadoria de Administração Geral (2016). *Demonstrativos de receitas e despesas.* Viewed January 8 2017. Tomado de https://usp.br/codage/?q=node/5. U de Chile: Dirección de Finanzas y Administración Patrimonial (2016). *Información pública.* Retrieved January 8 2017 from http://uchile.cl/portal/presentacion/informacion-publica/77241/presupuesto. UBA: Universidad de Buenos Aires. (2016). *Presupuesto 2015.* Retrived 9 January 2017 from https://df.uba.ar/es/institucional/pagina-del-director/51-institucional/pagina-del-director/7013-presupuesto-uba-2015. UNAM: Universidad Nacional Autónoma de México. (2015). *Agenda estadística 2015.* Retrieved 9 January 2017 from http://planeacion.unam.mx/Agenda/2015/pdf/Agenda2015.pdf

The growth of private higher education in Latin America

In the late 1960's and 1970's, private higher education systems became prominent in most Latin American countries. The rise of private education establishments was partly a result of social elites departing from public institutions—which became more and more available to the masses—to more exclusive institutions (Levy, 1995). Other causes were the saturation of the public sector due to increased demand for places in public universities stimulated by demographic growth, the search for other education options not offered in public institutions and a loss in prestige of public higher education institutions.

In 1960, an estimated 31 percent of higher education institutions in Latin America belonged to the private sector. By 1970, this percentage grew to 46 percent, and by 1995 54 percent of tertiary establishments in the region were private. The percentage of students enrolled in private institutions in 1960 was 15.2 percent, but by 1970 the number doubled to 30.5 percent. By the mid 1990's, the proportion of students enrolled in private higher education institutions reached 38.1 percent (García, 2007). This expansion has been supported strongly by the private sector as Ferreyra *et al.* (2017) pointed out.

In 2014, according to UNESCO (2017), an average of 43 percent of higher education students were enrolled in private schools in Latin America. However, analysing each country individually reveals that the private sector is more consolidated in some places than others, with Brazil and Chile, surpassing the regional average in terms of private higher education enrolment (Graphs 4 and 5).

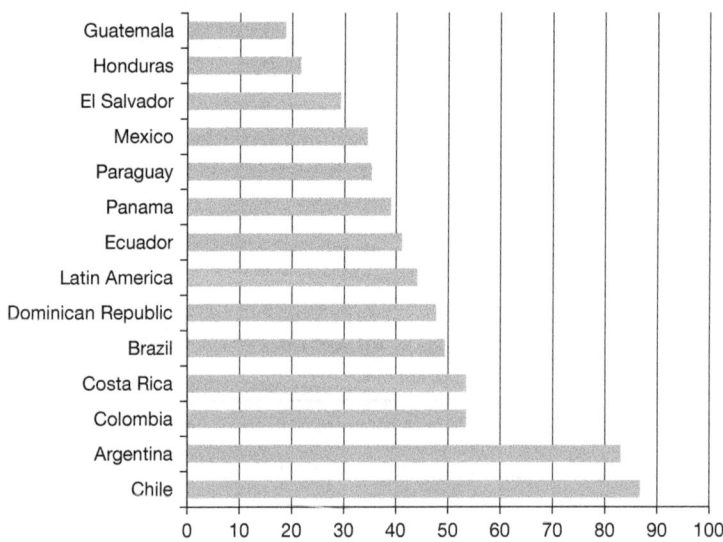

Figure 8.4 Gross enrolment ratio in higher education in Latin America (selected countries) (2014)

Is higher education in Latin America a public good? • 131

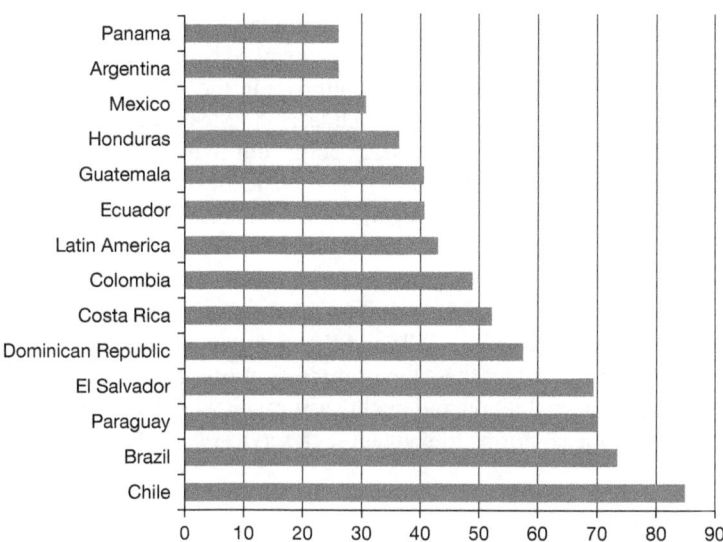

Figure 8.5 Percentage of the private higher education enrolment in Latin America (selected countries) (2014)

Source: UNESCO (2017). *Unesco Institute for Statistics*. Retrieved 20 February 2017 from http://data.uis.unesco.org/Index.aspx. Graph made by the authors.

Even though Chile reached nearly 84 percent higher education enrolment in 2014, this was largely due to a strong private sector, which accounts for more than 80 percent of enrolment in that country. Meanwhile, in countries like Brazil, Paraguay and El Salvador, where gross enrolment in higher education is below the regional average, the private sector remains strong. In Chile, on the other hand, the private sector is correlated with resources allocated to higher education; the growth of the private sector would appear to be a consequence of historical and political situations rather than simply a direct result of investment in higher education. Furthermore, in the Dominican Republic and El Salvador the strength of the private higher education sector coincides with a low percentage of public spending for higher education in those countries, which has created the ideal conditions for private sector providers to thrive.

Private higher education in Latin America has contributed to the diversification and stratification of the systems, although each case should be analysed individually, as some countries have more regulation of private institutions; for example, in some countries these institutions can access public funding and in other cases the private institutions can conduct activities that traditionally only public institutions have conducted, such as basic research. In several Latin American countries there are no major differences between for-profit and nonprofit higher education institutions like in the US. However, there are reports of an increase in for-profit private institutions. The most recent World Bank report on the region quotes Brunner and Ferrada (2011) who note that 'the expansion of the private sector can be partly explained by the fact that for-profit HEIs are now allowed in at least seven countries in the region' (Brunner and Ferrada, 2011). They are: Bolivia, Brazil, Chile, Haiti, Mexico, Panama and Peru (Ferreyra, *et al.* 2017: 100). Rama (2012) points out that the for-profit higher education sector has a presence in at least 65 percent of the Latin American region (Rama, 2012). Also, according to Levy (2011), Brazilian for-profit institutions account for 19 percent of total enrolment (p. 390). Unfortunately, there is little to no information about this sector in other countries. However, the participation of transnational for-profit universities such as Laureate have an important presence in Mexico, Chile and Brazil, but as Levy points out, Latin America was unprepared for these for-profit institutions in terms of not having a solid system of accreditation and quality assurance, as well as the absence of a complete set of legal norms to regulate such services (p. 390).

The issue of stratification

Most Latin American countries were conquered by the Spaniards who established universities as part of the process of colonisation, which means that the oldest universities in the Americas are in Latin America, not the United States or Canada. For instance, the University of Santo Domingo was established in 1538, the National University of San Marcos in 1551, the Royal and Pontifical University of Mexico in 1551, the Pontifical University of Cordoba in 1613, the Royal and Pontifical University of San Carlos Borromeo in Guatemala in 1676 and the Royal and Pontifical University of San Jeronimo in Cuba in 1721. Indeed, some of these universities became the National Universities in these countries where their traditions and importance are still relevant in the region. The Portuguese, on the other hand, had a different approach regarding higher education: Brazilian universities were created after the country obtained its independence, which was the case of the Federal University of the Amazonas founded in 1909 and the University of São Paulo founded in 1934. Before the founding of these universities, the only antecedent was the Royal Academy of Artillery, Fortification and Design.

Understanding the historical and current role of universities is necessary because many Latin Americans still perceive attending traditional universities to be more prestigious and important than attending other, newer types of higher education institutions. Of course, the rate of returns approach provides evidence that higher education in general is relevant economically speaking to the individual: 'the average returns to schooling are highest in the Latin America and the Caribbean region and for the sub-Saharan Africa region' [. . .] 'The returns are lower in the high-income countries of the OECD' (Pshacharopoulos and Patrinos, 2004: 112). The rate of returns in Latin America for higher education graduates is still signifcant. The higher education graduates can earn 104 percent more than those who only study secondary education. Actually,

Is higher education in Latin America a public good? • 133

attending college for just one year can improve a person's earnings by 35 percent in comparison to those who only study secondary education (Ferreyra *et al.*, 2017). However, not all higher education institutions are the same and the value of the diplomas varies per institution as in all countries.

To offer a better idea regarding the stratification of the higher education systems in Latin America, Graph 6 illustrates the percentage of non-universities offering higher education in selected Latin American countries. In places like Peru or Venezuela, the non-universities represent almost 40 percent of the total institutions. Some characteristics of the non-universities are: limited autonomy; limited academic programmes (sometimes they mostly offer short or technical programs); a small number of students and academics; lack of regulations in terms of accreditation and quality assurance; absence of research activities; and poor working conditions for academics (González, 2007). In countries like Colombia, these institutions have an important presence; for example, in 2003 about 18 percent of its students were enrolled in these types of institutions, but in 2013, this percentage increased to 50 percent (Ferreyra *et al.*, 2017). While these non-universities institutions do not necessarily offer poor quality education in their programmes, it is very possible that they have fewer resources, their application processes are less selective, they have less demand, and the range of programs is more limited compared to traditional universities.

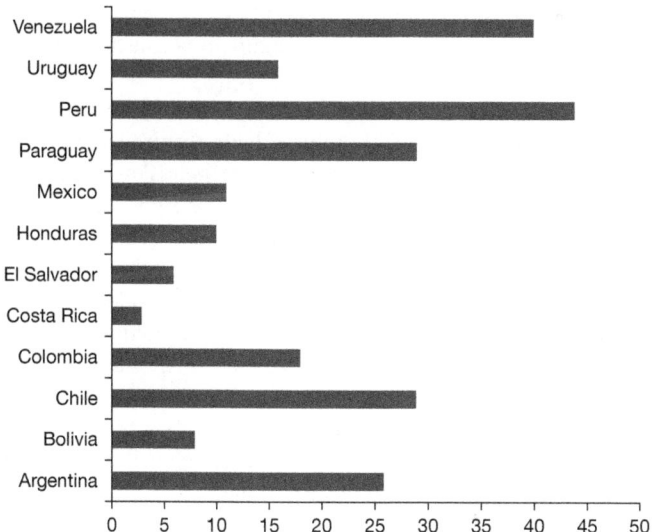

Figure 8.6 Percentage of the higher education enrolment at non-university higher education institutions in relation to the total enrolment in Latin America, 2003.

Source: González, H. (2007). Instituciones de educación superior no universitaria. En IESALC (Coord.). *Informe de la educación superior en América Latina y El Caribe 2000–2005. La metamorfosis de la educación superior.* Retrieved 16 April 2017 from https://goo.gl/0ksFWG

In contrast to the previous graph, Table 8.2 shows the percentage of enrolment in the most prestigious universities in five Latin American countries, which appear in the global rankings (Maldonado and Cortes, 2016). Even though the total higher education enrolment in Latin America constitutes 12 percent of worldwide higher education enrolment, the presence of Latin American higher education institutions in global universities rankings is not very high. In the case of Argentina, the three top institutions in such rankings, which are public universities, represent almost 30 percent of the total enrolment of the country since the access to the University of Buenos Aires is unrestricted but its dropout rate is very high. However, it is a considerable percentage, especially when compared to other countries. The enrolment of the three most prestigious public universities in Mexico represents 9 percent of the country's total enrolment. The Monterrey Institute of Technology and Higher Education, the top prestigious private institution according to the same rankings, only represents 1.4 percent of the total national enrolment. But other prestigious Latin American universities account for even less enrolment in their countries. For example, in Chile, the enrolment of the top three institutions amounts to 6.6 percent of the total national enrolment, and the two public institutions represent only 4.28 percent of the total enrolment. In Brazil the situation is even more dramatic since the enrolment of the three most prestigious institutions hardly represents 3 percent of the national enrolment of the country, and in Colombia, the two top public universities represent 2.64 percent of the national enrolment, which when added to the top private institution's enrolment increases to 3.57 percent.

Prestige matters to Latin American higher education institutions. The best example is the relevance that global rankings have acquired in the region, even when their presence there is still marginal. Nevertheless, in most cases, except for Argentina, these institutions do not constitute a significant proportion of national enrolments. These institutions presumably receive a considerable amount of public financing (see Table 8.2 below). Again, the question is to what extent the educational services they provide can be considered a public good or whether in the context of these societies they represent more of a private good. Naturally most of these institutions contribute in many other ways that go beyond serving students, for instance in terms of knowledge production and dissemination, offering cultural activities, creating spaces for critical and social thinking and so on, but as mentioned before, these contributions are still very blurry according to the current evidence and data.

In economic terms, having stratified systems is justified because 'returns from the types of higher education that traditionally have had restrictions on entry are markedly higher than returns from studies with free entry. This result in unquestionable (Aarrestad, 1972: 274). This basically means that if everybody had access to the same universities, the value of higher education would decrease; for example, lately the rate of returns for higher education graduates have decreased given the expansion of enrolment (Ferreyra et al., 2017).

Table 8.2 Total enrolment of selected universities in Latin America in relation to the total enrolment per country

Higher education institutions by country	Enrolment	Percentage in relation to total enrolment
Argentina	1 871 445	100
University of Buenos Aires	324 288	17.32
National University of la Plata	116 954	6.24
National University of Córdoba	122 522	6.54
Brazil	8 027 297	100
University of de São Paulo	86 000	1.07
State University of Campinas	34 652	0.43
Federal University of Rio de Janeiro	67 329	0.83
Chile	1 217 675	100
Pontifical Catholic University of Chile	28 311	2.32
University of Chile	29 883	2.45
University of Santiago de Chile	22 378	1.83
Colombia	2 109 224	100
University of Los Andes	19 658	0.93
National University of Colombia	51 161	2.42
University of Antioquia	4 711	0.22
Mexico	4 339 665	100
National Autonomous University of Mexico	225 495	5.19
Metropolitan Autonomous University	56 606	1.30
National Polytechnic Institute	113 176	2.60

Sources: The numbers include graduate students. Instituto Nacional de Estudos e Pesquisas Educacionais Anísio Teixeira. (2016). Sinopses Estatísticas da Educação Superior. Retrieved 16 April 2017 from http://portal.inep.gov.br/sinopses-estatisticas-da-educacao-superior. Universidad de São Paulo (2017). 80 anos de excelencia. Reviewed on April 16, 2017. Retrieved from http://usp.br/institucional/a-usp/historia/. Unicamp. (2017). Alunos. Retrieved 16 April 2017 from http://unicamp.br/unicamp/alunos. Universidade Federal do Rio de Janeiro. (2017). UFRJ em números. Reviewed April 16, 2017. Retrieved from: https://ufrj.br/docs/lai/ufrj-em-numeros-2013.pdf. Universidad Nacional Autónoma de México. (2017). Estudio Comparativo de las Universidades Mexicanas. Retrieved 16 April 2017 from http://execum.unam.mx/. Consejo de Rectores de las Universidades Chilenas. (2015). Proceso de admisión 2016. Retrieved 16 April 2017 from http://psu.demre.cl/publicaciones/2016/2016-15-08-06-universidades-cruch-y-adscritas. Consejo Nacional de Educación. (2017). Índices educación superior. Reviewed on April 16, 2017. Retrieved from http://cned.cl/public/secciones/SeccionIndicesPostulantes/Indices_Sistema.aspx. Secretaría de Relaciones Institucionales, Cultura y Comunicación de la UBA. (2012). Nuevo Sistema de Información Permanente para la realización de censos. Retrieved 16 April 2017 from http://uba.ar/comunicacion/noticia.php?id=3319. Universidad Nacional de La Plata. (2017). Anuario Estadístico 2016: Indicadores Comparados. Retrieved 16 April 2017 from http://unlp.edu.ar/indicadores. Universidad Nacional de Córdoba. (2017). La UNC en cifras. Retrieved 16 April 2017 from https://unc.edu.ar/sobre-la-unc/. Secretaría de Políticas Universitarias. (2017). Anuario de Estadísticas Universitarias. Retrieved 16 April 2017 from http://portales.educacion.gov.ar/spu/investigacion-y-estadisticas/anuarios/. Dirección de Planeación y Evaluación. (2017). Universidad en cifras. Retrieved 16 April 2017 from https://planeacion.uniandes.edu.co/universidad-en-cifras/universidad-en-cifras. Dirección Nacional de Planeación y Estadística UNC. (2016). Informe de gestión 2015. Retrieved 116 April 2017 from http://onp.unal.edu.co/ADMON_ONP/ADJUNTOS/20160212_160226_Informe_de_gestion_DNPE_2015.pdf. Ministerio de Educación Nacional. (2014). Estadísticas de educación superior. Retrieved 16 April 2017 from http://www.mineducacion.gov.co/sistemasdeinformacion/1735/articles-212350_Estadisticas_de_Educacion_Superior_.pdf.

Nevertheless, Marginson (2016) points out that in measuring 'the hierarchy of value in higher education – stratification in its different forms, is the keystone issue' [...] 'stratification interacts closely with competition, and reduction in one mostly leads to reduction in the other' (Marginson, 2016, Loc 4639). According to Marginson, if the value of higher education is not similar between institutions, this prevents higher education from contributing to society in terms of democracy, equality and solidarity (Marginson, 2016). Clearly the value of higher education in Latin America is not equal and there is a long way to go to achieve this goal.

Discussion: defining higher education as a public good: Stratification and inequities

According to Marginson (2016), one of the main obstacles in the discussion of higher education as a common good is the stratification of the system. When universities are highly stratified by prestige, size of the institutions, quality, rankings positions it is more difficult to argue that higher education is a common or public good. In fact, Marginson seems very convinced that the Nordic countries have found a better balance in terms of access to higher education institutions, as the difference among universities in countries like Finland or Norway is remarkably less than in countries like the United States or the United Kingdom. If Scandanavia is the ideal model, then the Latin American higher education systems are very far from it since our countries generally lack an institutional equilibrium. In Latin America, the top public institutions hardly constitute important proportions of the total enrolments, but the problem of access in terms of the general population is an even larger social problem for the whole region with some exceptions like Chile with 84 percent enrolment or Argentina with 80 percent (Maldonado and González, 2016). Regarding the large number of students who attend other institutions (the non-universities), the chances of accessing the top institutions are especially limited if they belong to the poorer segments of society.

As was mentioned before, Latin American higher education is facing many challenges: increased demand for the services; lack of control over private sector growth – particularly of the for-profit universities; strong inequity between the access of the poor and the rich; lack of relevance (in terms of social mobility and their academic programmes); and insufficient public resources.

In this context, it is interesting to note that most Latin American authors assume higher education is a public good without questioning its conceptual contradictions and theoretical implications. The very few who have discussed this, such as Da Silveira (2015) or Rodríguez (2014), follow Samuelson's position, but as Marginson (2016) argues, 'Samuelson's framework is useful in identifying minimum necessary public costs but not for exploring the potential for public goods above that baseline' (Loc 1923). Indeed, much of the debate on higher education has been informed by the work of Samuelson (1964) who defines public goods as being 'one or both ... non-rivalrous and non-excludable.'... Goods are non-excludable when the benefits cannot be confined to individual buyers, such as clean air regulation. Private goods are neither non-rivalrous nor non-excludable. They can be produced, packaged and sold as individualised commodities in markets.' (Marginson, 2016, Loc 1500). Samuelson concludes by saying that defining first whether a good is public or private cannot determine how to treat such a good, but apparently in the world of higher education, most people tend to take a position before deciding how to treat that good:

> The debate around the definition of higher education as a public good has many layers. From an economic point of view, defining something as a public good means that it should be available to others, just like the air people breathe, public parks and knowledge itself. Their use of the good does not preclude its use for others, according to classic economists.

However, higher education is not available to everyone, especially in developing countries, at least not in ideal conditions since higher education opportunities in most countries around the world are based on social class background. Thus, the matter of higher education as a public good is more or less answered but other questions remain: Do people have a right to higher education? Is it merely a public service? Should it be the state's responsibility? Or is higher education a private good with public benefits? (Mas-Colell, Whinston, and Green, 1995: 359)...

Marginson (2016) suggests a new way to look at this debate.

> 'It is accepted that higher education is a common public good, in which its private benefits are seen as a function of its public nature' (Loc 344) ... 'The common good is understood in terms of social solidarity, social relations based on universal human rights and equality of respect' (Loc 380) ... 'The first kind of common good is commonality across national borders, which is a global public good' (Loc 380) ... The second common good offered by higher education is the formation of common relationships and joint (collective) benefits in solidaristic social relations within a country—national public goods.
>
> (Marginson, 2016)

But why should the stratification of the Latin American higher education matter? In part, the answer is attached to the increasing worldwide dialogue on inequality and inequity. Recent economists who have addressed the issue of inequity consider that education and knowledge may be the key factors to fight these problems. Pikketty (2014) argues that during a long period of time the main force that can achieve more equity is knowledge dissemination and skills. Stiglitz (2012) and Atkinson (2015) also consider that inheriting privileges in education can be problematic. However, these authors, including Deaton (2013), do not go beyond this recognition that access to education and dissemination of knowledge can contribute to a reduction of inequities. But they do not suggest concrete ways to reach such goals; perhaps this is a task that people in higher education must do. In any case, stating that higher education will help to reduce inequities while not addressing the inequities that already define higher education, as is the case with Latin America, seems merely a rhetorical response.

Stiglitz (2012) for instance recognizes that parents with better and more resources can send their children to better schools, and as a consequence, these students have better chances to study at the top colleges (what he defines as 'intra inequity',). This is an excellent way to analyse what happens in many Latin American countries. 'From 2000 to 2013, access of the less privileged population to higher education increased by only 7 percent. On the contrary, the more privileged population increased its access to higher education by 6 in the same period (SITEAL, 2015)' (Maldonado and González, 2016). This growth will not be enough to reach a larger participation in the higher education sector from the most disadvantaged students. The gap will not be reduced between the rich and the poor at this pace. Clearly this is at least the case for Mexico, and probably other very unequal countries like Brazil, where the access to higher education is almost impossible for the poorest students, especially those from families in the lowest two deciles (or first quintile) of income whose chances to complete a college degree are practically zero (Solís, 2015). Currently about 10 percent of Mexican students who belong to the two lowest deciles of income have access to higher education versus about 60 percent of Mexican students who belong to the two highest deciles. Another example of this situation is represented by Chile and Brazil:

> "The majority of students enrolled in higher education in Latin American countries are still mostly from those families with the highest income". In Chile 62% of the highest income quartile population in tertiary education age are enrolled in higher education against only 21% of those from the lowest income quartile. In Brazil, about 47% of the highest income quartile population is enrolled in tertiary education, while only 5% of the lowest income quartile population is enrolled in tertiary education.
>
> (Heitor and Horta, 2014: 65)

Moreover, the types of institutions each segment can access should be analysed. One main question is the expenditure of higher education, especially for the poorest families whose educational expenses sometimes include costs of living, food and clothes in addition to tuition. The situation is even worse when the only chance for low income students in Mexico is to attend to low-quality private universities (mostly garage universities) after the most in demand and practically free public universities fail to accept them. To what extent does the heavy public subsidisation of higher education represent an equal policy in such unequal contexts? Students from the lowest income have a lower probability of accessing the better public institutions, while the most advantageous students – with more cultural, social and financial capital – have more chances to access the top public universities, even increasing expansion would be for the benefit of the most advantageous groups (Lucas, 2001; Márquez, 2012).

According to Beviá and Iturbe-Ormaetxe (2002) people who are able to complete higher education degrees will earn more income in the future and eventually, as most economists agree, will pay more taxes. But 'people whose children do not receive higher education however, should agree to help pay the cost of such education, providing that taxes are sufficiently high to ensure an adequate redistribution in favour of their own children at some time in the future' (p. 321). The problem is that this formula does not seem to be working in Latin America where inequalities appear to increase instead of closing the gap between rich and poor. This should be something that Latin American universities, particularly the oldest and most prestigious, start taking more seriously by proposing more efficient ways to address these inequities. Preserving the meritocratic approach does not help solve this problem. Indeed, there are countries like Brazil or Venezuela which have established affirmative action policies but more dissemination of the results of such policies would help improve the higher education debate.

Final remarks

Last but not least, Hazelkorn and Gibson (2017) mention that the most important thing in this debate, more than technically defining whether higher education is a public or a private good, is to analyse from where and how people define higher education as a public good, what the main concepts are and the main implications of such concepts. This chapter is an attempt to contribute in that sense of the debate surrounding the expansion of higher education, with particular reference to the growth of the private sector and in particular of the for-profit institutions, the problems regarding stratification, and a conceptual discussion on whether it is possible or not to consider higher education as a public good in Latin America or at least to start uncovering the many layers of the problem.

One key question is whether higher education can be discussed as a public good or common good when the access to higher educaion is divided into layers; when the most prestigious universities mostly depend on the capital of their students: cultural, social, economic and political. This is the main problem when the public and the private sectors are analysed in one of the most unequal regions in the world. The public system is very important and the role of public higher education institutions is crucial to many social sectors in Latin American societies. However, when the very stratified access is considered along with all the real barriers that exist for the poorest or less privileged students to access the top public institutions with the best programmes, it is valid to ask: who is the public sector serving? When the value of a degree in the market and in the eyes of the society is so different, how is it possible to talk about higher education as a common good?

Finally, if rhetorically higher education is a public good that must be financed by the State and to which access must be equal, in reality Latin American societies are facing important challenges regarding highly stratified higher education systems that reproduce many socio-economic inequities of the region. The continuous growth of private higher education – and particularly of for-profit institutions, with lack of control of the quality of their academic programmes is not helping such imbalances. Therefore, there is a need to continue discussing conceptually this idea of higher education as a public good in different regions of the world, but also to analyse the growth of new providers and the way they are shaping this debate.

References

Aarrestad, J. (1972) 'Returns to higher education in Norway', *The Swedish Journal of Economics*, 74, 263–280.

Atkinson, A. (2015). *Inequality: What can be done?* Cambridge, MA: Harvard University Press.

Balán, J. and Trombetta, A. (1996) An agenda of problems, policies and debates on higher education in Latin America, *Prospects*, XXVI(2): 387–412.

Beviá, C. and Iturbe-Ormaetxe, I. (2002) 'Redistribution and subsidies for higher education', *Scandinavian Journal of Economics*, 104(2): 321–340.

Da Silveira, P. (2016). ¿Qué hay de púbico y qué hay de privado en la educación? En Revista colombiana de Educación (70): 201–219. Reviewed on 10 February 2017. Retrieved from http://scielo.org.co/pdf/rcde/n70/n70a10.pdf

Deaton, A. (2013) *The great scape: Health, wealth and the origins of inequality*, Princeton: Princeton University Press. (check title)

Ferreyra, M. M., Avitabile, A. C., Botero, Á. J., Haimovich, P. F. and Urzúa, S. (2017) *At a crossroads: Higher education in Latin America and the Caribbean*, directions in development—human development, Washington, DC: World Bank.

Goldrick-Rab, S. (2016) *Paying the price: College costs, financial aid and the betrayal of the American dream*, Chicago: Chicago University Press.

González, H. (2007) Instituciones de educación superior no universitaria. En IESALC (Coord.). *Informe de la educación superior en América Latina y El Caribe 2000–2005. La metamorfosis de la educación superior*. Retrieved 16 April 2017 from https://goo.gl/0ksFWG

Hazelkorn, E. and Gibson, A. (2017) Public goods and public policy: what is public good, and who and what decides? *Centre for Global Higher Education working paper series*, (18). Reviewed 2 May 2017. Retrieved from http://www.researchcghe.org/perch/resources/publications/wp18.pdf

Heitor, M. and Horta, H. (2014) 'Further democratizing Latin America: broadening access to higher education and promoting science policies focused on the advanced training of human resources', *Journal of Technology Management and Innovation*, 9(4): 64–82.

Levy, D. (1995) *La educación superior y el estado en Latinoamérica: desafíos privados al predominio público*. Mexico: CESU-UNAM / Flacso México / MA Porrúa.

Levy, D. (2011) 'Public policy for private higher education: a global analysis', *Journal of Comparative Policy Analysis: Research and Practice*, 13(4): 383–396.

Lucas, S. (2001) 'Effectively maintained inequality: education transitions, track mobility, and social background effects, *American Journal of Sociology*, 106(6): 1642–1690. Retrieved from: http://jstor.org/stable/10.1086/321300?seq=1#page_scan_tab_contents

Maldonado-Maldonado, A. (2017). La inequidad en la producción y el uso del conocimiento ¿dónde queda América Latina? In Universidad de Ciencias Aplicadas y Ambientales (UDCA) y Asociación de Universidades de América Latina y el Caribe para la Integración (AUALCPI). *Construcción de espacios regionals: inclusion social latinoamericana*. Tomo II (pp. 57–70). Bogota: Universidad de Ciencias Aplicadas y Ambientales (UDCA) y Asociación de Universidades de América Latina y el Caribe para la Integración (AUALCPI).

Maldonado-Maldonado, A. and Cortes, C. (2016) 'Latina American higher education, universities and worldwide rankings. The new conquest?', in E. Hazelkorn (ed.), *Global rankings and the geopolitics of higher ducation. understanding the influence and impact of rankings on higher education, policy and society*, London/New York: Routledge Taylor and Francis Group, Serie: 'International Studies in Higher Education' pp. 162–177.

Maldonado-Maldonado, A. and Verger, A. (2010) 'Politics, UNESCO, and higher education', *International Higher Education*, 58(Winter): 8–9.

Maldonado-Maldonado, A., González, R. and José, H. (2016) 'Higher education expansion in Latin America', in *Encyclopedia of international higher education systems and institutions*, Springer. Retrieved from: https://link.springer.com/referenceworkentry/10.1007/978-94-017-9553-1_55-1

Marginson, S. (2016) *Higher education and the common good*, Melbourne: Melbourne University Press. [ebook].

Márquez, A. (2012) 'El costo de estudiar en México', *Perfiles educativos*, 34(136): 190–194. Reviewed on 7 October 2014. Retrieved from: http://ses.unam.mx/integrantes/uploadfile/rrodriguez/CreditosEducativosEnMexicoNo.pdf

Mas-Colell, A., Michael, D.W. and Jerry, R.G. (1995) *Microeconomic theory*, New York: Oxford University Press.

Organización de Estados Iberoamericanos (OEI). (2017) Declaración Final de la Conferencia Regional de Educación Superior en América Latina y El Caribe. Conferencia Regional de Educación Superior 2008. Reviewed on 2 February 2017. Retrieved from http://oei.es/historico/salactsi/cres.htm

Pikketty, T. (2014) *Capital in the twenty-first cen*tury,Cambridge, MA : Harvard University Press.

Psacharopoulos, G. and Patrinos, H. A. (2004) 'Returns to investment in education: a further update, *Education Economics*, 12 (2): 111–134.

Rodríguez, R. (2014) Ser o deber ser: La educación superior como bien público. *Campus Milenio*. Reviewed 4 December 2016. Retrieved from: http://campusmilenio.mx/index.php?option=com_k2&view=item&id=1949:ser-o-deber-ser-la-educacion-superior-como-bien-publico&Itemid=140

Samuelson, P. (1964) 'Public goods and subscription TV: correction of the record', *The Journal of Law & Economics*, 7 (October): 81–83.

Sá, M. C. (2016) 'The rise and fall of Brazil's science without borders, *International Higher Education*, 85(Spring): 17–18.

Sistema de Información y tendencias Educativas en América Latina (SITEAL). (2015) Escolarización en América Latina 200–2013. Reviewed 2 February 2017. Retrieved from: http://siteal.iipe.unesco.org/sites/default/files/rec_siteal_2_2015_04_28.pdf

Solís, P. (2015) Mayor cobertur educativa. La misma desigualdad social. *Distancia por tiempos. Blog de Educación de la Revista Nexos*. Reviewed 2 January 2017. Retrieved from: http://educacion.nexos.com.mx/?p=55

Stiglitz, J. (2012) *The price of inequality*, New York: WW Norton & Co.

UNESCO. (2009) *World conference on higher education: The new dynamics of higher education and research for societal change and development, Communiqué*, Paris: UNESCO. Reviewed 2 February. Retrieved from: http://unesdoc.unesco.org/images/0018/001832/183277e.pdf.

UNESCO (2012) *Situación Educativa en América Latina y el Caribe. Hacia una educación para todos 2015.* Reviewed on 3 January 2017. Retrieved from http://unesco.org/new/fileadmin/MULTIMEDIA/FIELD/Santiago/pdf/situacion-educativa-mexico-2013.pdf

UNESCO (2017). *Unesco Institute for Statistics.* Reviewed on 20 February 2017. Retrieved from http://data.uis.unesco.org/Index.aspx

9

Higher education development in China
Fast growth and governmental policy since the Chinese economic reform of 1978

SHUMING ZHAO AND YIXUAN ZHAO

Introduction

The world has witnessed the great achievements of China's economic and social development since the opening up to the outside world in 1978. The rapid growth of the economy brings opportunities for the development of China's higher education system. Recently, the global education groups British QS and Universitas 21 recorded rankings of higher education systems and China's higher education system is ranked respectively eighth and fifth (China News Network, 6 November 2015), which shows the global recognition of China's higher education system.

The fast growth of Chinese higher education since the 1978 economic reform

Expansion of the higher education system

In the twenty first century, Chinese higher education has made a leapfrog development. In 2016, China had an enrolment of 74,860,000 students at colleges and universities, and there were 2,879 colleges and universities. The number of higher education institutions increased from 598 in 1978 to 2879 in 2016, while the number of undergraduates in regular higher education institutions grew from 165,000 in 1978 to 70,420,000 in 2016, and the number of teachers grew from 206,300 to 1,572,600.

China started expanding the enrolment of college students from the late 1990s. In 2001, more than 1.14 million undergraduate students graduated from Chinese colleges and universities. In 2017, about 7.95 million undergraduates will graduate from Chinese universities. Figure 9.1 shows the number of college graduates from 2001 to 2016.

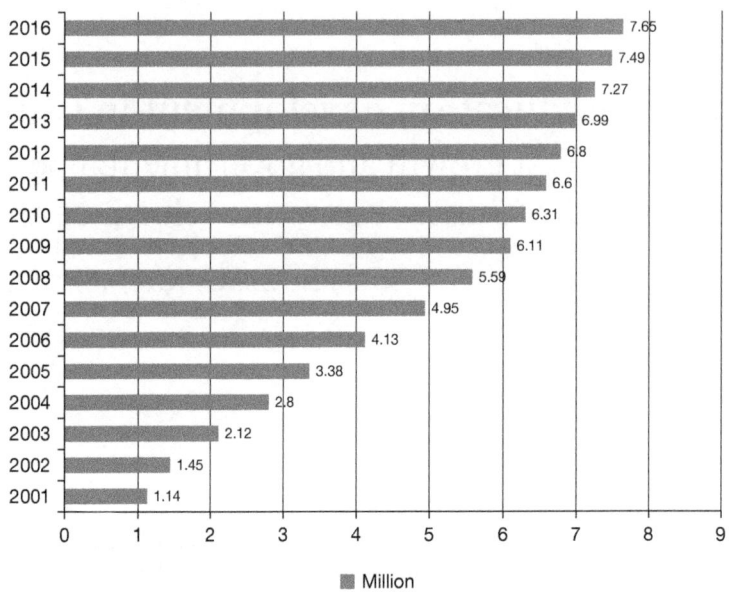

Figure 9.1 The number of college graduates in China
Source: http://mnw.cn/news/china/1194094.html

The development of Chinese postgraduate education

Since the economic reform and opening up to the outside world in 1978, graduate education has made great progress. In 2015, China's number of postgraduate students at colleges and universities reached 1.9 million, about 20 percent higher than in 2010. At the same time, the engagement of graduates in scientific and technological innovation has continued to improve.

Postgraduate education pays more attention to cultivating practical skills and ability. Before the 8th Five-Year Plan (1991–1995), higher education institutions in China had only academic degree programmes and taught purely theoretical knowledge. There was a lack of professional education programmes. Since the 8th Five-Year plan in 1991, China started MBA programmes with nine business schools. The emergence of professional postgraduate programmes showed that Chinese higher education began to change from focusing on academic research and talent training to combining academic knowledge with professional education to cultivate professional practice abilities. Now more than 236 business schools are offering MBA programmes, and sixty universities have been offering EMBA programmes with an enrolment of 40,000 students each year, of which about 8000 are EMBA students. China has a total enrolment of 540,000 MBA students including 60,000 EMBA students. About 300,000 MBA including 40,000 EMBA students have graduated and received their degrees.

In addition to MBA programmes, there are about forty professional degree programmes, such as Master of Public Administration (MPA), Master of Professional Accounting (MPAcc), Master of Education (M.Ed.), Master of Public Health (MPH) and Juris Master (JM).

The international influence of Chinese graduate education keeps rising. In 2015, there were twenty-five universities in the Chinese mainland entering into the UK top 500 QS world university rankings, with more than 600 disciplines among the top 1 percent of Essential Science Indicators (ESI) in the United States, ranking sixth in the world (China News Network, 6 November 2015). Another manifestation of the rising international influence of Chinese postgraduate education is the rising number of international students in Mainland China. According to the Ministry of Education, about 397,635 international students from 202 countries and regions are studying in China in 2015. International postgraduate students in China reached 50,000 in 2014, more than double the number in 2010. (Liu, 2016)

Educational fairness: from equity as the starting point to educational quality

Enhancing the quality of education has been a common goal for countries all over the world. However, establishing basic education development does not necessarily increase education fairness as people increasingly demand high-quality education. The Chinese government insists that promoting fairness in education should be taken as a basic education policy. As for the regional distribution of colleges and universities, in 2000 there were 554 higher education institutions in central and western areas, while in 2014 the number became 1,363, increasing 2.46 times. In April, 2015, the Chinese Ministry of Education issued a notice to certify the special plan of enrolment in poor rural areas. It arranged to enrol 50,000 students in 832 poor counties and ten provinces, such as Hebei and Henan, where the admission rate of key colleges and universities is lower than that in other areas (Xinhua Net, 3 April 2015).

The improvement of scientific research level

During the 12th Five-Year Plan period (2011–2015), higher education institutions had undertaken 60 percent of the 973 National Science Research Projects, more than 80 percent of research projects sponsored by the National Natural Science Foundation of China, and over 85 percent of the National Philosophy and Social Science projects. The research output has been growing rapidly. In 2014, higher education institutions won more than 70 percent of the three-major science and technology awards in China. Original and innovative ideas such as 'abnormal quantum hall effect' emerge continuously. The improvement of scientific research ability and discipline construction drives Chinese higher education institutions to move forward in international academic rankings.

Nearly 600 disciplines are in the top 1 percent of the world's homogeneous subjects, globally ranking sixth. More than fifty subjects are in the top one thousand. (Zhai, 2016)

The contribution of higher education to economic construction and social progress

In April 2016, Chinese Ministry of Education launched China's Higher Education Quality Report which shows that the development of China's higher education basically keeps pace with that of the national economy. Since 2000, in order to meet the needs of local economic development, the Chinese government adjusted the layout of higher education so as to coordinate regional and socio-economic development. Local governments issued policies to promote local higher education institutions' support of the economy. For example, Sichuan Provincial government proposed incentive packages to attract high-level talents, the improvement of innovative talents training modes and incentive policies to promote the transformation of scientific and technological achievements (Sichuan Daily, 9 July 2016).

Higher education's development supplies human resources and advanced technology for China's economic growth and social progress. China successfully launched its first heavy-lift Long March 5 carrier rocket from Wenchang Space Launch Center, Hainan Province on 3 November 2016, marking a new milestone in the country's space industry (China Long March 5 Carrier Rocket, 2016). Chinese high-speed railway construction is considered as a wonder of economic development. All above are inseparable from achievements in scientific research and technical support from higher education institutions.

The influence of internationalization

Through internationalization students can learn compulsory academic knowledge though access to teachers, and students have a larger platform to demonstrate their educational achievements. The university's education activities have become internationalized. More universities have hired international faculty members to teach courses and participate in joint research. At the same time, Chinese colleges and universities have been sending faculty members and students abroad. In 2015, the total number of Chinese students studying abroad reached 523,700, an increase of 13.9 per cent compared to 2014 There are a growing number of Chinese who have studied abroad, as well as an increase in the number of students who returned to China after they completed their studies.

Meanwhile, internationalization also shows in enrolment of more foreign students thereby building an inclusive university culture. In 2015, more than 397,635 international students from 202 countries and regions were studying in China. While there has been a slight decrease in the number of international students from Europe, America and Oceania, there is an increasing number of students from Africa.

The rapid development of higher education is inseparable from government policy guidance and support

1978–1983: the recovery period (from starting economic reform and opening up to the outside world to the 1984 commodity economy)

After 10 years of destruction during the Cultural Revolution (1966–1976), the devastated country had to be rebuilt. In 1977, by restoring the college entrance examination system as a major symbol, China began the arduous process of change and ideological liberation. Since then, according to Deng Xiaoping's proposal, a series of higher education policies have been resumed and established the: restoration of postgraduate education system, the establishment of degree system, large-scale dispatch of overseas students and strengthening of key universities. These major policies have stimulated the vigour and vitality of higher education.

In 1978, China implemented the economic reform and opening-up to the outside world policy, shifting from the highly centralized planned economy to gradually the commodity economy in 1984 and opening up fourteen coastal cities to the outside world. The policy determined economic development as the centre of China's development. In September 1982, the twelfth Chinese Communist Party Congress identified educational work as the strategic focus of economic development. In 1983, Deng Xiaoping wrote the inscription for Beijing Jingshan School: 'Gear education to the needs of modernization, the world and the future'. Under this guidance, the reforms of higher education quietly started.

1984–1992: the change period (from commodity economy to socialist market economy)

In 1984, China started the semi-commodity economy system and 1985 was a special landmark year in the history of China's higher education policy. In May of that year, with the promulgation of the 'Decision of the Central Committee of the Communist Party of China on the reform of the education system', the institutional reform had become the focus of higher education policy. In the reform of the macro-management system, China's central government had strengthened provinces, autonomous regions and municipalities to co-ordinate higher education, and expanded the autonomy of colleges and universities. In the reform of the educational system, three levels were determined which include the central, provincial (including autonomous regions and municipalities directly under the Central Government, such as Beijing, Shanghai, Tianjin and Chongqing) as well as cities under provinces and the Chinese government explored the mode of cross-sector, cross-regional joint schools, which changed the situation that the schools had been only undertaken by the government. In the reform of the enrolment system of colleges and universities and the reform of the distribution system of graduates, the method of uniform enrolment of HEIs all according to the state plan and the distribution of all the graduates assured by the state were changed. In terms of the internal management system in universities, president responsibility, faculty appointment and personnel system reform were changed to commence a process of reform.

At the same time, the structural reform of higher education became a major strategic policy. In the reform of the hierarchical structure, higher education changed the unreasonable situation of colleges and universities to accelerate the development of college education. In the reform of discipline structure, Chinese government accelerated the development and support of emerging departments and specialties such as finance, politics, law and management, supporting the growth of these emerging disciplines and interdisciplinary education. In the reform of formal structure, through the development of higher vocational education and adult higher education, China promoted the diversification of higher education.

In 1992, with Deng Xiaoping's speech during his famous Southern Tour and the fourteenth Party Congress as a symbol, China's reform, opening up and modernization entered a new historical period. The establishment of a Socialist Market Economic System and the speeding up of socialist modernization put forward new demands for the reform and development of China's education. The '211 Project' was aimed at raising about 100 universities and key disciplinary areas as a national priority for the twenty-first century and was the largest scale and highest level attention accorded to higher education since the founding of the People's Republic of China. The project is not only a major incentive for China to implement the strategy of national rejuvenation through science and education, but also a systemic reform project of higher education. 'Rejuvenating the country' as the value of this period to lead, strongly pushed the development of China's higher education into the fast lane and opened the prelude to the development of higher education at the turn of the twenty-first century.

1993- today: the flourishing period (from the establishment of market economy to the present)

Since China adopted the Socialist Market Economic System in 1992, China has abolished the highly centralized economic system. In higher education, in China before 1993, all college students were assigned to jobs according to the planned economy. Since 1993 all college students have to find their own jobs. The selection process between each graduate and organization has been adopted. A human resource management system has been established in all organizations in China (Zhao, 1995).

China entered a new stage of building a well-off society in an all-round way by accelerating the building of socialist modernization. Under the guidance of the 'rejuvenating the country through science and education' strategy, the Chinese government has promulgated a number of important educational regulations and policies and mapped out a grand blueprint for the reform and development of cross-century education. With the promulgation of 'Higher Education Law' (1998) as a starting point, the construction of higher education policy has entered a new stage of comprehensive rejuvenation and prosperity. A series of policies on the rejuvenation of higher education have impacted the development of higher education, including promoting the popularization of higher education, intensifying teaching reform in colleges and universities, accelerating the pace of first-class university construction and improving the system reform of higher education. The policies brought Chinese higher education unprecedented development and prosperity.

On the basis of the '211 Project', in accordance with Chinese former President Jiang Zemin's proposal during the centennial celebration of the founding of Peking University, 'the nation must have many first-class universities at advanced world level in order to realize modernization" China has been determined to fully support first-class universities, such as Peking University, Tsinghua University, Nanjing University and other top universities to create high-level universities. His speech was delivered at Peking University on May 1998, so that the project was named '985 Project'. The '211 Project' and '985 Project' have been implemented, focusing on the construction of 112 colleges and universities in the '211 Project', including thirty-nine universities in the '985 Project' with a cumulative investment of RMB110 billion yuan (about US$17 billion). With the 20-year sustained focus on construction, the overall level of colleges and universities in the '211 Project' and '985 Project' and the level of disciplines have been improved significantly. The gap between China's high-level universities and world-class universities has been greatly reduced. In China, the key disciplines with distinctive characteristics and advantages have prepared the universities as a base for solving the major problems in economic, scientific and social development. On 5 November 2015, the State Council issued the 'the overall program to co-ordinate the first-class universities and first-class disciplines'. 'Double first-class construction' is an integration and heritage building on the basis of achievements and experiences of '211 Project' and '985 Project'.

Nowadays, China's economic development has entered a new normal economic stage. Chinese President, Xi Jinping emphasized that universities should be strengthening education, enhancing the quality of human capital, and applying attention to scientific and technological progress and comprehensive innovation. In 2015, the State Council fully deployed the deepening of innovation and entrepreneurship education reform, and raised the policy-oriented reform to the national strategic level, to meet the requirements of economic and social development. At the same time, to a certain extent, this move slowed the employment pressure. The Ministry of Education, the National Development and Reform Commission and the Ministry of Finance promulgated the 'guidance on directing some local universities to become applied and professional education institutions' to promote the development of transformation.

The characteristics of marketization of China 's higher education

The decentralization government administration. Since the 1980s, marketization of China's higher education gradually started with the reform of the market economy. Since higher education managed by the government is becoming less and less suited to the needs of the society, the central government gradually decentralized the right of management of higher education to local government, improving the enthusiasm of the local government to run schools and continuously expands the autonomy of the university. Colleges and universities are allowed to develop the school's principles and policies according to the needs of the society and market. It can be seen that the central government has changed the policy of highly controlling higher education in the past and tried to abandon the role of direct control, so assisting the marketization of higher education.

The diversification of funding. Another characteristic of the marketization of China's Higher Education is the reduction in the proportion of national investment, and the increase in the proportion of investment in the field of higher education from non-government sectors. In order to seek a wide range of school financing channels and improve the conditions of schools and faculties, higher education institutions launched a variety of financing and income-generating activities. To promote the transformation of technological achievements and the industrialization of academic achievements, universities established their own businesses. Moreover, the universities offer training courses to organize adult education to attract more students. In order to attract more financing and loans, universities are closely seeking to strengthen cooperation with industry and commerce.

In addition to self-financing activities, universities also collect tuition fees from students. And in the mid-1980s, as long as the students could meet the requirements of the entrance examination, these students could obtain enrolment to college with free tuition. By the mid-1990s, the central government began to adopt the 'user pays' principle, which meant that consumers (parents, students and prospective employers) should spend money on the purchase of educational services, whose demand for education determines the needs of producers (schools, administrators and teachers), while the government is gradually reducing the funding of public education. Now, all students are required to pay tuition. Students also can get scholarships, grants and loans conditionally.

The improvement of efficiency and benefits of running schools through competition. The emergence of the '211' project is a typical embodiment. The 'project' expects top universities to play a leading role and normal universities to follow the lead to achieve the purpose that 'focus on the rapid improvement of the quality of education and scientific level, making it the backbone of higher education system'. And therefore, central government planned to focus on the construction of about 100 colleges and universities in the twenty-first century, and support these colleges and universities with more funding projects, faculty development programmes, more funds for buildings and equipment etc. In order to be able to enter the 100 universities, colleges and universities launched a teacher, tuition, research and employment at all levels of fierce competition. In colleges and universities, there is competition for resources among faculty members, human resource management and distribution systems in order to meet the needs of promoting high quality in teaching and research, which in turn is conducive to the improvement of the school's own strength to deal with the market competition.

The strengthening of education with economic development. China's education system is deeply affected by the political system. For a long period, education serving politics had been an important educational policy in China. Educational goals, educational systems, curriculum settings, educational finance and the right to be educated are all directly affected by political factors. As higher education is an important superstructure, the nation is particularly strict with higher education and the government was directly involved in top universities and the higher education process, including higher education funding, higher education curriculum and work distribution of college graduates. Since the economic reform and opening up to the outside world in 1978, the central government shifted its focus to economic construction, and has paid more attention to the development of education. Education, especially higher education, is regarded as an important foundation for economic development and comprehensive social progress and an important tool for comprehensive national strength. Higher education development is associated with economic development. Therefore, the university's subjects and curriculum began to focus on economic and market demand, with emphasis on applicability and technicality. At the same time, the relationship between university graduates and the nation has undergone a fundamental change. In the past, college students were provided education for free; upon graduation, all college students were assigned to jobs. Since China adopted Socialist Market Economic System in 1992, college students have to pay for schooling. They have the freedom to choose which colleges and universities they apply to and what programmes they want to study. Upon graduation, they also have the freedom to find their own jobs.

Evaluation of marketization of higher education in China

The marketization of China's higher education, the 'user pays' principle, and the limited role of private investment in schools, demonstrate the limits to the government's investment in education and financing, but this does mean that higher education institutions are totally out of the government's control. Although the state no longer directly controls the management of colleges and universities, there still exists a variety of forms of government intervention. Obviously, it is difficult for the government alone to meet the growing demand for higher education. The state has abandoned its role as the sole provider of educational services and allowed non-state providers to enter the field of education, and permits shared responsibility for the provision of educational services. However, unlike Western countries, China is still dominated by public universities in providing services for higher education and the private sector only plays a limited and marginal role. Higher education institutions created by entrepreneurs and other social organizations, are far smaller than the traditional public colleges and universities in terms of school size, teachers, research level, or the market share and competitiveness. Both the main sponsors and the main service objectives of China's higher education are still the responsibility of the Chinese government. Colleges and universities operating to service the community are not really in place, in comparison to community colleges in the United States. The recognition of the concept of customer service has not become a leading value in Chinese higher education.

Current problems faced by Chinese higher education: drawbacks of the existing talent cultivation mode

In his speech entitled 'The Advantages of Research-intensive Universities' at the 'Peking University Centennial Forum of Presidents', Gerhard Casper (1998), former president of Stanford University, pointed out, 'High-tech companies in Silicon Valley alone recorded earnings of 85 billion dollars in 1995, and according to one estimate, 62% of those earnings can be traced back to companies whose founders had connections to Stanford. They have created hundreds of thousands of jobs'. If the innovation capacity of a country's universities is not strong, that country cannot ultimately change the national economic growth mode. In today's knowledge economy, if there is no world-class university in a country, it will not become a real world power.

First-class universities cannot do without first-class students. Viewing university enrolment as the first link in the chain of personnel training, will directly affect the quality of university personnel training. The past years have witnessed a large expansion of colleges and universities. Many schools, however, have focused on expansion, neglecting quality improvement. Motivated by interest, universities blindly followed, expanding cheaper, lower-cost specialties, such as law, management and education. This phenomenon has caused the homogenization of higher education institutions. In addition, the lack of surveys on market demand contributed to disequilibrium between talent cultivation and social needs, resulting in the waste of higher education resources.

Many Chinese universities lack interest in the training model, showing a disconnection between enrolments and training link. In fact, enrolment and the personnel training should be inseparable. Recruiting students of different potential and different strengths, universities should have a corresponding teaching programme to match. At the same time, universities need to enrol with careful and personalized selection, while designing different training programmes. As Professor Li Peigen, the former president of Huazhong University of Science and Technology, emphasized:

> The current university education is basically for the present service. It lacks independent insights and thinking, and unconsciously regards the students as products on the educational product line. It is a challenge in the future for higher education to lead students to deal with the development of science and technology and society through education.
> (China Youth News, 25 May 2016)

As China moves into the 'new normal' economic development stage, college graduates have faced problems of finding good jobs during the economic slowdown. It is widely agreed that higher education institutions regard improving students' personal interests and research abilities as a main goal, while innovative, practical and integrated talents are more important to economic and social development. There is a great need for applied and innovative talents in every industry in China. Whereas, balancing the pursuit of high quality academic activities while promoting students' practical skills, innovation ability and social responsibility could be the biggest challenge that the Chinese government is now facing.

HEI's lack of autonomy

In recent years, the momentum of the traditional model of China's economic development dropped, and a number of outdated factories and production models began to be forced out. The Chinese government has realized the importance of economic restructuring, and thus vigorously promotes innovation-based economic growth model and fully attaches importance to the important role of colleges and universities in the national innovation system. The Chinese government put forward a series of important policies, such as the 'Outline of National Medium and Long-term Educational Reform and Development Plan' (2010–2020) to guide the construction of higher education. The construction of key high-level research universities is an important strategic measure for China to improve its comprehensive national strength and increase its scientific and technological innovation capacity. This initiative has invested funding in China's top universities to build world-class universities through the '211 Project' and '985 Project', and the process has achieved initial success. However, while accelerating China's economic growth model, China is not determined to make a thorough reform of the university's management system, so as to give enough autonomy to universities.

The university autonomy and academic freedom are considered to be important conditions for academic excellence. In fact, the autonomy of colleges and universities in China is still very limited. Colleges and universities have a high degree of dependence on the government, and there is still a considerable distance between the expectation of 30 years ago that advocated colleges and universities would be running autonomously according to the law. In the framework of the government-led resource allocation system and evaluation system, the vitality and initiative of the university itself as an independent institution is far from being exerted. In the '211 Project' and the '985 Project', the launch to the implementation and evaluation are entirely government-led. As an independent academic organization, the university is more subject to administrative power, and passively responds, which inevitably leads to the implementation of the project, the construction of universities and discipline were forced to operate by the government's strong intervention and limitation. At the same time, the Chinese government put one-sided emphasis on the construction of universities to meet the needs of economic construction, and set a 'timetable' for building up world-class universities, inevitably leading to quick success and instant benefits.

The modernization demands of scientific and technological progress and economic development put forward higher demands on the innovation and flexibility of higher education institutions and their educational concepts, policies and implementation. (Daly, 2015) With China's social and economic transformation, the situation that China's higher education system is facing has become increasingly more complex, and a higher level of strategic management to deal with various factors is needed. With the ever-changing external situation and the ever-increasing new missions, the role of universities is becoming more diversified. In addition to nurturing talent to adapt to social and economic development, Chinese higher education needs to cultivate high-end talents with a sense of innovation and abilities to lead for scientific and technological progress. How to stimulate the inner innovation vitality of universities is now the most important question for Chinese universities to explore in the new management mode. China's colleges and universities need to further reform the management model, allowing universities to have more autonomy in order to compete soundly in the market-oriented system. It is necessary to establish a reasonable performance appraisal system to guide the healthy development of colleges and universities for flexibility in response to the external opportunities and challenges.

Unbalanced development and single funding source

China has developed an unbalanced higher education system. The top universities have received generous funding, and many now compete favourably with the best institutions in the world. In contrast, many small local colleges and universities are not funded adequately and do not have the same benefits. As a result, these institutions are usually of lower quality, and their graduates are not as well-prepared for the labour market, thus the graduates have difficulties in finding jobs. This situation comes from China's unbalanced higher education funding system.

Under the present financial system, the appropriation process of higher education is a typical dual appropriation model: the higher education institutions have the educational authority; but the relevant financial departments directly control the financial resources of higher education and have financial rights. This funding system is rigid because the higher education sector and the financial sector do not properly position themselves, distorting the relationship between the higher education sector and the financial sector. China's educational reform in 1985 put forward a reasonable positioning of the relationship between universities and the government financial sector which was aimed at expanding the autonomy of colleges and universities, but, today, this vision has not yet been achieved.

Chinese public universities rely mainly on government funding and government investment in the share of total expenditure is 61.9 percent. Private universities mainly rely on tuition fees to maintain operations, and the tuition proportion of total expenditure ranges up to 82.67 percent (Zhou, 2014a). Due to this executive-led allocation of resources, there is uneven development, a single source of funding and other issues concerning Chinese universities. This funding method has a strong administration, and is not conducive to the transformation of functions. Besides, transparency, fairness and stability of college funds cannot be guaranteed. The lack of a public finance allocation system in higher education, makes the allocation of financial resources the 'unilateral act' of the government, so that the amount of higher education financial appropriation can only be determined based on the government's financial capacity, rather than on the demand for higher education, which literally determines and reduces the efficiency of the use of higher education financial funds.

The financial input of higher education lacks impartiality, and its allocation benefit is difficult to justify. Due to China's implementation of hierarchical management system for universities, scientific research institutions, relying solely on the 'basic expenditure budget plus project budget' funding approach, broadens the financial allocation gap and lacks impartiality. Due to the limited financial resources of higher education and the current funding model based on the number of college students and the number of research projects to divide the budget allocation of funds, this circumstance will inevitably lead to those larger, more powerful key universities, such as the '211 Project' and '985 Project' having a larger share of financial resources. Correspondingly, the vast majority of other colleges and universities share very limited financial resources. So it is an inevitable result that the gap between key universities and the vast majority of ordinary universities will widen. From the angle of maximizing efficient use of financial resources, such inefficient allocation of financial funds is not conducive to the improvement of higher education.

It is not enough to have only a few high-quality elite universities. A successful system of higher education should have reasonable quality at all levels, improving the training to ensure that all graduates are better prepared to enter the labour market. An unbalanced funding system is unable to bring about a balanced education system.

Private education in a weak position

Private education provides more access to higher education. As of May 2015, there were 2553 national colleges and universities (including 447 private universities, 275 independent colleges and 7 Chinese-foreign cooperatively-run institutions). Private education has accounted for 28.55 percent, and has become an important component of China's higher education system (Ministry of Education, 21 May 2015). However, none of the first-class higher education institutions are private schools. Problems exist with the status and quality of private education.

Although private education has broken the single structure of education, due to the allocation of resources, it is still in a weak position. Since the government holds the resources, it develops public education as a priority, offering certain policy options. Under the protection of the national policies and the planning system, public colleges and universities not only have stable sources of continuing funds, faculty members and teaching equipment, but also have guarantees that potential students have access to graduate employment, as well as guarantees regarding the status and treatment of faculty members. Private colleges and universities are not only weak in in terms of power, but also have little social recognition.

Second, on the planning layer, governments at all levels have not completely included private education into the overall economic and social development plan. Due to the lack of proper planning, in some areas, the distribution of local private education is irrational. Institutions of the same type and the same pattern are redundantly constructed, resulting in a serious waste of resources. Some areas have an 'overheating' phenomenon of private education. Investors have poured into the market for private education, without appropriate understanding of both education and market rules.

In addition, some independent institutions have been emerged in China that have became obstacles in the development of private education by competing for policy resources. Independent colleges usually referred to as secondary colleges, which is the result of cooperation of ordinary universities with the social forces according to the new mechanisms and the new model. Social organizations or individuals outside the public institutions use non-state financial funds, running the institutions to implement undergraduate academic education in the name of some public universities. These colleges become a means of making a profit for public institutions. This kind of college blurs the difference between pure public institutions and purely private colleges. It is much easier for them to obtain administrative support than pure private institutions, with the so-called policy that encourages common development. Thus, it is quite easy for such institutions to occupy a considerable market share of private education, and set more obstacles for the real private schools to step forward. To some extent these institutions consolidate the strong position of public institutions, which escalates the imbalance between pure public institutions and private colleges, and ultimately makes the situation of private education weaker.

Outlook for Chinese higher education: talent cultivation mode updating teaching methods

At present, the largest gap between Chinese colleges and universities and the world-class international universities is in teaching approaches. As economic globalization deepens, universities will need to place more emphasis on innovation and strengthening question-inquiry teaching methods in order to cultivate students' innovative consciousness, spirit and ability. At the same time, attention needs to be given to learning experiences that promote students' ability to solve practical problems. Building world-class universities will require an open and inclusive environment that respects multi-cultural differences and values by cross-culture communication. Universities need to focus on how to expand students' international horizons and promote overall competitiveness in the globalized world today. Moreover, there is a need for greater diversity and choice in education. It is essential to teach students according to their aptitude, and to create more personalized learning opportunities and learning experiences. National economic development requires the labour force to be more adaptive, so in the future Chinese higher education should enhance students' ability for learning new knowledge, adjusting to new environments and solving new problems. Overall, the teaching ideas of higher education should reflect the needs of society and the economy, reflect the spirit of the times and embrace a different alignment, following the common law of education, and combined with China's reality.

Adjusting and optimizing the discipline structure

Chinese colleges and universities should make an effective discipline development plan that clarifies the future direction for each discipline, according to the national development needs and technological trends, combined with school orientation and discipline advantages. Top universities are charged with the responsibility of cultivating scarce high-quality talents for China. The talent training should be more practical and actively adapt to national and regional development needs. In fact, higher education is an interdisciplinary field incorporating insights and methodologies from different social science disciplines. In this case, traditional disciplines should be updated and upgraded, focusing on the knowledge integration of different disciplines and seeking new directions for professional disciplines. China is seeking to adapt the content of higher education to the development of new technologies, new industries, new formats and is constantly improving the quality of the personnel training of traditional disciplines.

Perfecting the quality certification system

From a global perspective, the success of a country's education cannot only be defined by its own national standard. It depends on the performance of that country's education system on the world stage. Due to different cultural traditions, economic levels and social systems, in some respects there is no comparison in education between different countries, but in many ways the quality of education can be compared. Therefore, the establishment of the quality certification system is critical. Chinese colleges and universities should expand their international horizons; strengthen exchanges and cooperation with top world universities. To this end, China should steadily carry forward the progress on the establishment of comparable indicators which are of international standard, so that evaluative criteria of education not only has Chinese characteristics, but also considers quality relative to top universities in other countries. A scientific quality certification system would provide a sound basis for policy making.

The management mode: decentralizing power to universities

Chinese universities have been regarded as subsidiary components of the government instead of as independent legal entities. The Chinese government directs and manages universities mainly through the administrative system by using administrative directions and supervision. As part of the national plan, university objectives, tasks, staff size and funding, post setting, personnel appointment and removal are all administered by the government department. The universities' financial systems, personnel systems and social welfare systems are basically the same as government agencies, and all universities have a certain administrative level. This government management system leads to the situation in which responsibility is not clear and the universities lack autonomy.

Expansion and implementation of autonomy among universities first requires separation of the government and universities. To promote the modernization of higher education governance, universities should insist on control of decision-making and on implementation of the separation of powers. Through the clear demarcation of the relationship between the higher education service and the government. The university should be transferred from the traditional administrative affiliation into a modern contractual relationship to the government. In addition, the expansion and implementation of university autonomy requires the government to actively explore the negative line management. The so-called negative line management model refers to the government stipulating what matters in higher education are 'national affairs' and it needs to control, in addition to the list of restricted areas that universities are allowed to steer. The essence of the negative line management model is to insist on the principle of 'entities can do anything which are not prohibited by the law'. All measures of government management that are inconsistent with the autonomy of universities must be in the form of a list. The negative government list must comply with the principle of 'legal reservation', that is to say, the government cannot increase the control items or impose new obligations on universities unless there is explicit authorization of law, namely 'government departments must not do anything unless it is mandated by the law' (Zhou, 2014b).

The funding mode: transformation of government functions

The key to China's establishing a public finance system for higher education is to transform the government functions, and allow the market to allocate resources. The Third Plenum of eighteenth CPC Central Committee pointed out that the next step is to improve various policies such as government subsidies, government purchases of services, student loans, funding awards, incentives and other institutional donors to encourage social forces to participate in educational operations. This is essentially intended to introduce market forces in the field of higher education. The government empowers the individuals and institutions that compete in the market to run colleges and universities, essentially establishing a service-oriented government. In the public market, higher education services can be undertaken by NGOs, and the government does not have to direct colleges and universities. The higher education system's commitment to public welfare requires the vigorous cooperation of the government, the public and enterprises. The providers of public services can be chosen in accordance with the market principles of efficiency. These providers may be either public universities or private universities. The government should transform its role as a direct Higher Education Services provider to becoming the supervisor, and the evaluator, as well as making the rules for resource allocation.

Diversification: supporting the development of private education

In the future, as the Chinese government addresses its support for private education, it is necessary first to clearly define the management system. It should made specific the respective division of roles and responsibilities of the government at all levels as well as those of other social organizations in the promotion of private higher education. The moral responsibilities and legal liabilities of the government should be known to society. For example, the Chinese government could refine and improve its financial support for the promotion of private higher education, and provide the support policies for land taxation, loans and other supportive policies, creating a favourable environment for the healthy development of private higher education through various laws and regulations. The Chinese government should learn from experiences and lessons in the United States, Germany, Japan and other countries and build a sound system of financial support for private colleges and universities as soon as possible, using the method of tax incentives, land concessions, financial assistance, loans, grants and other economic means to regulate the development of private higher education. When the Chinese government takes the macro-control of private higher education, it should grasp the relationship between macro-control and university autonomy, and minimize direct intervention in college affairs and allow colleges and universities to develop in accordance with educational rules.

Conclusion

China, as the world's most populous country, is an important part of global higher education. China's higher education system has its own uniqueness because of its particular historical context. Since the economic reform and opening to the outside world in 1978, China's higher education has been greatly developed and expanded, but there remain systemic challenges and opportunities to be addressed in order for colleges and universities to improve the quality of teaching, research and social service. In examining the future of higher education in China, the Chinese government's policies and initiatives remain important in order to enable universities to educate students and ensure that graduates make future contributions to society.

References

Casper, G. (1998) Speech at the Peking University Centennial Celebration: 'The Advantage of the Research-Intensive University': The University of the 21st Century [R], 3 May1998.
China Education Daily, 29 October 2014.
China Long March 5 Rocket, 3 November 2016. Available online at http://hxen.com/word/xinwen/2016–11–04/448738.html
China News Network, China's 25 Universities are Included in 2015 Top 500 World-class Universities [N], 6 November 2015. Available online at http://chinanews.com/gn/2015/11–06/7610269.shtml
China News Network, Number of China University Graduates [N], 23 May 2016. Available online at http://mnw.cn/news/china/1194094.html
China Youth News, 25 May 2016. Available online at http://news.ifeng.com/a/20160525/48839907_0.shtml
Daly, R. (2015) *Keynote Lecture at the China Education Symposium 2015 Conference [R]*, Harvard University, Graduate School of Education, 4 May 2015.
Decision of the CPC Central Committee on the Reform of the Educational System[R]. Website of the Ministry of Education of the People's Republic of China, 27 May 1985. Available online at http://moe.edu.cn/publicfiles/business/htmlfiles/moe/moe_177/200407/2482.html

Deng, X. (1993) *Selected works of Deng Xiaoping*, Volume 3 [J].
Higer Education Law. *The Fourth Session of the Standing Committee of the Ninth National People Congress*, 29 August 1998.
Jiang, Z. (1998) Speech at the 100th Anniversary Celebration of Peking University [R], 4 May 1998, Website of the Ministry of Education of the People's Republic of China. Available online at http://moe.edu.cn/jyb_sjzl/moe_177/tnull_2475.html
Liu, Y. (2016) Speech at the 32nd Meeting of the Academic Degrees Committee of the State Council [R], 8 March.
Ministry of Education. Special Enrollment Program Targeting Rural Poor Areas in 2015 will Recruit 50,000 Students [N], Xinhua, 3 April 2015. Available online at http://news.xinhuanet.com/edu/2015-04/03/c_1114868508.htm
Ministry of Education of the People's Republic of China. The List of Colleges and Universities Nationwide [EB/OL], 21 May 2015.
National Bureau of Statistics of China. Available online at http://data.stats.gov.cn/index.htm and Statistical Communique on the Development of Education in China in 2015, Ministry of Education. Available online at http://moe.edu.cn/srcsite/A03/s180/moe_633/201607/t20160706_270976.html
Report on China's Higher Education Quality: No.1 of Scale in the World [N], People, 9 April 2016. Available online at http://bbs1.people.com.cn/post/1/1/2/155441052.html
Sichuan Daily. 9 July 2016.
Sina News Network. The number of Chinese graduate returnees have reached 26.11 million, 12 April 2017. Available online at http://news.sina.com.cn/c/2017-04-12/doc-ifyeayzu7635538.shtml
Xinhua Net. 3 April 2015.
Xiong, R. Sichuan Introduced 'Talent New Deal' Boosting Comprehensive Innovation [N], Sichuan Daily, 2016-07-09001.
Zhai, Z. (2016) Analysis on Hotspots of Chinese Higher Education in 2015 [Z], Website of the Ministry of Education of the People's Republic of China, 4 January 2016. Available online at http://moe.edu.cn/jyb_xwfb/s5148/201601/t20160104_226815.html
Zhai, Z. (2016) 'The new step of higher education in China [J]', *Chines Higher Education Research*, 1: 1–3.
Zhao, S. (1995) 'MBA education in China', *Journal of Higher Education*, 4: 83–87 and 98.
Zhao, S. (1995) *Human resources management in Chinese enterprises*, China, Nanjing: Nanjing University Press.
Zhou, G. (2014a) 'From governance to management: re-orientation of university regulations [J]', *Journal of Educational Science of Hunan Normal University*, 2.
Zhou, G. (2014b) 'The modernization of China's higher education governance: current situation, problems and countermeasures [J]', *Chines Higher Education Research*, 9: 16–25.
Zong, H. (2014) In 2013, 82.2% of SCI papers published by Chinese authors (the first author) were from colleges and universities [N], China Education Daily, 292014. http://news.sciencenet.cn/htmlnews/2014/10/306350.shtm

10
Whither the Japanese system of higher education? Higher education as a public and private good – differentiation and realignment

FUMI KITAGAWA AND AKIYOSHI YONEZAWA

Introduction

What is distinctive about the Japanese higher education system is the coexistence of three higher education sectors; the 'national', the private' and the 'local public'; each with a different legal status. Each sector is impacted upon by different privatization forces and varying degrees of state control (Kitagawa and Oba, 2010; Yonezawa, 2013a; Huang, 2016). Since the inception of the modern higher education system in the nineteenth century, the statuses of Japanese universities have been stratified according to their historical origins and established reputations.

There is a clear distinction in the public funding allocation process between national and local public and private universities. The national and local public sectors are founded by the central government and local authorities respectively. Japan's private sector comprises the vast majority of both the total number of institutions and student enrolments, particularly at the undergraduate level – a common phenomenon in East Asia across South Korea, Taiwan and the Philippines (Altbach and Umakoshi, 2004), unlike the United States and many European nations (Huang, 2016). In Japan, private higher education has taken an important role for absorbing the demand for higher learning, which is unmet by the public higher education provision. Especially since the 1960s, the number of the students enrolled in private universities has increased dramatically, including those of the first baby-boomer generation born after World War II (Yonezawa, 2013b). While university academics in Japan including those of private universities in general have had relatively high commitment to research activities (Arimoto *et al.*, 2008), only a few Japanese private universities (those with a long history and prestige) are visible in world class research. Moreover, the basic and big sciences that require massive investment, have been almost monopolized by around ten top national universities (Yonezawa, 2016).

Arguably, Japanese higher education has benefited from the historical collaboration between the public and private sectors, with strong privatized financing over the decades to get to the stage of approaching near 'universal access' to higher education (Trow, 2006). Similar to many of the developed economies, Japan has been facing recent acute pressure to reduce the public financing of higher education by shifting the financial burden to individual households. As of 2016, there are 777 universities and colleges in Japan of which 600 (77.2 percent) are private institutions. Among the public institutions, there are eighty-six national universities and ninety-one local public universities founded by prefectures and municipalities. In addition, there are specialized schools and colleges that provide more vocational types of degree (341 junior colleges and fifty-seven colleges of technology) and diplomas (2817 professional training colleges).

Rising competition with other Asian nations and their universities has forced the Japanese government to place higher education high on the national policy agenda in order to maintain its strategic competitiveness. Both the Japanese government and these universities have aspired to elevate their status as 'world class' universities (Yonezawa, 2013a). The 'top' national Japanese universities have been recognized as being among the top of the university rankings in Asia since the end of the 1990s. The University of Tokyo claims to be the nation's highest in global ranking, which ranks thirty-fourth in the QS World University Rankings as of 2016/17. Close behind are Kyoto University (joint thirty-seventh) and Tokyo Institute of Technology (fifty-sixth) (QS World University Ranking, 2016).

Currently, there are several interrelated demographic and economic challenges facing Japanese higher education. First, Japan's population of 18-year-olds dropped from 2.05 million in 1992 to 1.19 million in 2011. A further decrease of the 18-year-olds population is expected after 2018, and it will drop below 1 million around 2031 and down to 0.5 million by 2050. The percentage of those who advance to university education has recently rather stabilized around 50 percent of the population. The gross enrolment rate in higher and post-secondary education institutions, including junior colleges, colleges of technology and professional training colleges, currently amounts to nearly 80 percent of the age cohort (Huang, 2016). However, competition for students is expected to become more intense as the youth population shrinks, leading to the reduction of tuition revenue as well as the merger and closure of institutions. Against such trends, the government is keen to attract more international students by globalizing Japanese higher education. It has recently set a target of having 300,000 foreign students in the country by 2020, while the 100,000 mark was achieved in 2003.

The second challenge, for the higher education system is concerned with, the strained state of public finances. The cumulative national debt increased from 76.7 percent of GDP in 1997 to an estimated 250.35 percent of GDP in 2016, which is the highest public debt among member countries of the OECD. Government subsidies for both national and private universities are declining due to the continuing cuts in public finances. It is expected that the government will take a measure to restructure both public and private universities by encouraging mergers (Japan Times, 12 April 2016). The burden of the governmental debt is also sometimes politicized by the unstable and populist financial policies to stimulate the national economy and counter the long term decline in the size and aging of Japan's national population.

The third related challenge is concerned with the affordability of higher education for students in Japan. The total amount of student loans has greatly increased in recent years through the usage of national bonds. There has been a recent political debate triggered by the fear of 'defaulting' on these student loans. There is a recognition that national, public and private universities in Japan have failed to provide affordable education to their students. A recent government initiative, to set up a new grant-in-aid scholarships that do not have to be repaid is seen as a policy to enable young people to continue higher education without the burden of repaying their debts. Nevertheless, there remain a number of unresolved issues also regarding the amount of available resources, student eligibility, and the equitable distribution of scholarships in order to sustain educational opportunities and thus to reduce the financial burden on the students.

In the context of this historical background and these societal challenges, this chapter investigates the impact of recent higher education funding policy in Japan and how that has affected the nature of the higher education system, and also the implications for its being seen as either a 'public or private good'. It is interesting to examine the case of Japan, a historically diversified and differentiated national system, which has been changing rapidly with recent national 'top-down' policy reforms, followed by more recent and new 'bottom-up' institutional initiatives. Following this Introduction, the next section discusses the changing dynamics of both public and private funding for the Japanese higher education system in comparison with other OECD countries. The third section, illustrates the policy reform processes over the last two decades, including the incorporation (or an introduction of a corporate based administrative agency model) of the national universities and the continuing differentiation within the system given shrinking public funding and the changing domestic higher education market. The chapter discusses the current wave of new policy initiatives that aim to pick the 'elite' national universities to create 'world-class' universities. The chapter concludes by discussing the continuing challenges and tensions for Japanese higher education, which have redefined and realigned constantly the nature of higher education as both a public and private good – and which may provide a model for the future university in Japan and beyond.

The public and private nature of the Japanese higher education system – its history and recent reforms

Historically, the national universities have constituted the core of the elite sector in the Japanese higher education system and have been protected by the state.

However, the national university sector itself consists of diverse institutions whose functions and components are significantly different in terms of their history, even though they all have had the same legal status since the education reform just after the World War II. There were seven imperial universities, which were historically treated as 'elite institutions' by the government. Official recognition of these institutions as elite 'imperial universities', ceased in 1949. Since then the Japanese government, at least officially, has treated all the national universities equally, while they have sought to protect top research universities from the 'massification' of higher education (Yonezawa, 2007). These differences have been considered 'discriminatory' primarily by the national universities which were founded in the post-1945 period. The government has been concerned with how these differences could be justified (Amano, 2008). These seven, along with a small number of other distinguished national universities and a few research-intensive prestigious private universities, constitute what are currently referred to as the 'top research universities' in the Japanese higher education system.

In 2004, a radical change was introduced to Japanese national universities based on the National University Incorporation Law (2003), which granted them more autonomy from government (for details of the reform process and evaluation, see: Oba, 2005 and Yamamoto, 2004). Formerly, they were operated as governmental organizations based on the Act for the Establishment of National Schools. This law intended to promote more active and socially engaged institutions with greater organizational diversity and distinctiveness, and indirectly promote inter-university competition (Woolgar, 2007). Due to the incorporation of national universities in 2004, every national university is now established as a legal entity in its own right according to the framework laid down in the National University Incorporation Act. Since 2004 the eighty-nine newly established National University Corporations (NUCs) have received two types of grants from the national government: grants for operating costs and subsidies for capital expenditures. NUCs have full discretion on how to use the grant, while the flexibility of the capital subsidy is constrained. The government announced in 2003 that operational grants would be reduced by 1 percent each year for all NUCs. Each institution has been expected to develop supplementary income sources which may or may not include increases in tuition fees, competitive research funding, and income from industry. This allocation model reflects the fact that the government cannot finance the basic infrastructure for conducting core and large-scale scientific research solely relying on public budgeting.

As already mentioned, the finance of Japanese higher education sector is influenced by its historical disposition consisting of three sectors, with a particularly large private sector. The proportion of public expenditure on higher education in Japan is lower than many other OECD countries. Public spending on tertiary education as a percentage of all public spending as of 2013 is just below 2 percent, much below the OECD average (OECD, 2016). By sector,

Table 10.1 Three types of HEIs with public budgetary allocation (Japanese yen) Source: MEXT, 2016; Huang, 2016; collated by the authors.

Types of HEIs	National	Public local	Private
Numbers (2016)	86	91	600
Budgetary allocation from MEXT (2011)	1,202 billion	NA	321 billion
(2015)	1,094 billion	NA	315 billion

the central government allocated over 90 percent of national universities' funding, especially prior to March 2004 when all national universities became national university corporations. This ratio is expected to have declined after more than a decade since the major reform.

More than half of 'local public' universities' income comes from grants from the local authorities, which is in line with their mission to be more responsive and relevant to the demands of local economic development, community, and industry. In addition to income from tuition fees from students, local public universities receive a limited amount of funding from the national government, through MEXT (the Ministry of Education, Culture, Sports, Science and Technology). This includes competitive funding for educational programmes. There has been a continuing decline for 'local public' universities in the proportion of public expenditure since the early 2000s (Huang, 2016).

In contrast, for almost all private universities the main source of financial revenue is tuition fees. Although the central government has provided some financial support to private universities since 1973, the proportion of public subsidies makes up less than 20 percent of their total revenue (Huang, 2016). In recent years, about 10 percent of their total expenditure is being supported by the national government through 'The Promotion and Mutual Aid Corporation for Private Schools of Japan' (PMAC), a special administrative corporation.

In the 2015 fiscal year, the budgetary allocation for the operational funding of national universities was 1,094 billion Japanese yen, while the national budgetary support for private universities remained at 315 billion yen, in total.

As the following sections show, the public funding for higher education has become even more highly concentrated on the top national public universities.

Further differentiation of the system and concentration of resources: creation of the world class university

The last two decades have witnessed a series of higher education policy reforms, which have re-enforced the institutional differentiation within the already diverse system. In the 1980s, Japan experienced a substantial change in the direction of national financial policy from welfare state towards neo-liberalism. Under the budgetary ceilings set for the recovery from the budgetary imbalance within the welfare state policy in 1970s, the public support towards higher education has also been faced with budgetary stringency. The operational expenditure of private universities that started in 1970s had already stagnated under the continuous increase of total expenditure. In order to strengthen competition among universities, new types of budgetary funds and project-based funds were expanded during the 1990s (Asonuma, 2002), while the governmental budget toward national universities stagnated. Top universities such as the University of Tokyo started a national campaign by arguing the needs to support research and education activities by the national universities in order to sustain the national economy based on science and technology.

In addition to the financial allocation, during the 1990s, the government reorganized the top national universities to strengthen graduate schools at both the doctoral and master levels (*daigakuin jutenka*). In 2003, professional graduate programmes (*senmonshoku daigakuin*) were newly introduced by the Ministry of Education, Culture, Sports, Science and Technology (MEXT) to respond to changing skill needs in the so called 'knowledge-based society' (Ushiogi, 1997). As a result, all former imperial universities and other top universities separated academic staff from the undergraduate based faculties and relocated them in graduate schools. This is seen as a way to separate the research and teaching functions at research-intensive universities, and seven former imperial universities were given priority to go through with this re-organization.

With rapid changes in the internal and external environments, particularly the pressure on public financing, both the government and universities in Japan have undergone a major re-examination of the allocation of public resources to the higher education sector. The changing policy rationale to strengthen elite universities can be summarized as follows: '... invisible differentiation is becoming more difficult, and justification through visible evidence of performance is becoming more influential' (Yonezawa, 2007). Over the last two and half decades, the allocation of traditional public research funding has shown greater concentration on a small number of 'elite' universities further accelerated by the concentration of 'competitive' research funding. This has resulted in an increasingly differentiated and hierarchical higher education system.

The launch of the twenty-first century Center of Excellence (COE 21) programme, in 2002, can be seen as a marked shift in Japanese higher education policy regarding the status of its elite institutions. The selection for the scheme was based on performance and research potential, with 274 COE units from ninety-seven universities selected in the three consecutive fiscal years of 2002, 2003 and 2004 (MEXT, 2006). The main activities supported under this programme included: an invitation to attract top foreign researchers to work in Japan, support for young researchers (doctoral and post-doctoral fellowships), collaboration with foreign research groups, symposia and workshops, and the provision of new equipment and space for research. The emphasis was on 'strategic research training' and 'competition', particularly at the graduate level in the sciences, engineering and medical research, which played to the strengths of national universities.

The Japanese government's efforts to foster world-class research were accelerated by the establishment of a series of new support programmes during the past decade. In 2007, the Global COE programme replaced the COE 21, with the number of selected Global COE research bases now much smaller than those of COE 21, while the amount of grant money for each research base is expected to increase substantially. In terms of selection criterion, the potential sustainability of research beyond the programme and the emphasis on educating and training young researchers (thus 'research bases' (*kenkyu kyoten*) rather than 'project units') was stressed. But rankings among the top universities based on the number of selected COE research units merely reinforced the existing hierarchy of Japanese higher education institutions (Kitagawa and Oba, 2010).

Adding to this, in September of 2007, MEXT announced the 'World Premier International Research (WPI) Centre initiative' to support five research bases for the next 10–15 years, with approximately 500 million to 2 billion Japanese yen per base annually. Four former imperial universities, namely, Tohoku, Tokyo, Kyoto and Osaka Universities, and the National Institute for Materials Science (NIMS), were selected. Since the first round projects have closed, continuous calls for a limited number of new projects have been heard.

The world-class university policies became deeply embedded in both national policy and the university management system over the decade (Oba, 2008; Yonezawa, 2007). Such an institutionalization of world-class university policy has progressed at the levels of national policy and university policy (Yonezawa, 2013a). Maintaining world-class universities is a very costly operation needing continual support from the government and concentration of such efforts is

Table 10.2 Japanese government funding initiatives to support 'elite' universities in the 2000s

2002	21st COE programme (COE 21)
2003	Enactment of the National University Corporation Law
2004	Incorporation of national universities
2007	Global COE programme; World Premier International Research Center (WPI) Initiative
2009	Global 30 programme
2013	Programme for promoting the enhancement of research universities
2015	Top global university project
2016	Categorization in budgeting the operational funds for national universities
2017	Distinguished National University Corporation

limited to a small number of institutions (Altbach, 2003; Baker, 2007). A question that may be asked is why public funds should support the development of world-class universities in Japan. At the national policy level, the government has encouraged universities to voluntarily choose different functions, including conducting world-class education and research (see Kitagawa and Oba, 2010). To achieve such policy objectives, the government has developed a series of project funding schemes promoting top-level world class research. The funds related to world-class research and education were awarded primarily to a limited number of comprehensive research universities, which arguably compensated for the budgetary cut in the operational expenditure subsidy of a selected number of national universities.

In 2009, the government commenced a new policy initiative, whose goal was to select thirty universities as 'Core Universities for Internationalization' (Global 30). The Global thirty project was meant to support educational activities related to internationalization. The size of the fund was rather limited (between 100 and 400 million yen per university annually), and the universities had to provide matching funds in order to implement the project (see Yonezawa, 2011). Under the Aso Cabinet, between 2008 and 2009, the first thirteen universities (seven national – Tohoku University, Tsukuba University, the University of Tokyo, Nagoya University, Kyoto University, Osaka University and Kyushu University; and six private – Meiji University, Sophia University, Keio University, Waseda University, Doshisha University and Ritsumeikan University) were selected. Apart from Tsukuba University, every national university selected is a former imperial university, and all the private universities are located either in Tokyo or Kyoto, the major cities with a strong university concentration (Yonezawa, 2013a).

Further changes are ongoing as the current government has been building up a new higher education system (Yonezawa and Shimmi, 2015). First, as a part of Science and Technology policy, the government started a Programme for Promoting the Enhancement of Research Universities in 2013, aimed at encouraging the capacity development of research management for realising world-class research. In this programme, the government selected seventeen national and two private universities as well as three national research institutes. Each university received from 200 to 400 million Japanese yen per year, and strengthened the research management function by employing the university research administrators. Second, the government started Top Global University projects as a ten year project to improve the global competitiveness among universities. Adding to twenty-four universities with unique international profiles, thirteen (eleven national and two private) comprehensive research universities were selected to be 'globally competitive', in line with the Prime Minister's initiative to encourage around ten Japanese universities ranked within the global top 100. Third, the government introduced three categorical options in achievement goals when the national universities started the six year plan as a request for the operational budgeting by the government in 2016. The government has requested national universities to choose from three categories, namely, 'internationally competitive in all the major fields', 'internationally competitive in some fields', 'serving local needs' in their mid-term goals with an evaluation scheme starting in 2016.

Lastly, in 2017, the government is going to nominate a few national universities as 'distinguished national university corporations' that can act and compete globally. This can be seen as a historical policy change, given the persistence since the World War II of explicitly promoting differentiation among the former imperial universities. It should be noted, however, that the financial incentives as part of such designated distinguished status are very limited. This implies that in order to get designated prestigious 'elite' status, the government requires universities' own efforts of capacity building – including developing external funds through international research fund raising, income generation through university-industry cooperation, and philanthropy activities.

Towards the entrepreneurial university model? Converging public and private domains?

Since the 2004 incorporation of the national universities, the Japanese government has continuously reduced the operational grants for national universities. Each institution has been expected to develop supplementary income sources, which may or may not include increases in tuition fees, competitive research funding and income from industry. In response to this decrease in public funding, the higher education sector has been in close collaboration with the government and deeply engaged in efforts to build tighter university – business relationships in the belief that positive outcomes can and will emerge. In Japan, as in many other countries, policymakers and university managers have eagerly embraced the discourse surrounding 'the entrepreneurial universities' (Clark, 2001) and have sought to further generate external income generation. Like other countries, government officials have urged national universities to diversify their revenue sources by emulating the 'entrepreneurial university' model and stimulate academic entrepreneurship to promote university – industry links as a means to stimulate economic growth (see Etzkowitz, 2015).

The development of Japanese university-industry collaborations since the late 1990s has been characterized by growing cooperation not only between universities and industry, but also between the two ministries: METI (the Ministry of Economy, Trade and Industry) and MEXT (the Ministry of Education, Culture, Sports, Science and Technology); especially with regard to enhancing intellectual property and local industrial-cluster strategies. It has been pointed out that Japan's cluster programmes are strongly concentrated on the development of new technology and university-industry links (Kitagawa and Woolgar, 2008), and there is a noticeably weak integration of cluster efforts with other regional initiatives to upgrade education, training and finance (Shapira,

2008). At the institutional level, universities have developed interface capabilities, both as an internal faculty and academic administrative development and in response to external encouragement and subsidies, such as establishing Technology Transfer Offices (TTOs) (Kneller, 2010; Woolgar, 2007).

However, research commercialization and securing income from industry through knowledge transfer activities, still remain peripheral to many academic communities in Japan, where 80 percent of R&D is performed in industry. Nonetheless, it is noted that in recent years, there has been steady growth in the commercialization of research from universities and collaboration with industry. Top national universities have succeeded in increasing their total revenue by diversifying their income sources, also trying to improve their international profiles (Yonezawa, 2013a). The top ten Japanese universities with the highest research income from external sources (joint and commissioned research with industry and other organizations) consist of the seven former imperial universities, the Tokyo Institute of Technology, and two private universities – Keio and Waseda (Kitagawa and Oba, 2010). Nevertheless, whether or not national universities are truly becoming 'entrepreneurial' is debatable and hard to see (see Huang, 2016). For instance, at the University of Tokyo, Japan's top university, the share of external collaborative research income and endowment accounts for 25 percent, while the government subsidies and research grant, respectively account for 32.8 percent and 10 percent (University of Tokyo, 2016).

In recent years, the 'world class university' policy drives have been accentuated as part of Prime Minister Abe's efforts to revitalize the Japanese economy, injecting more dynamism and innovation into the economy through a greater focus on research and development, and improving the competitiveness of universities. Furthermore, in addition to the world class research university agenda, there is an imperative for universities to make their graduates match the needs of employers. Many businesses in Japan have cut back their training programmes and are looking to universities to fill the gap. As businesses become more global, companies are seeking workers with better social and organizational skills, and the ability to work in teams in the global knowledge society. One of the positive solutions is, arguably, to deepen the university industry collaboration for facilitating human resource development by combining industrial skills and academic knowledge.

Creating excellence by the concentration of research funding in a limited number of 'world class' universities may have some other consequences – functional diversification may lead to greater institutional differentiation (see Kitagawa, 2008, 2009). While the former imperial universities and a certain number of national universities have a national and international orientation, many other universities have a smaller and more regional or local focus. For example, national universities in non-metropolitan areas increasingly see themselves as contributing to regional development as central to their core institutional missions. With fewer public resources available for higher education, there will be a need to place a higher priority on responsiveness to local and regional needs, and on demonstrating its usefulness to society in order to receive public support. Thus, universities in general increasingly see contributing to regional development as their mission, but actual institutional contexts varies substantially, conditioned by the geographical location, the historical relationships the university has been building with the local actors, and the relationships between national, local public and private universities in the area.

There is no one size model in which fits all such public-private partnerships including forms of university-industry collaboration. Recent policy drives such as Global 30 and business-university research collaboration seem to provide at least one model targeting a particular type of university response to current policy challenges. Such a top-down institutionalization of the Triple Helix model of university-industry-government relationships (Etzkowitz and Leydesdorff, 1997) can be seen as part of the recent policy drive towards the privatization of the public system and of recent policy-driven privatization of the public system in Japan. The different types of universities – national, private and local – all need to find their own models to respond to the new challenges posed by the Triple Helix models.

Functional differentiation or institutional isomorphism?

Historically, different types of universities have had different functions, resources, networks and spatial aspirations within diversifying national higher education systems (Teichler, 1999, 2004). The change process is influenced by a number of factors including their history, the national system of higher education, culture, geographical location, resource base, status, leadership, stakeholders and ambitions. Eades (2005) pointed out the changing division of labour between the three sectors of HEIs: in Japan up to 1998, the tripartite division between national and local, public and private universities, was rather clear and can be summarized as follows:

> 'national universities should meet the needs of the nation, local public universities should meet the needs of the local communities that established them and private universities should be mainly responsive to the market'.

Arguably, such a historical division has become more complex through 'deliberate erosion' (Eades, 2005) of the difference between the three sectors as the pace of national university reform accelerated. Such erosion of institutional functions is underpinned by a survey results based on the perceptions of university senior managers (Kitagawa and Oba, 2010). This study that was conducted over a decade ago in March 2006, targeting all universities in Japan, including national, private and local public, revealed the institutional responses at three levels of senior academic managers (presidents, faculty deans and department heads (DHs)). The study asked the senior managers views concerning the differentiating functions of universities and where they think their institutions were placed strategically. As a whole, the pre-war universities aimed at raising or maintaining their standing by performing the roles of 'world-class research and education centres', while the postwar institutions tended to give priority to 'community-based' functions. However, these divisions are not now so clear-cut, with both pre-war and post-war universities intending to enhance a number of different roles and functions. The majority of universities, regardless of their legal status (namely, national, local public, or private) or institutional type (comprehensive, multidisciplinary, or single faculty), intend to enhance more or less their roles in almost all functions studied in the survey.

The private universities have been increasingly seen as competitors of national universities for seeking public budgetary allocation. The government subsidies for the operational budgets of national universities had decreased, even among top universities. All universities are encouraged to look for non-public sources of income. Furthermore, the government has introduced new grants for students, responding in 2016 to the overreliance on student loans. This is also adding further tensions in relation to the budgetary allocation between the national and private universities.

At the university level, different models of institutional governance and management need to be aligned better in order to identify processes and impacts of functional differentiation. The top universities, especially national universities, have implemented governance reforms during the incorporation process since 2004. At the same time, they have developed their own management structures by establishing original and distinct action plans. The management reforms of national universities since the 2000s have been followed by the private universities, including the increased stress on institutional research and strategic planning. At an institutional level, strategic resource allocation for selected strategic functions have been the key to managing the differentiation of the higher education system (Kitagawa and Oba, 2010).

Recent higher education reforms by the government seem to be reinforcing the processes of so-called 'institutional isomorphism' (DiMaggio and Powell, 1983), making existing differences between national and local, public and private universities less substantial. On one hand, we can argue that the diversified funding mechanism with which each university may be willing to choose suitable functions within the system is a prerequisite for an effective higher education system. On the other hand, there must be appropriate incentive mechanisms for institutions to diversify their functions. In order to manage differentiation in any higher education system, issues concerning both a university's internal governance and management and questions related to external governance of the system as a whole need to be addressed: For example, policy incentives may need to be created which foster networks and alliances of universities across different functions and also universities and their partners at multiple levels in society.

Conclusion

This chapter presented the recent reform process in Japanese higher education, concerning the tensions emerging within the system due to the ever tightening of public resources, and the growing concentration of resources upon few 'world-class' universities. After the incorporation of national universities in 2004, the last decade has witnessed a series of higher education policy reforms, which have re-enforced the institutional differentiation within the already diverse system. Although the government stresses that universities should voluntarily choose appropriate functions, in reality, the policy seems to leave little room for choice, largely because the distribution of competitive research funding is highly skewed in favour of a few elite universities. While many of the universities wish to be world-class centres, only a limited number of universities – essentially a few elite universities, which have been created throughout the history of the Japanese higher education system – have the resources to do so.

There are two simultaneous forces at work: first, the 'mismatch between societal expectations and institutional capacities to deliver', and second, the extent to which 'external demands are reshaping or even undermining the very nature of the university' (Perry, 2006). Japanese universities have reacted to the recent 'competition' and 'differentiation' policy promoted by the government, by developing their own institutional strategies and intermediary organizational capabilities. Overall, one could argue that there is a widening gap between the objectives of government policy and the resources available for its implementation at the institutional level. Increased competition among universities is expected to give rise to further questioning of the difference in governmental funding between national universities and between national and private universities.

We argued earlier that the Japanese higher education system has benefited from historical collaboration between the public and private sectors, with a strong privatized financing through student tuition fees over the decades, to arrive at the state of nearly universal access to higher education. The current challenges and tensions for the Japanese higher education system need to be understood with the evolutionary perspective that drives such a diverse system, which has constantly redefined and realigned the nature of higher education as both public and private good.

References

Altbach, P. G. (2003) 'The costs and benefits of world-class universities', *International Higher Education*, 33(Fall): 5–8.

Altbach, P.G. and Umakoshi, T. (eds) (2004) *Asian universities: Historical perspectives and contemporary challenges*, Baltimore, MD: Johns Hopkins University Press.

Amano, I. (2008) *Future of national universities and their incorporation: Between independence and inequality*, Tokyo: Toshindo, (in Japanese).

Arimoto, A., Cummings, W. K., Huang, F. and Shin, J. C. (eds), (2008) *The changing academic profession in Japan*, Dordrecht: Springer.
Asonuma, A. (2002) 'Globalisation and higher education reforms: The Japanese case', *Higher Education*, 43: 127–139.
Baker, D. P. (2007) 'Mass higher education and the super research University', *International Higher Education*, 49(Fall): 9–10.
Clark, B. (2001) 'The entrepreneurial university: new foundations for collegiality, autonomy and achievement', *Higher Education Management*, 13(2): 9–24.
DiMaggio, P. J. and Powell, W. (1983) 'The iron cage revisited: institutional isomorphism and collective rationality in organizational fields', *American Sociological Review*, 48: 147–160.
Eades, J. (2005) 'The Japanese 21st center of excellence program: internationalisation in action?', in J. S. Eades, R. Goodman and Y. Hada (eds), *The 'big bang' in Japanese higher education: The 2004 reforms and the dynamics of change*, Melbourne: Trans Pacific Press.
Etzkowitz, H. and Leydesdorff, L. (eds) (1997) *Universities and the global knowledge economy: A triple helix of university-industry-government relations*, London, England: Pinter Publishers.
Huang, F. (2016) Changes and challenges to higher education financing in Japan, Centre for Global Higher Education working paper series, no10. Available online at http://researchcghe.org/perch/resources/publications/wp10.pdf
Japan Times (2016) Japan's public and private universities face major shake-ups and mergers as student numbers fall, 12 April 2016. Retrieved from http://japantimes.co.jp/news/2016/04/12/national/japans-public-private-universities-face-major-shakeup-mergers-student-numbers-fall/#.WNeq72czWUk
Kitagawa, F. (2005) Constructing advantage in the knowledge society – roles of Universities reconsidered: the case of Japan, *Higher Education Management and Policy*, 17(1): 45–62.
Kitagawa, F. (2008) (Post) 'Mass higher education and Japanese elite universities', in T. Tapper (ed.), *Structuring mass higher education; the role of elite institutions*, London: Routledge.
Kitagawa, F. (2009) 'University – industry links and regional development in Japan: connecting excellence and relevance?', *Science, Technology and Society*, 14(1): 1–33.
Kitagawa, F. and Oba, J. (2010), 'Managing differentiation of higher education system in Japan: connecting excellence and diversity', *Higher Education*, 59: 507–524.
Kneller, R. (2010) *Bridging islands: Venture companies and the future of Japanese and American industry*, Oxford, England: Oxford University Press.
MEXT. (2016) Statistical abstract 2016. Available online at http://mext.go.jp/en/publication/statistics/title02/detail02/1379369.htm
Oba, J. (2005) 'The incorporation of national universities in Japan: initial reactions of the new national university corporations', *Higher Education Management and Policy*, 17(2): 105–125.
Oba, J. (2008) Creating world-class universities in Japan: policy and initiatives, *Policy Futures in Education*, 6(5): 629–640.
OECD. (2016) *Education at glance*, Paris: OECD.
Perry, B. (2006) Science, society and the university: a paradox of values, *Social Epistemology*, 20(3): 201–219.
Teichler, U. (2004) Changing structures of the higher education systems: The increasing complexity of underlying forces, UNESCO forum occasional paper series paper no. 6 Diversification of higher education and the changing role of knowledge and research (3–16). Retrieved from http://unesdoc.unesco.org/images/0014/001467/146736e.pdf
Trow, M. (2006) 'Reflections on the transition from elite to mass to universal access: Forms and phases of higher education in modern societies since WWII', in J. Forest and A. Philip (eds), *International handbook of higher education*, New York: Springer, pp. 243–280.
University of Tokyo. (2016) Budgeted Revenue for 2015. Retrieved from http://u-tokyo.ac.jp/en/about/finances.html
Ushiogi, M. (1997) 'Japanese graduate education and its problems', *Higher Education*, 34: 237–244.
Woolgar, L. (2007) 'New institutional policies for university–industry links in Japan', *Research Policy*, 36: 1261–1274.

Yamamoto, K. (2004) 'Corporatization of national universities in Japan: revolution for governance or rhetoric for downsizing?', *Financial Accountability & Management*, 20(2): 153–181.

Yonezawa, A. (2007) 'Japanese flagship universities at a crossroads', *Higher Education*, 54(4): 483–499.

Yonezawa, A. (2011) 'The "Global 30" and the consequences of selecting "world-class" universities in Japan', in Nian Cai Liu, Qi Wang and Ying Cheng (eds), *Paths to a world class university*, Rotterdam: Sense Publishers.

Yonezawa, A. (2013a) 'Challenge for top Japanese universities when establishing a new global identity: Seeking a new paradigm after "world-class"', in J.C. Shin and B.M. Kehm (eds), *Institutionalization of world-class university in global competition*, Springer, pp. 125–143.

Yonezawa, A. (2013b) 'The development of private higher education in Japan since the 1960s: A reexamination of a centre-periphery paradigm', in A. Maldonado-Maldonado and R.M. Bassett (eds), *The forefront of international hgher education: A festschrift in honour of Philip G. Altbach* Springer, pp. 189–200.

Yonezawa, A. (2016) 'Can East Asian universities break the spell of hierarchy?: The challenge of seeking an inherent identity', in C. Collins, M.N.N. Lee, J.N. Hawkins and D.E. Neubauer (eds), *The Palgrave handbook of Asia pacific higher education*, Palgrave Macmillan, pp. 247–260.

Yonezawa, A. and Shimmi, Y. (2015) 'Transformation of university governance through internationalization: challenges for top universities and government policies in Japan', *Higher Education*, 70(2): 173–186.

11
How inexorable is the shift from the public to the private funding of higher education?

DAVID PALFREYMAN, TED TAPPER AND SCOTT THOMAS

Introduction

The purpose of this volume has been to place in different national/regional settings the apparently almost universal shift from the public to the private funding of higher education systems. This generalization, however, needs to take into account the fact that some systems have had entrenched within them for many years a combination of both public and private funding, and that nearly all nations have had at least some examples of both privately and publicly funded higher education institutions in their midst, while in some countries – notably Germany – the policy battle is still not resolved. Variation in outcomes is aided by the fact that both public and private funding can assume different forms. Perhaps the most dramatic form of private funding is the imposition of student tuition fees, but what also needs to be noted is the endeavour of many institutions to enhance their endowment income with the resources sometimes raised for the specific purpose of supporting innovative academic programmes. It is also a fact that the balance between private and public funding has oscillated over time and that there is no certainty that this oscillation has come to an end. Moreover, although this volume is built around an examination of the recent increase in private funding, there is no certainty that this will continue indefinitely in all countries. Thanks to demographic trends, political development and evolution in the content and purposes of higher education, the balance between the public and private funding of higher education will evolve over time. It is our belief, however, that the main trajectory in the near future will be an increase in private funding and that will be more dependent upon institutional initiatives rather than action by governments, but that all funding will be regulated by the state to achieve government-defined public policy goals.

This chapter is organized around analysing the impact of the extension of the private funding of higher education as it evolves in three different contexts:

- where there is already an established pattern of mixing private and public funding
- where there is a policy shift that dramatically increases private funding in order to move to a mass system of higher education
- where the increase in private funding is aimed at restructuring radically the existing model of higher education

The chapter will conclude with an interpretation of what light these developments throw upon the future of higher education as a policy arena worthy of political attention.

The three developments

a. Extending private funding where it is already established policy

In several nations, private funding has for some time already been an established feature of the higher education system. In Japan, Australia and the United States student access has been expanded through privately-funded universities and the charging of student tuition fees. In Australia, there was an established political consensus about the funding of social goods; and so when governments on the left politically, moved towards the public funding of fees, this was seen in some quarters as breaking an established norm about the provision of social goods. However, contemporarily the charging of student tuition fees, albeit underwritten by a widely admired system of income-contingent student loans, appears to constitute the current political consensus. In Japan, the funding debate has centred more upon public support for research, as the nation struggles to encourage the emergence of a stratum of so-called 'world-class' universities; while student access for many years has been underwritten by the privately funded universities which dominate the higher education system and have been responsible for securing something approximating 'universal access to higher education'. In the United States, there has always been clearly identifiable public and private sectors with a blurring of the divide as publicly founded institutions are now more likely to charge tuition fees while research in both sectors is sustained by research grants from state-funded institutions and the corporate sector.

There are interesting parallels between developments in the United States and in the United Kingdom. The United States was the first nation to arrive at a system of mass higher education and this was essentially underwritten by the public funding of the states' institutions. The belief was that this helped to enhance positive social and political values, whereas in the UK public funding, as seen in 1963 Robbins Report, was more about the need to sponsor social mobility in the drive towards forming a more socially inclusive society. In both countries, even if the rationale for public expenditure on higher education remains, a counter-ideological thrust has arisen which sees higher education institutions as providing more of a private than a public good. In the UK, this ideology took root strongly in the 1980s – the Thatcher years. Although excepting overseas students, her governments, thanks mainly to opposition from her own backbench members of parliament, were unable to impose tuition fees upon home-based students. The UK fees regime was formally instigated by the first Blair Government, although in 2017 General Election the Labour Party's manifesto proposed the abolition of student fees and a return to public funding. But perhaps more important than any ideological shift has been a revamping of policy priorities. In both the US and the UK, a number of policy concerns are now seen as meriting greater public funding than expenditure on higher education. Thus although, unlike Poland and most Latin American nations, both the US and the UK could afford to underwrite financially a mass system of higher education, the political will to do so has declined and perhaps is in the process of evaporating.

Both the movements towards and against the private funding of higher education have given rise to significant political conflicts between national and more local units of governance. In Germany, we have the fraught situation in which the federal government imposes student fees while some states abolish them at least for their own home-based students; while in the United States some states underwrite tuition costs for their home-based students while permitting their universities to impose them on out-of-state students. In the UK, we have national governments imposing different fee obligations upon students depending upon which country in the UK (England, Scotland, Wales or Northern Ireland) is their home residence. We are looking at more than an ideological battle; one that is also deeply embedded in local political terrains with governments favouring their own residents.

b. Embracing private funding and establishing mass access to higher education

In Poland and Latin America, we find governments embracing the move towards mass higher education but not funding it publicly and instead relying upon privately funded institutions to fulfil their policy goals. In fact there has been a general move in all the systems analysed in this volume to promote the expansion of access to higher education, at least in part, through the charging of tuition fees. There was nothing explicitly malevolent about such a policy direction in either Poland or the Latin American countries because governments simply lacked the resources to underwrite an expansion of access to higher education. The consequence, however, has been the emergence of a plethora of privately funded institutions which occupy a clearly marked lower niche within their national systems and unlike – as has to some extent been occurring in Japan – these institutions are highly unlikely to evolve to the point where they can be said to be research universities, and should that occur it will require almost certainly a change in government policy and the injection of public funding.

c. Private funding and changing the purpose of higher education

In some countries, the move to expand private funding to increase access to higher education is but one move in a package of innovations that are seen as necessary to change the overall character of the higher education system – it is more than a means of simply expanding access to higher education. China provides an excellent example of this strategy where the move towards private funding is part of a package of reforms geared to constructing a system that makes the universities more receptive to serving the perceived socio-economic needs of the country while granting them greater control over their own development.

More generally marketization impacts upon the pattern of student demand to which institutions need to respond if they are to sustain their financial security. Universities need to be sensitive to the fact that demand for different areas of knowledge declines and expands with, in recent years, seemingly a general drift towards disciplines which appear likely to ensure good job prospects for their students. This trend transcends all the national developments incorporated in this study and has led to a general shift in the balance of institutional power as academic authority declines in the face of the increased authority exercised by university leaders and managers. Currently in the United Kingdom, we see moves to make the levels of student fees that institutions charge in part dependent upon student satisfaction with their degree programmes. Thus increasingly institutional survival may become dependent upon where and what students choose to study, while in England institutional financial stability may also become dependent how their students rate their degree programmes. There is universal state regulation of the market, and as we have noted this can lead to benign regulation strategies, as with Australia's income-contingent loans scheme; but in England, once the Higher Education and Research Act 2017 is fully implemented, it could force a significant change in the overall academic map of UK higher education[1].

China provides an excellent example of the purposeful and direct use of a move towards private funding as part of a general package of change – as opposed to the recent and indirect moves in the UK. In China, the change process is geared not simply to expanding the higher education system but constructing a model that makes the universities more receptive to serving the perceived social and economic needs of the nation while granting the universities greater control over their own development, supposedly enhancing institutional autonomy while guiding the purposes of higher education. As is generally the case the question is what should be the balance between institutional autonomy and the pressures that are exerted by the state and the market. University management and leadership are now everywhere more to the fore but face the unenviable task of balancing the demands of the internal institutional pressures with the pressures emanating from the state and market. What makes the task potentially so difficult is that these pressures may well pull in different directions. There may be a strong move within universities to preserve established academic maps but a failure to change may result in institutional insolvency that then forces even more radical change. Marketization not only requires more developed institutional management, it also requires more system planning and a state-regulated market could be a more effective way of achieving these goals than direct forms of state control.

The policy and political significance of the shift from public to private funding

While the move from the public to the private funding does not mean that there is automatically less state intervention in the regulation of higher education, it does mean that there is a declining interest in higher education as a policy issue. This is particularly true of the United States with its well-established mass and very diversified system of higher education. Other social issues come to assume (for example, health care) greater political significance. If market funding, in the form of student tuition fees, can go a long way to underwriting the financial costs of higher education and if it can be regulated and fine-tuned, in order to ensure the imposition of state-defined policy goals, then why should universities be given large amounts of public funding and afforded political capital? Examples of the fine-tuning of policy are to be found in the following nations: The decisions of UK governments of differing political persuasions to impose tuition fees – initially upon only overseas students while excluding both EU and home-based students, and to make special concessions to students enroling in the so-called STEM (science, technology, engineering and mathematics) subjects; The imposition of tuition fees by those US state universities, initially upon out-of-state students, while sustaining free tuition for instate residents ; Or in the disproportionate awarding of public research funding to elite Japanese and German universities in the endeavour to establish a cadre of world-class universities.

In Germany, on the contrary, we see that the debate about the public funding of higher education remains a critical political issue, although so much of the conflict there has been entwined with the question of who determines higher education policy – the federal government or the states. The universal threat to university systems is not only from the likelihood of a decline in public funding but also generated by the increasing marginalization of higher education as a policy issue, perhaps sometimes sustained by parties more concerned with retaining their political images rather than with a deep interest in trying to define the purpose of the university. Interestingly, even when higher education policy issues continue to generate conflict between levels of governance within political systems as seen particularly in Germany and in the UK (and to a lesser extent in the US) this is again invariably more about political interests attempting to secure their own support base rather than any substantial analysis about the purposes of higher education and how it should be structured and funded to achieve those purposes.

In all the countries incorporated in this volume, it is the move towards the imposition of student tuition fees to underwrite the costs of higher education teaching that has proven to be the most controversial form of marketization. It has generated the deepest political conflicts, and most often placed the interests embedded in higher education systems at odds with the wider society, incumbent governments and established state structures. These conflicts have often been sharp even in those countries in which a combination of the public and private funding of higher education – Australia, Japan and the United States – has been a longstanding norm. What is less contentious, and appears to be becoming more prevalent are institutional endeavours to raise private funding. Such endeavours are long-established (especially in the US) and are a manifestation of institutional autonomy rather than a sign of bowing to politically imposed policy objects or to the whims of the market, although in fact such institutional moves may well complement both state and corporate initiatives.

It is market funding that seemingly enriches the institution – sponsoring research, underwriting new programmes or providing scholarships – whereas tuition fees are perceived as imposing a financial burden that hits the poorer members of society the hardest. These perceptions are only likely to change when access to higher education is not socially divisive and when it is perceived as securing both a public good and as well as advancing individual opportunities, with Japan, Australia and the US – with their long-established traditions of dual funding – pointing to the way forward.

Higher education institutions should be perceived as organizations that perform important societal functions, above all the organization of high status knowledge; and need public funding if only to support policy goals that enable them better to fulfil those functions by widening social access, defending the presence of a wide range of knowledge areas, and enabling the move towards a knowledge-based economy. Higher education needs to move beyond its current widespread entrapment in the politics of funding and focus on securing these key policy goals regardless of its funding base.

The changing scenario

In Poland, we see that whereas private funding has increased access to higher education and led to the emergence of a mass system, a national demographic trend means that demand is now in decline. The consequence is the amalgamation of some privately funded institutions coupled with the outright closure of others; student demand is simply not there to sustain institutional longevity. A similar trend is noticeable elsewhere, particularly in Japan. The consequences of a declining birth rate have a significant impact upon the demand for higher education that is not fully countered by either the widening of social access to the university or by extending the opportunity to older age groups who may enter as mature students. This will cause particular problems for those universities and those academic disciplines in which there is a sharp decline in student demand. The obvious response is an expansion of institutional management and system planning, which raises the possibility of moving from the imposition of standardized student tuition fees to variable fees with levels determined by the institutions rather than politically at the national or state levels. This means a move towards a reflective marketized system, which, short of a return to substantial public funding, may be the only way to ensure the survival of some institutions and certain disciplines. Or, as in Poland, the alternative may be a drastic rationalization of provision. Of course such a situation could bring about a return to substantial public funding as the only way to avoid such a crisis in academia. However, although some national systems of higher education have broad societal respect and their representative associations retain some political authority, there is no guarantee they could secure policy outcomes that would ensure their long-term survival. And if they did that would it be on terms that many of them would find acceptable? While in Poland, it may be the privately funded institutions that are currently facing retrenchment, there is the likelihood, as Japanese experience demonstrates, of such pressure being applied to the more prestigious publicly funded institutions everywhere – and whether government policy would respond to their needs in a more generous manner remains to be seen. However, as the US and UK experiences demonstrate governments have a complex range of policy issues to handle which they may well consider are more worthy of public funding than higher education. But if the price of salvation is that institutional policy direction is controlled by the state and that there is no meaningful academic autonomy, then perhaps closure is preferable to surviving on imposed terms. However, with respect to Poland and across Latin America the analysis is that private funding was used for the purpose of bringing about a mass system of higher education. The question could now be whether, in conjunction with judicious public funding and intelligent regulation by the state, the university as we have known it can be saved? As our chapter on MOOCs suggests it is possible that the more things change, the more they remain the same!

Note

1   Only England will feel the impact of this legislation because it is only the Higher Education Funding Council for England that is under Westminister's control; with universities in Wales, Scotland and Northern Ireland controlled by their own legislatures.

Index

Aarrestad, J. 134
Abe, Prime Minister (Japan) 171
A Global Week of Action for Free Education (Germany) 119
Alexander, F. 49
Allen, J. 38
Altbach, P.G. *et al.* 95, 100, 107, 162, 189
Amaral, A. 93, 98
Anderson, F. 54
Anderson Report (UK) 72–73
Anderson, Z. 38
Antonowicz, D. 91, 94, 103
Archibald, R. B. 33
Asonuma, A. 167
Atkinson, A. 137
Australian Bureau of Statistics 68
Australian higher education reviews 50–52; Mills review 50; Murray review 50
Australian hybrid fees regimes: fees/grants mix 50–52; from private to public funding 52–53; growth of private providers 57–60, 67; tuition fees in public universities 60–61
autonomy in Chinese higher education 153–154

BAFoG (Germany) 113
Bain, A. 51
Baker, D. P. 169
Balán, J. 124
Barr, N. 90, 91
Barrilleaux, C. 31, 32
Basic Constitutional Law (Germany) 112–16
Beazley, K. 57

Becker, W. E. 40
Belfield, C. R. 90
Belkin, 39
Bellas, M. L. 39
Ben-David, J. 20
Bender, M.C. 38
Berdahl, R.O. 21, 22
Berkman, M. 32
Berry, F. S. 24, 26
Berry, W. D. 24, 26
Bevia, C. 139
Beyle, T. 31
Bill & Melinda Gates Foundation 36
Blair Government (UK) 3, 179
Bond, Alan 57
Bowen, H.R. 39
Bozeman, B. 20
Bradley, D. 58, 62
Brandeis, Louis 19
Brill, C. 81
British *QS* rankings 143,145
Brown, Roger 41
Buckingham, J. 52
Burke J. C. and Associates, 23

Cakitaki, B. 52, 57, 59, 62, 63
Callender, C. 101
Castles, Francis 63
Center of Excellence (Japan) 167, 168
Centre for Higher Education Development (Germany) 116
changing pattern of higher education funding in the UK 84–88
Chapman, B. 55
Cherastidtham, I. 60, 61, 63, 66
China News Network 143, 145

China Youth News 153
Ciarimboli, E. B. 20, 24
Clark, Burton 20, 170
Coaldrake, P. 56
Cohen-Vogel, L. 35
Colavecchio, S. 39
College Board (US) 22, 37
Commonwealth Scholarship Board (Australia) 50, 51
Complete College America initiative 36
Conley, V. M. 39
Conservative Government, 1979 (UK) 79–80
Contemporary reform initiatives in Chinese higher education, 156–160
Converging public and private higher education domains in Japan 170–172
Coper, M. 49
Correia, F. 93
Cortes, C. 134
Cultural Revolution (China) 147

Dalglish, T. K. 29
Daly, R. 154
Da Silveira, P. 136
Dawkins, John 63
Dearing Report (UK) 76, 80
Deaton, A. 138
Deaton, R. 23, 30, 33, 35
Debray *et al.* 36
decline in the Polish higher education sector 107–108
defining private provision (Poland) 96–98
Deng Xiaoping 147, 148
Department for Business, Energy and Industrial Strategy (UK) 88
Department for Business, Innovation and Skills (BIS) (UK) 78, 80
Department for Education (UK) 75, 88
Department of Education and Science (UK) 74
Department of Education and Training (Australia) 50, 57, 59, 60, 61, 65, 66, 68
Desrochers, D. M. 22
DiMaggio, P. J. 173
Distinguished national university corporations (Japan) 170
Division between grant income/student fees in Australia 51, 53, 54, 55, 58
Dougherty, K. J. *et al.* 23, 32, 33, 35
Doyle, W. R. 25, 26, 27, 31, 33, 35

Drivers of higher education policy in the US states 22–37
Duckett, S. 52
Duderstadt, James 22
Dye, T. R. 26

Eades, J. 172
ecology of state higher education policymaking in the US 24–37
Education at a Glance 118
Education Commission of the States (US) 36
Education Reform Act, 1988 (UK) 73–74, 79–80, 85
Ehrenberg, R. G. 27
enrolment in most prestigious Latin American universities 134
enrolment in selected Latin American universities by country 135–136
enrolment in non-university higher education institutions in Latin America 133
enrolments in private education in Poland 97
Etzkowitz, H. 172
expansion of higher education system through privatization: Japan 162–164; Latin America 130–132; Poland 93-95
expansion of systems: Australia 49–52; China 143–145; Latin America 125–128; Poland 81–93, 95; UK 72–73
expenditure on education in selected Latin American countries, 126–127
expenditure on science and technology in selected Latin American countries, 128
external/internal privatization (Poland) 90–91

federalism, more control by the federal government: Germany 114–118; US 21–22
Feigenbaum, H. 90
Feldman, D. H. 33
Ferreyra, M. M. 124, 132, 133, 134
Finkelstein, M. J. 39
Forsyth, H. 50
Fox, B. 23
Fraser, M. 53
Fraser, Malcolm 52–53
Fryar, A. H. 93
funding changes in English higher education over time 84–88

Index • 187

funding of English higher education as driven by: desire to create knowledge society 82–93; economic turmoil 79; equity considerations 81–82; expansion in student numbers 81; ideological change 79–80
funding of German higher education 119–120
funding of Latin American universities 129

Gandara, D. 31, 34, 37
Garritzmann, Julian 48, 62, 63
Geiger, R. L. 91, 95, 96
Georgia Budget and Policy Institute 34
Gerhard, Casper, 152
German 'excellence initiative' 122
German Rector's Conference 116–118
German states and imposition of tuition fees 117–118
Gibson, A. 139
Glenny, L. A. 20, 23, 28
Global Center of Excellence (Japan) 168, 160
Goldman, William 41
Goldrick-Rab, Sara 129
Gomez, R. R. 93
Gonzalez, R. 133, 136, 138
Goodin, R. E. 92
government guidance of higher education policy in China 147–150
Gray, V. 33, 34
Griffith, C. 28
Griswold, C. P. 26, 27
gross higher education enrolment in selected Latin American countries 130
gross private higher education enrolment in selected Latin American countries 131
GUS (Central Statistical Office, Poland) 92, 97, 99, 100, 102, 104

Hall, C. 36
Handbook of Research for Education and Technology 9
Harper, William Rainey
Haroun, H. *et al.* 81
Harrison, N. 81
Hawke Labor Government (Australia) 53–54, 60
Hazelkorn, E. 139
Hearn, J.C. 19, 20, 21, 23, 24, 25, 26, 27, 28, 30, 31, 32, 33, 34, 35, 36, 38, 39, 40

Heitor, M. 138
Heller, D.E. 26, 30, 35 101
HELP loan scheme (Australia) 67
Hicklin. A. 33
Higher Education Act, 2004 (UK) 76
Higher Education and Research Bill (UK) 180
higher education as a private good (Germany) 120–122
higher education as a public good, Latin American analysis 136–139
higher education as a regulated market (UK) 74–78
higher education as constitutionally a publicly funded system (Germany) 112–113
Higher Education Contribution Scheme (Australia) 54–55, 65, 66
Higher Education Funding Councils (UK) 74–75, 78, 183
Higher Education Law, 1998 (China) 149
Higher Education Pact (Germany) 120
Higher Education Quality Report (China) 146
higher education system, stratification of, in Latin America 132–136
higher education, tensions in the delivery of 7–10
Hillman, N. W. 30, 32
historical legacy of mixed patterns of higher education funding: Australia 48–49; Germany 113–114, 119–120; Japan 164–166; US 19–22
Hochschulrektorenkonferenz 2015 (Germany) 120
Holbrook, T. 31
Holdsworth, J. M. 21
Hollis, P, 32
Horta, H. 138
Hossler. D. *et al.*, 27, 40
Howard government (Australia) 60
Huang, F. 162, 166
Hurlburt, S. 22

Illich, Ivan 8
impact of economic performance on higher education funding (UK) 73–74
impact of internationalization on Chinese higher education 146–7
impact of marketization on Chinese higher education 150–153
incentive-based budgeting systems (US) 40

income-contingent loans: Australia 53–54, 59–67; UK 84–88
increasing differentiation in Japanese higher education 172–172
Independent Commission against Corruption (Australia) 60
independent learning 7–10
Inside Higher Education 12
internal national policy differences on student tuition fees: Australia 49–57; Germany 118–120; UK 72–74; US 22–24, 27–34
Iturbe-Ormaetxe, I. 130
Ivy League universities 14

Japan Times, 164
Japanese funding initiatives to support elite universities 166–170
Jobs for the Future initiative (US) 36
Johnstone, D. B. 93, 95, 107

Keegan, Desmond 9
Kehm, B. 114, 116, 122
Kemp, David 56, 58, 59
Kim, T. 98
Kinmonth, E. H. 98
Kinne, A. 23
Kitagawa, F. 162, 168, 169, 171, 173
Kneller, R. 171
Krause, N. 116
Kwiek, M. 90, 91, 92, 93, 94, 95, 96, 105

Labor Governments (Australia), 63, 66
Labor Party (Australia) 49, 54, 62, 63 65, 68
Labour Party's 2017 General Election Manifesto (UK) 179
Lacy, T. A. 26, 29, 32, 35
Langer, L. 31
Latin American and the Caribbean Regional Higher Education Conference 2008, 124
Leslie, D. W. 22
Levin, H. M. 90
Levine, A. D. 35, 98
Levy, D. C. 90, 91, 92, 95, 96, 99, 100, 106
Leydesdorff, L. 172
Liberal-Country Party coalition (Australia) 49–50
Liberal Democrats (UK) 77
Liberal Government (Australia) 51, 52, 62, 63-64, 65-66
Liu, Y. 145

Local Education Authorities, student grants (UK) 72
Lomax-Smith, J. 62, 65
Lord Browne of Madingley Report (UK) 76–77
Lowery, D. 33, 34
Lowry, R. C. 30, 33
Lucas, S. 139
Lumina Foundation for Education (US) 36

Macintyre, S. 53, 55
Main Council for Higher Education (RGSW, Poland) 94
Maldonado, A. 124, 128, 134, 138
Malec, J. 105
Marginson, S. 66, 121, 136–7
Marine, G. M. 27
Marques, Juliana 9
Marquez, A. 139
Martin, L. *et al.* 50
Mas-Colell, A. 137
Master Plan for the Higher Education of California 7
McAllister, I. 52
McGettigan, A. 87
McGuinness, A.C. 20, 22, 30
McLendon, M.K. 20, 21, 23, 25, 26, 28, 30, 31, 32, 33, 34, 35
McMahon, W. 39
Meier, K. J. 31, 32, 33
Menzies, Robert 50, 62
METI (Japanese Ministry of Economy, Trade and Industry) 170
MEXT (Japanese Ministry of Education, Culture, Sports, Science and Technology) 166, 167, 168, 170
Meyer, J. W. 21
Milan, M. C. 39
Ministry of Education (China) 156
Ministry of Science and Higher Education (MNISW, Poland) 98, 106
Mistretta, M. A. 35
Mohr, L. B. 24
Mokher, C. 25, 30, 32, 33, 35
MOOCs 6–18; delivering MOOCS 10–11, 14, 15; The future of MOOCS 14–16, 183; what are MOOCs? 10–14
Moore, M. G. 8
Moore, R. 52
moves to secure higher education as a public good in the US states 37–41

Index • **189**

Mumper. M. 28
Murray, K. *et al*.57

Nair, C. S. 95
National Archives (Australia) 53, 54
National Development and Reform Commission (China) 150
National Natural Science Foundation of China 145
National Research Council (NCN, Poland) 99, 100, 101,108,
National Student Clearinghouse (US) 14
National Tertiary Education Union 60, 62
National University Incorporation Law (Japan) 165
Neave, G. 93
Nelson, B. 56
Ness, E. C. 25, 30, 31, 32, 33, 34, 35, 37
Newfield, C. 21, 37
Nicholls, J. 55
Nicholson-Crotty, J. 31, 32
Norton, A. 52, 54, 55, 56, 57, 58, 59, 60, 61, 62, 63, 65, 66

Oba, J. 162, 165, 168, 169, 171, 173
Obama administration and federal oversight of US higher education 21
OECD 52, 63, 64, 85, 86, 98, 118, 121, 128, 132, 163, 164, 165
Office for Students (UK) 78, 88
Ordorika, I. 93
Organizacion de Estados Iberoamericanos (Latin America) 124
Orr, B. 57

Paatrinos, H. A. 132
Pact for Research and Innovation (Germany) 120
Pascarella, E. T. 39
Pasternack, P. 12
Pawlowski 104
Paying the Price 129
Pell Grant (US) 36
Perna, L. W. 22
Perry, B. 174
Pikketty, T. 137
Pinheiro, R. 91, 94
Plibersek, T. 66
policy differences on fees at US state level, 19–22, 24,32
policy differences on fees of German political parties 119

policy divides on tuition fees between governments and their universities: Germany 119–122; Japan 174; UK 74–78; US 22–25
policy shifts on the funding of UK higher education 74–78
Pomianek, T. 105
Powell, W. 173
President Xi Jinping (China) 149
Priest, D. M. 40, 93, 107
privatisation of higher education, overall opposition to 3–5
Professor LI Peigen 153
programme for promoting the enhancement of research universities (Japan) 169
Projects (China): *211 Project* 149, 151, 153,154, 155; *985 Project* 149, 153, 154, 155
Promotion and Mutual Aid Corporation for Private Schools of Japan 166
Pshacharopoulos, G. 132
public funding of higher education, supportive reasons for 1–3
Pusser, B. 22

Quality Assurance Agency (UK) 78
QSL-money (Germany) 118

Rama, 132
Reckhow, S. 36
reforming Chinese higher education 156–150
Research Assessment Exercises (UK) 74
Research Excellence Framework (UK) 83
research funding by university, Poland 101
Research and Innovation strategies (UK) 78, 88
resistance to the public funding of private higher education institutions in Poland 103–106
Resource Accounting and Budgeting (UK) 87
Rick Perry (Texas Governor) 38
Rick Scott (Florida Governor) 38
Rippner, J. 31, 37
Robbins, S. B. 38
Robbins Report (UK) 73, 178
Rodriguez, R. 136
Roskam, J. 51

Sa, M. C. 129
Samuelson, P. 136–7
Sanyal, B. C. 95, 107
Schleicher, Andreas 121
Schmidtlein, F. A. 21
Schugurensky, D. 20
Schumpeter. Joseph, 40
Schuster, J. H. 39
Shah, M. 95
Shen, F. X. 33
Shimmi, Y. 169
Sieminska, R. 91
Silicon Valley 152
Simons, M. 53
Smith, A. A. 21
Snyder, M. 23
Socialist Market Economic System (China) 148, 151
Solia, P. 138
Southern Regional Education Board (US) 36
Squire, P. 32
St. John, E. P. 40, 93, 107
State Accreditation Commission (PKA, Poland) 94
'Starving the Beast' 37
State Higher Education Executive Officers Association (US) 36
state variations in the higher education system (US) 29–30, 39–40
Stedman, L. 56
STEM subjects 23, 38, 82, 86, 181
Stiglitz, J. 137, 138
stratification in higher education in Latin America 124–135, 139–140
Supreme Court (US) 19
Szczepanski, J. 91

Tandberg, D. A. 25, 28, 30, 31, 32, 33, 34, 35
Tannock, P. 57
Teacher, T. 51
Teaching Excellence Framework (TEF) (UK) 78, 88
Teichler, U. 172
Teixeira, P. 93, 95, 98
Terenzini, P. T. 39
Tertiary Education Quality and Standards Agency (Australia) 58, 59
Texas Association of Business 34
Thatcher Governments (UK) 3, 78–80, 179
Thelin, J. 23

Thomas, S. 36
Thomason, A. 40
Thrun, Sebastian 10 11
Toutkoushian, R. K. 32, 39
Tracey, H. 49
trend in the balance between public/private funding (Poland) 99–102
Triple Helix models (Japan) 172
Trombetta, A. 124
Trow, M. 163

Umakoshi, T. 162
UNESCO 125–126, 130, 131
United States as having a higher education system? 19–22
Universities/Higher Education Institutions: Antioquia 135; Australian Catholic University 57; Beijing Jingshan School 147; Bologna 7; Bond 67; Buenos Aires 129, 135; California 7, 22; Chicago 8; Chile 129, 135; Duke 12; Federal University of the Amazonas 132; Federal University of Rio de Janeiro 135; Georgia State Institute of Technology 13, 14; Harvard 10, 11, 12, 14; Indiana 40; Keio 169; Kyoto 163, 169; Los Andes 135; Manitoba 10; Metropolitan Autonomous University 135; Michigan 22; Minnesota 40; MIT 10, 12, 13; Monterrey Institute of Technology and Higher Education 134; Nagoya 169; Nanjing 149; National Autonomous University of Mexico 129, 135; National Institute for Material Sciences 168; National Polytechnic Institute 135; National University Cordoba 135; National University of Columbia 135; National University of la Plata 135; National University of San Marcos 135; National University of Santo Domingo 135; Notre Dame (Australia) 57, 58; Open University 9, 10; Osaka 168, 169; Oxford 7; Paris 7; Peking 149, 152; Pennsylvania 11, 40; Pontifical Catholic University of Chile 135; Pontifical University of Cordoba 132; Ritsumeikan 169; Royal Academy of Artillery, Fortification and Design 132; Royal and Pontifical University of Mexico 132; Royal and

Pontifical University of San Carlos Borromeo 132; Royal and Pontifical University of San Jeronimo 132; Sao Paulo 129, 132, 135; San Jose State 12; Santiago de Chile 135; Southern California 40; Stanford 11; State University of Campinas 135; Tohoku 168, 169; Tokyo 163, 167, 168, 169, 171; Tokyo Institute of Technology 163; Tsinghua 168; Tsukuba 160; Waseda 169; Western Australia 49; Wisconsin 22; Texas 22
University Grants Committee (UK) 72
Ushiogi, M. 167

Vanstone, A. 55, 65
Verger, A. 124
Vincent-Lancrin 98
Von Humboldt 6

Wakeham *Review of STEM Provision*(UK) 82–83
Walczak, D. 91
Walker, J. L. 24
Warshaw, J. B. 20, 24, 26, 32, 35, 39
Watson, L. 58
Western Interstate Commission on Higher Education (US) 36

Whitlam government (Australia) 52, 62, 63–64,
widening participation in German higher education 113–114
Willcox, S. 52
Woolgar, L. 165, 171
World Bank 131–132
World Conference of Higher Education 2009, 124
World Premier International Research Centre Initiative (Japan) 168
Wong, K. K. 33
Woodhouse, K. 23
Woznicki, J. 99
Wran, N. 65

Xinhua Net 145

Yamamoto, K.165
Yonezawa, A. 98, 162, 163, 165, 167, 168, 169, 171
Young, S. P. 30, 35

Zhai, Z. 146
Zhao, S. 148
Zhou, G. 155
Zumeta, W. 22, 23, 27, 30

Taylor & Francis eBooks

Helping you to choose the right eBooks for your Library

Add Routledge titles to your library's digital collection today. Taylor and Francis ebooks contains over 50,000 titles in the Humanities, Social Sciences, Behavioural Sciences, Built Environment and Law.

Choose from a range of subject packages or create your own!

Benefits for you
- Free MARC records
- COUNTER-compliant usage statistics
- Flexible purchase and pricing options
- All titles DRM-free.

Benefits for your user
- Off-site, anytime access via Athens or referring URL
- Print or copy pages or chapters
- Full content search
- Bookmark, highlight and annotate text
- Access to thousands of pages of quality research at the click of a button.

REQUEST YOUR FREE INSTITUTIONAL TRIAL TODAY

Free Trials Available
We offer free trials to qualifying academic, corporate and government customers.

eCollections – Choose from over 30 subject eCollections, including:

Archaeology	Language Learning
Architecture	Law
Asian Studies	Literature
Business & Management	Media & Communication
Classical Studies	Middle East Studies
Construction	Music
Creative & Media Arts	Philosophy
Criminology & Criminal Justice	Planning
Economics	Politics
Education	Psychology & Mental Health
Energy	Religion
Engineering	Security
English Language & Linguistics	Social Work
Environment & Sustainability	Sociology
Geography	Sport
Health Studies	Theatre & Performance
History	Tourism, Hospitality & Events

For more information, pricing enquiries or to order a free trial, please contact your local sales team:
www.tandfebooks.com/page/sales

Routledge
Taylor & Francis Group

The home of
Routledge books

www.tandfebooks.com